TROUBLED
RELATIONSHIPS

FAMILIES IN TROUBLE SERIES

Series Editors: CATHERINE S. CHILMAN,
ELAM W. NUNNALLY, FRED M. COX
all at University of Wisconsin—Milwaukee

Families in Trouble Series is an edited five-volume set designed to enhance the understanding and skills of human services professionals in such fields as social work, clinical psychology, education, health, counseling, and family therapy. Written by recognized scholars from several academic disciplines, this impressive series provides practice guidelines, state-of-the-art research, and implications for public policies from a family systems perspective. No other book or integrated series of books provides such an authoritative overview of information about the wide range of economic, employment, physical, behavioral, and relational problems and lifestyles that commonly affect today's families.

VOLUMES IN THIS SERIES:

Volume 1
Employment and Economic Problems

Volume 2
Chronic Illness and Disability

Volume 3
Troubled Relationships

Volume 4
**Mental Illness, Delinquency,
Addictions, and Neglect**

Volume 5
Variant Family Forms

TROUBLED RELATIONSHIPS

Families in Trouble Series, Volume 3

Edited by:
Elam W. Nunnally
Catherine S. Chilman
Fred M. Cox

SAGE PUBLICATIONS
The Publishers of Professional Social Science
Newbury Park   Beverly Hills   London   New Delhi

To our spouses, children, and grandchildren

For information address:

SAGE Publications, Inc.
2111 West Hillcrest Drive
Newbury Park, California 91320

SAGE Publications Inc.
275 South Beverly Drive
Beverly Hills
California 90212

SAGE Publications Ltd.
28 Banner Street
London EC1Y 8QE
England

SAGE PUBLICATIONS India Pvt. Ltd.
M-32 Market
Greater Kailash I
New Delhi 110 048 India

Printed in the United States of America

Library of Congress Cataloging-in-Publication Data

Families in trouble : knowledge and practice perspectives for
  professionals in the human services / edited by Catherine S.
  Chilman, Fred M. Cox, Elam W. Nunnally.
    p. cm.
  Includes bibliographies and indexes.
    Contents: v. 1. Employment and economic problems—v. 2. Chronic
illness and disability—v. 3. Troubled relationships—v.
4. Mental illness, delinquency, addictions, and neglect—v.
5. Variant family forms.
    ISBN 0-8039-2701-0 (v. 3) ISBN 0-8039-2702-9
(pbk.: v. 3)
    1. Problem families—United States. 2. Family social work—United
States. 3. Problem families—Counseling of—United States.
4. Problem families—Government policy—United States. I. Chilman,
Catherine S. II. Cox, Fred M. III. Nunnally, Elam W.
HV699.F316   1988   88-6539
362.8'2'0973—dc19   CIP

FIRST PRINTING 1988

Contents

Introduction to the Series

ELAM W. NUNNALLY, CATHERINE S. CHILMAN,
AND FRED M. COX

MAJOR PURPOSES AND CONCEPTS

The major purpose of this series of books is to enhance the understanding and skills of human services professionals in such fields as social work, education, health, counseling, clinical psychology, and family therapy so that they can more effectively assist families in trouble. There is no need to elaborate here that many of today's families are in serious trouble, as rising rates of divorce, unmarried parenthood, poverty, and family violence suggest. The stresses imposed by a rapidly changing society are creating severe strains for families and their members. There are also positive aspects of these changes, however, including improved health care and freedom from backbreaking toil, as well as increasing knowledge about family-related problems and ways to minimize them.

Thus, to reduce the negatives that are afflicting families and to enhance the positives, it is important to marshal the social and psychological knowledge and practice wisdom now available to enrich professional family-related practice, policies, and programs. The editors fully recognize that current knowledge is all too meager; much more needs to be developed. However, let us use the knowledge we do have while the search for more continues.

This series proposes to function as a basic knowledge, theory, and practice resource of the highest scholarly and professional quality. It is directed to practitioners and graduate students in the human service professions who work with troubled families. It emphasizes families in trouble, rather than families in general. As far as the editors can ascertain, no other book or integrated series of books combines an authoritative overview of information about the wide range of economic, employment, physical, behavioral, and relational problems and lifestyles that commonly affect today's families.[1]

This is especially true with respect to books that link up-to-date, research-based knowledge about common family-related problems to implications both for clinical practice and for policy and program development and implementation. For the most part, publications and curricula for the human services tend to be presented in discrete, specialized units. In the family field, for instance, knowledge from the social and behavioral sciences is often presented in a separate course with its own texts that emphasize basic knowledge and theory, with little or no mention of the applications of this knowledge and theory to professional practice. Quite different courses and texts deal with clinical practice applications, often with little reference to the related knowledge and theory base. Another set of courses and texts deals with planning and policy strategies for programs to meet individual and family needs, with little reference either to clinical practice techniques or to basic knowledge and theory foundations on which program and policy development should rest.

Thus, professionals tend to have serious difficulty forming clear links along the continuum of theory, knowledge, policies, programs, and clinical practice. Yet professional services cannot be adequately designed and delivered unless these links are made and applied, in an integrated way, to meeting the needs of families and their members.

Family Systems Perspective

A family systems perspective forms the fundamental conceptual scheme of this series. Families are seen as small, open systems, deeply affected by their internal, interpersonal dynamics and by the many aspects of the external environment with which they interact. From the internal dynamics perspective, everything that happens to one member of the family affects all members. The internal systems of families can vary in a number of ways, some of them dysfunctional. For example, the members of some families are so tightly and rigidly interconnected, or "fused," that members have virtually no sense of personal identity. Flexible changes of family patterns in order to meet changing conditions from within and from outside the family then become virtually impossible. Moreover, in such instances individual family members find they cannot extricate themselves from the poorly functioning family system.

In addition, some families form dysfunctional subsystems, such as a closed partnership between a father and son in competition with a closed mother-daughter partnership. Such alignments tend to undermine the parents' marriage and the development of sons and daughters as maturing individuals.

Some families with interpersonal problems, such as poor husband-wife relationships, deny their real difficulties and displace them onto another family member, such as a child, who may then become the problem-laden scapegoat for both parents.

There are many other variations on the internal systems theme, briefly sketched here. The chief point is that efforts aimed at treating individual members of families are often fruitless unless the operation of the whole family system is better understood and included in treatment plans, as well as in programs and policies. Moreover, individual treatment, without regard to family system dynamics, may increase rather than decrease the problems of the whole system and its members.

In seeking to understand family systems, it is also important to study the many "family actors"—older, middle, and younger generations and interactive members of the extended family such as grandparents, aunts, uncles, brothers, sisters, steprelations, former spouses, and close friends.

It is also essential to consider the development of families and their dynamics over the life span, with the recognition that family interactions, concerns, and tasks vary at different life cycle stages and crucial transition points such as marriage, childbirth, launching children into schools and jobs, retirement, illness, and death.

Family structures and lifestyles vary, especially at this time in society when a variety of family forms is becoming more common, including single-parent, divorced, widowed, separated, reconstituted, gay or lesbian, extended, foster and adoptive, and two-career families; cohabiting, never-married couples who may also have children; childless couples; and, of course, the traditional two-parent nuclear family with one or more children. Each of these family forms has its own particular strengths and vulnerabilities.

When families have particular problems such as unemployment, low income, chronic physical illness or death of a member, chemical dependency, mental illness, conflict with the law, and so on, their strengths are likely to be seriously undermined. The nature and extent of the stresses they experience will be affected by a number of factors, including family system characteristics and family developmental stage. It is crucially important, therefore, to consider family-related problems, such as those mentioned above, in a family-focused context rather than in the more usual framework that seeks to treat or plan for individuals without appropriate consideration and understanding of the complexities of family dynamics, both internal and external.

External factors affecting families are all too frequently overlooked or brushed aside by human service professionals, especially those in clinical practice. Viewing families ecologically, as open systems, leads to the recognition that many factors in the environment have a strong impact on them. These factors include the state of the economy, employment conditions, the availability of needed resources in the community, racism and other forms of discrimination, and so forth. When environmental conditions are adverse and community resources are inadequate, the stresses on families escalate, especially for families of relatively low income and low educational and occupational status. It then becomes the responsibility of professionals to help vulnerable families develop strategies to deal more effectively with these stresses. Professionals may also need to serve as advocates to assist families in obtaining available resources and to work with other local, state, and national groups to promote improved conditions and resources.

In light of the above, the proposed series includes overview chapters about existing and needed policies and programs that are directed toward more effective problem management in support of family well-being. It is hoped that this material will serve as a stimulus and information base for professionals in their larger community responsibilities.

CONTENT

With these purposes and concepts in mind, the editors offer a series of five books, each of which has the following underlying structure (a) research-based theory and knowledge about each topic, (b) suggested guidelines for methods of family-centered practice, and (c) implications for public programs and policy. At our invitation, recognized specialists from their respective fields have prepared chapters dealing with particular aspects of this overall plan. Specific problem areas that are often associated with trouble for families are covered in the five books. Volume 1, *Families with Problems with Work and Financial Resources,* discusses employment and income. Volume 2, *Families with Physically Impaired Members,* deals with physical illness and disabilities. Volume 3, *Families with Disturbed Family Relationships,* covers that problem area. Behavior that the community finds unacceptable is discussed in Volume 4, *Families with Mental Disorder, Addiction, Delinquency, and Neglect.* Volume 5, *Families with Problems Related to Alternate Lifestyles,* covers participation in alternative family forms that are sometimes accompanied by difficulties for the families involved.

We recognize that not all problem topics are covered. Space constraints require that we select a set of subjects that seem to be most widespread and most apt to be related to serious troubles for families. We also do not cover all major methods of human service delivery. Our discussion is limited, for the most part, to methods of direct practice in the provision of social and psychological services. The reasons for this limitation are (a) the editors' expertise lies in the social/psychological area, (b) we believe these practice approaches to be of major importance in assisting families, and (c) the majority of human service professionals today are in direct practice.

Although we believe the methods of social planning, administration, and legislative advocacy, to name a few, also are essential to the human services enterprise, adequate coverage of these topics is beyond the scope of the present series.

Underlying Concepts

Definition of the Family

We define a family to mean two or more people in a committed relationship from which they derive a sense of identity as a family. This definition permits us to include many nontraditional family forms that are outside the traditional legal perspective, including families not related by blood, marriage, or adoption. This broad definition is essential if we are to recognize the full variety of family forms found in modern society.

"Families in Trouble" versus "Troubled Families"

We begin with the premise that most, if not all, families are apt to encounter stresses at one time or another in their lives. Due to these stresses they may, from time to time, be "in trouble." This concept is quite different from that which proposes that some families are inherently troubled, largely because of their own internal problems.

We build on the work of such systems theorists as Bertalanffy (1968), Buckley (1967), and Bateson (1972, 1979); family stress and coping theorists such as Hill (1949), Olson and McCubbin (1983), and McCubbin, Cauble, and Patterson (1982); and such clinical theorists as Haley (1963, 1976), Minuchin (1974), Watzlawick, Weakland, and Fisch (1974), and Satir (1967, 1983). We amplify their concepts to

develop a multifaceted set of interrelated principles which are reflected to one degree or another in the various chapters.

In so doing, we weave together knowledge and theory from a
number of the social, behavioral, and biological sciences and integrate them within a family systems framework. Although such a
complex approach may seem overly ambitious, we believe it is important, especially if knowledge and theory about families are to be
effectively applied to the fields of practice, programs, and policies.

Our basic theoretical position is that the reactions of family systems and their members to stressful experiences depend on the
following major interacting factors:

1. The nature, severity, and duration of the stress and its effects on each
   family member and the family structure.
2. The perception of each member of the family system (which often
   includes the extended family) of what the stress is and what it means
   to each member in terms of that person's beliefs, values, and goals.
3. The size and structure of the family (such as number, gender, and
   spacing of children); the marital status of the parents; the presence of
   other kin or friends in the household.
4. The stage of family development and age of each member.
5. The psychological characteristics of each family member (including
   personality and cognitive factors).
6. The physical characteristics of each family member (such as state of
   health and special physical assets and liabilities).
7. The previous life experiences that each family member brings to the
   present stressor event. For instance, a series of losses of loved ones
   during childhood and adolescence can make a parent, as an adult,
   particularly sensitive to another severe illness or death.
8. The characteristics of the family system, including the clarity or
   ambiguity of its boundaries, the rigidity or flexibility of behavioral
   patterns, the existence of subsystems and their nature, the degree of
   fusion or distancing of relationships, interaction with external systems, and patterns of communication, plus social, psychological, and
   material resources available from within the family and its network.
9. Social, psychological, and material resources available to families
   from communities. This includes not only the existence of a wide
   variety of community services and resources that are potentially supportive of the well-being of families and their members, but the recognition that families are apt to vary in their access to community
   resources depending on such factors as the degree of social stratification, racism, ethnocentrism, and power politics within the community.

In summary, the above formulation proposes that families are not inherently "stable" or "healthy" or, conversely, "unstable," "troubled," or "sick," but that most families encounter external or internal stresses at different points in the life span of each member. These stresses vary from one family to another depending on many factors in the environment and within the family. Families also differ in their capacity to cope with these stresses; their coping capacities depend on the nature of these stresses, plus a complex of family system and structure variables together with the social, psychological, and physical characteristics of each member.

To differing degrees, human service professionals can be of important assistance to families and their members at times when stressful events threaten to overwhelm their coping capacities. This assistance may consist of direct treatment, resource mobilization, or efforts to improve public policies or programs, all central topics covered in this series. These efforts are most apt to be effective if the professional approaches his or her work objectively, rather than judgmentally, and with a high level of competence solidly based on the best available scientific knowledge and skills derived from that knowledge, also a major focus of this series.

Our choice of authors was made partly on the basis of their reputations for scholarly or clinical achievements and partly on the basis of their affinity to a systems approach to understanding families and their environments. All of our invited authors were requested to relate their contributions to a systems frame of reference. We have not excluded other theoretical views, however, and the reader will find articles which contain, for example, learning theory and behavioral concepts as well as systems thinking.

We chose a systems paradigm as the orientation for these volumes for several reasons. First, this paradigm readily permits one to view the interplay of individual, family group, and community or societal factors in understanding how troubles arise for families and how families cope. Second, the systems paradigm is hospitable to developmental analyses of families and their difficulties and strengths. Third, at this juncture some of the most fruitful research studies and most exciting clinical developments reported in the scholarly and clinical literature are systems oriented.

We have asked the authors of the various chapters to pay careful attention to the available research in their fields and to view this research in a critical fashion so that they can make distinctions between what knowledge has been clearly established, what has been only partially established, and what still exists largely in the area of clinical impressions and speculation. Although much more and better research, both basic and applied, is needed on most of the topics covered in this series, the needs of families are such that it is essential for human service professionals to proceed in the most effective way they can, on the basis of what knowledge and theory is available. It is also essential for researchers to continue with the many studies that are needed, for them to disseminate their results, and for practitioners to study the research in their fields as new information becomes available. The editors have made a serious attempt to ensure that the present series brings together, in summarized and applicable form, the most pertinent, up-to-date research available on the various topics that are covered here.

Topics Included Throughout the Series: Racism, Ethnocentrism, and Sexism

As sketched above, each of the five books in the series deals with a set of issues that often cause trouble for families. Although the titles of the volumes do not include the subjects of racism, ethnocentrism, and sexism, we recognize that these factors are of central importance and have a profound impact on the whole of our society, as well as on many individual families and their members. Because these factors tend to have pervasive effects on numerous aspects of family lives, we incorporate a discussion of them as an integral part of many of the topics covered, including chapters on poverty, employment, interpersonal difficulties within families, variations in family forms, family-community conflict, and implications both for direct practice and public policies and programs.

NOTE

1. As of this writing (early 1987), there appears to be one partial exception to this statement. A recent two-volume text by McCubbin and Figley, *Stress and the Family* (1983), includes some of the topics that we have dealt with. However, the following important family-related subjects are not included in that book: poverty, long-term unemployment, alcoholism, marital and parent-child conflict, family violence, cohabitation, gay and lesbian lifestyles, nonmarital pregnancy and parenthood, chronic illness or disability of a parent, delinquency and crime, and aging. Moreover, the material on treatment in these volumes is rather sketchy and that on programs and policy almost nonexistent.

Preface
TROUBLED RELATIONSHIPS

Most Americans rate family relationships as a top priority in their lives, and most experience problems in marriage and/or parent–child relationships at one time or another. It is not surprising therefore that human service professionals are often asked for help with various forms of troubled family relationships: marital, postdivorce, and parent-child difficulties; family violence; and sometimes the need for substitute care of children. This volume is designed to help professionals become more effective in their efforts to assist families with relationship problems. It provides research-based knowledge of the major factors involved in troubled family relationships and offers suggestions for professional practice as developed by experienced family clinicians. The reader also will find suggestions about social policy and legislation that need consideration in order to create a more favorable environment for family life in America.

Candyce Russell provides an overview of research and theory concerning difficult marital relationship issues, and Judith Wallerstein addresses the issues that arise following a divorce, with particular reference to impact on children. Murray Straus and Richard Gelles review research and theory related to family violence, and James Whittaker and Anthony Maluccio discuss issues associated with placement of children out of their natural homes. Catherine Chilman presents research and theory pertaining to difficulties in parent–child relationships.

Family treatment for each of the above areas is presented by Insoo Berg, focusing on marital interaction; Eve Lipchik, focusing on parent–child relations; Scott Fraser, focusing on family violence; and Douglas Sprenkle, focusing on treatment related to divorce. Catherine Chilman provides an analysis of public policy processes relating to families, and Margaret Nichols examines the impact of family law.

Students will find the volume an indispensable introduction to family relationship issues and helping processes. Experienced practitioners will find the volume helpful in updating their knowledge base and expanding their repertory of treatment approaches.

Acknowledgments

We extend our gratitude to a number of people whose help has been of enormous importance in the development of this five-volume series:

To the Johnson Foundation that graciously extended the hospitality of its Wingspread Conference Center in Racine, Wisconsin for a two-day planning meeting of most of our authors at the start of this book project.

To the Milwaukee Foundation of Milwaukee, Wisconsin, that generously provided funds to meet some of the costs of the above-named planning conference.

To MaryAnn Riggs, Word Processor Extraordinary, who, with unusual skill and pertinacity, typed many of the chapters and prepared the bibliographies in standardized formats.

To Carolyn Washburne, expert technical editor, who polished the writing of each chapter promptly and efficiently.

To all of our authors who cooperated gallantly with this project and who tolerated the frequently heavy revisions suggested by the series editors who have consistently held to the ideal of a high-quality product that would be of important use to human service professionals, both as students and practitioners.

To families everywhere whose strengths and whose vulnerabilities have provided the basic inspiration for this series.

Elam W. Nunnally
Catherine S. Chilman
Fred M. Cox

Marriages under Stress:

1

A RESEARCH PERSPECTIVE

CANDYCE S. RUSSELL

Theoretically, under conditions of high stress and limited resources, any marriage is vulnerable to showing signs of distress: high levels of marital conflict, emotional distancing, detouring conflict through a child, or a pattern of one spouse underfunctioning and the other overfunctioning (Kerr, 1981). While individual neuroticism (Libman, Takefman, & Brender, 1980) and maturity (Cole, Cole, & Dean, 1980; Dean, 1966) tend to be associated with marital adjustment, clinic couples often score within normal ranges on neuroticism scales (Libman et al., 1980). We also know that within the same marriage across time, perceived marital quality is not constant. For instance, Feldman (1971) and Ryder (1973) both report drops in aspects of perceived marital quality immediately following the birth of the first child. Life presents a series of both predictable and unexpected stresses. It is not surprising that marriages respond to these events with one or more of the signs of distress mentioned above.

This chapter is limited to empirical literature on intact first marriage. It makes no claim to being exhaustive but will represent, in particular, three models for examining marriage: stress and coping, social exchange, and family life cycle. These models are relevant to couples who seek counseling as well as to those who do not. Thus, clinic couples are not presented as having a psychology unique to themselves. Furthermore, each of these models has generated a fair amount of empirical research.

It is important to note that because the focus of this chapter is on *intact* marriages, the nearly 5% of marriages that end in the first year of marriage are not addressed. A third of divorcing couples are married between 1 and 4 years, and many of these couples are unsampled in the research that follows (*Monthly Vital Statistics Report*, 1983). There is every reason to believe that marriages that end early are different from those which survive the first year. Early divorcing couples tend to be younger, poorer, and less educated than those who divorce in later years.

A STRESS AND COPING PERSPECTIVE

Compared to nonclinic couples, those who become clinic clients have been found to report almost twice the frequency of stressful life events in the 3 years before referral and a significant increase in stress the year immediately preceding referral (Bird et al., 1981). These authors conclude that a significant association exists between stressful life events and marital dysfunction and that a clinical assessment of life events can play a meaningful role in evaluation and plans for treatment. In particular, they found changes in family structure and/or changes in family interaction to be major sources of stress for their clinic couples.

The literature reviewed below links stressful life events to individual stress via, among other factors, a breakdown in the support function of marriage. The chapter concludes with a discussion of the nature of marriage as a mental health resource for its participants and what aspects of being married may support individual well-being.

Using depression in one of the partners as an indicator of distress, Mitchell, Cronkite, and Moos (1983) present data on a model of stress and coping that links negative stressor "events" (e.g., temporary lay-off) and chronic "strains" (e.g., financial difficulty) to depression via coping responses and family support. Coping responses are defined as "cognitions and behaviors that people use to modify adverse aspects of their environments as well as to minimize the potential threat arising from such aspects" (p. 435).

Using a sample of 157 clinically depressed patients and their spouses and a control group of 157 community couples, Mitchell et al. (1983) found the depressed patients to be at a disadvantage relative to control subjects on each variable in their model: They reported more stress, fewer personal coping resources, and lower levels of family support. Negative life events, coping, and family support each related directly to levels of depression, whereas long-term stresses were related to depression indirectly via their relationship to low levels of family support. Of the variance in symptoms, 29 to 44% was explained by the model. Of course, the cross-sectional nature of the study limits interpretation regarding direction of effect. Stress and support may be related to depression because depressed spouses cause negative events and alienate sources of support. Mitchell et al. (1983) conclude that the relationships among stress, support, coping, and personal functioning are probably reciprocal.

Spouses of depressed patients in the Mitchell et al. (1983) data fell between their depressed partners and control couples in level of stress, coping, and family support. It is possible that the strain of having a depressed spouse reduces the other spouse's ability to provide support and, over time, increases that partner's own level of stress.

Corroboration for this interpretation comes from a short-term longitudinal study conducted by Yager, Grant, and Balus (1984). Every other month over a 3-year period, data were collected from 40 male psychiatric outpatients and their wives and 75 nonpatient couples. Among the control couples symptoms in either partner were significantly predicted by the level of each one's *own* life events as well as by the symptom level of the spouses during the preceding two months. However, using clinic couples, symptom levels were related only to *self* life events, not partner's. This suggests that over time spouses of symptomatic partners may withdraw and strive to "immunize or desensitize" themselves to their spouses' symptoms. Another possible interpretation is that there is a dynamic balance in the relationships of clinic couples such that only one partner can be symptomatic at a time. At lower levels of distress (those seen in control samples), such a "seesaw" of symptom balance may not be necessary.

The marital relationship is especially stressed under conditions of unemployment or underemployment. Economic uncertainty is related to marital instability via shifts in marital power, domestic violence, division of labor, and effectiveness of parental authority and discipline (Voydanoff, 1983). Voydanoff (1983) reports that unemployment is less stress producing where the unemployed partner is not blamed for the unemployment and when he or she is not perceived as a failure in the provider role. The family's level of cohesion and adaptability and their links to extended kin and broader social supports are additional resources in reducing the stress of unemployment. Among blacks these resources, together with a pride in the black heritage and participation in all-black social groups, help black couples to cope with the stresses of prejudice, low levels of education, and high rates of unemployment (McAdoo, 1982).

Pearlin and Schooler (1978), in a classic study of the structure of coping, compare coping strategies for their effectiveness in three sets of relationships: marriage, parenting, and employment. Unlike employment, where personal control may be low, active problem solving was associated with successful coping in marriage. In a later study Ilfeld (1980) corroborated these findings by reporting that "optimistic action" as a coping style was more predictive of low marital stress than any other variable studied, including personality factors, other current social stressors, a lack of consensus between the partners, and background differences between the spouses.

Finally, Menaghan (1982) reports on a panel analysis of a large metropolitan data set examining the effectiveness of four marital coping strategies: negotiation, optimistic comparison, selective ignoring, and resignation. People with current marital problems were less likely to report using negotiation or optimistic comparisons and were more likely to use selective ignoring and resignation. Negotiation, though not associated with reduced feelings of stress, was associated with fewer *later* problems. Optimistic comparison, on the other hand, was associated with both lower distress and fewer later problems.

Marriage provides a structure to life that plays an important role in producing or maintaining individual psychological well-being (e.g., Andrews & Withey, 1965; Campbell, Converse, & Rodgers, 1976; Hughes & Gove, 1981). For men just *being* married carries some protection, probably because marriage often brings to the male certain instrumental benefits such as meal preparation, house cleaning, and so on. However, for both spouses, but especially women, the *quality* of the marriage carries an important additional protective function (e.g., Gove, Hughes, & Styer, 1983; Renne, 1971). Companionship, intimacy through mutual self-disclosure, and sex may be contributors. But Gove et al. (1983) suggest the structure of marriage goes beyond to create a "private world" that provides meaning and support to the individual.

Gove et al. (1983) and Gerstel and Gross (1984) suggest that the mental hygiene function of marriage includes a way of thinking about self as a "part of a whole" that goes beyond reciprocal self-disclosure and congruence betwen verbal and nonverbal messages. Withdrawal from the "private world" of marriage may be one of the hallmarks of distressed marriages, particularly those that present with dysfunction lodged within one individual. Furthermore, this withdrawal may be most likely to happen during times of heightened stressors external to the marriage.

AN EXCHANGE PERSPECTIVE

Researchers working from a social exchange perspective have identified several characteristics that distinguish distressed from nondistressed marriages. Among these are (a) greater perceived inequity, (b) lower rates of pleasing and higher rates of displeasing behaviors, (c) greater contingent reciprocity of negative behaviors (reactivity), and (d) stronger relationships between displeasing behaviors and daily satisfaction—all true of distressed as compared with nondistressed marriages (e.g., Davidson, 1984; Davidson, Balswick, & Halverson, 1983; Jacobson, Waldron, & Moore, 1980; Levenson & Gottman, 1983; Margolin, 1981; Margolin & Wampold, 1981).

Levenson and Gottman (1983) have even been able to document a greater physiological "linkage" and reactivity among a sample of distressed as compared with nondistressed couples. Furthermore, those differences were more pronounced when interaction was high in conflict (discussing a marital problem) as opposed to low in conflict (discussing events of the day). Heart rate, skin conductance, pulse transmission time, and somatic activity were the behavioral indicators used. In addition, self-reports of affective responses were gathered retrospectively via videotape recall. Although the authors do not comment on this, their findings are very consistent with Bowen Family Systems Theory. One of Bowen's goals in therapy is to reduce intensity and keep things calm so that partners can choose to respond from a basis of reasoning rather than reacting from a basis of emotion.

Observational studies of distressed and nondistressed couples have documented differences in how the two groups overtly resolve conflict tasks (e.g., Billings, 1979; Birchler, Weiss, & Vincent, 1975). In general, unhappy couples use more negative (e.g., put-downs) and fewer positive (e.g., supportive statements, "I" statements, reflection, etc.) communication behaviors. Markman (1979, 1981) has presented longitudinal data that indicate that negative communication behavior is predictive of later relationship unhappiness. Taken as a whole, these studies suggest that effective communication and conflict-resolution skills are important correlates, if not predictors, of marital happiness.

Recently, however, a number of studies have suggested that cognitive/perceptual factors may be at least as important as behaviors exchanged in resolving marital conflict and maintaining relationship happiness (e.g., Dhir & Markman, 1984, Floyd & Markman, 1983). These researchers note that spouses may perceive their partners' behaviors as positive or negative regardless of the degree of positiveness judged by trained outside observers (Floyd & Markman, 1983). Thus, the authors suggest that interventions designed to increase positive and decrease negative behaviors should be individualized to fit the couple's unique interpretations. In particular, they caution that the couple's attributions about the motivations for change may be important (i.e., "the therapist made you do it").

Besides documenting that distressed couples are especially reactive to one another, reciprocate negative behaviors, and often perceive negatives where others would not, social exchange researchers have investigated the relationship of frequency of interaction (especially companionate activities) and exchange of positive sentiment. Homans (1961) theorizes that the more often persons interact, the more likely they will be to find rewards they can share. They are also more likely to agree about how they see the world, which is rewarding in that it reduces cognitive dissonance ("If people I like see things differently than I do, maybe there is something wrong with me"). Furthermore, the more two people like each other, the more likely it is that they will invest time and energy in the relationship and that they will risk self-disclosure and intimacy. Thus, interactional frequency and positive sentiments are related in a circular fashion. Palsi (1984) reports an investigation of two of these hypotheses with respect to marriage: (a) There will be a positive relationship between frequency of marriage companionship activities and feelings of marriage well-being, and (b) joint activities will be more highly related to marriage well-being than parallel activities. Joint activities are defined as those that require the individual to be responsive to a partner and/or involve self-disclosure, whereas parallel activities do not require such high levels of personal involvement. Their cross-cultural data from Australia, London, and Los Angeles basically support their hypotheses and the earlier work of Orden and Bradburn (1968), who used data from large metropolitan areas of the United States. However, Palsi (1984) also notes that parallel activities retain some association with marriage well-being and should not be ignored for their contribution.

Equity theory maintains that being overbenefited or underbenefited in resource exchange should cause distress for relationship partners. Davidson, Balswick, and Halverson (1983) present data on affective self-disclosure between spouses that support those notions. In particular, 162 couples living in university married student housing reported lower levels of marital adjustment the greater the discrepancy in the partners' reported affective self-disclosure. Furthermore, this finding held both for individuals who reported giving more disclosure than they received and vice versa. Using the same university population, Davidson (1984) reports similar results on a more global measure of relationship "inputs" and "outputs" but cautions that while it is appealing to believe that perceived inequities lead to lower levels of marital adjustment, it is not unlikely that a maladjusted marriage may influence one's sense of equity. In fact, Murstein and MacDonald (1983) have suggested that couples may shift from a "commitment orientation" to an "exchange orientation" when the relationship is going poorly and slowly return to a commitment orientation as it begins to appear that exchanges are once again equitable.

Murstein and MacDonald (1983) define exchange orientation as the "weighing of behavior according to the rule that the value to A of a behavior expressed by A for the benefit of B should be reciprocated by what A perceives as an equally valued behavior on the part of B for A's benefit" (p. 298). Murstein, MacDonald, and Cerreto (1977) developed a scale to measure exchange orientation and predicted that it would be negatively related to marital adjustment. This prediction was supported in a sample of 34 husbands. However, the relationship for wives was not significant. Predictions were also made about pairs of exchange-exchange (E-E), exchange-nonexchange (E-NE), and nonexchange-nonexchange (NE-NE) couples. EE couples were predicted to score the lowest on marital adjustment. This was found to be true for EE husbands but not for EE wives.

In their most recent work Murstein and MacDonald (1983) also define and measure commitment (C): "A tendency to place the relationship with the spouse beyond the effect of any given negative act and to feel a sense of permanency about the relationship" (p. 299). This variable was expected to relate positively to marital adjustment. Furthermore, they predicted that the more the spouse possesses the desirable qualities of commitment and nonexchange, the greater the individual's positive marital adjustment. Using a nonrandom sample of 40 couples married a minimum of 3 years, both of these hypotheses were supported. Nevertheless, men scored significantly higher on "exchange" and lower on "commitment" than did women. The author notes that this finding is consistent with other research that reports men divorce alcoholic wives sooner than women divorce alcoholic husbands. This pattern is understandable given the fact that women's status is more often affected by marriage than is men's status. Thus, it is reasonable that women would be more attentive to their partner's needs and wishes. The direction of causality between C and E orientations and marital adjustment cannot be established with these studies. Most likely the association is reciprocal.

It is important to note, however, that Murstein and MacDonald caution counselors that while exchange in specific areas of conflict may be helpful in resolving an already *existing* conflict, teaching a philosophy of exchange in marriage may not be helpful. To do so might have the effect of sensitizing otherwise commitment-oriented spouses to short-term inequities that would lead to lower levels of adjustment. Additional evidence for this position comes from Sabatelli and Cecil-Pigo (1985) who report that in a large sample of randomly selected married individuals, degree of relational commitment (low levels of monitoring of alternatives and high levels of cohesion and solidarity) was related to high levels of relationship satisfaction. Yet, perceived equity in the distribution of outcomes within the relationship accounted for the largest percent of variance in levels of commitment reported by both men and women. Thus, it appears that committed spouses perceive equity when asked about it but do not routinely attend to "equity counts."

Equity within marriage, besides being related to marital adjustment, is often further related to individual symptoms of depression and affective disturbance (Hoover & Fitzgerald, 1981; Merikangas, Ranelli, & Kupfer, 1979; Schafer & Keith, 1980; Vanfossen, 1981). Hoover & Fitzgerald (1981) report that the depressed women in their sample were more likely than the controls to see themselves as yielding to their husbands after a disagreement and reported that their husbands seldom changed their opinions. Data from husbands indicated that they were unaware of the perceptions of their wives. In a clinic outcome study of nine married depressed or hospitalized female patients, Merikangas et al. (1979) report observed increases in the patient's influence or power in marriage over the course of treatment, resulting in a more equal balance of power. These two studies taken together would suggest that perceived (or actual) marital powerlessness may contribute to or help maintain depression, especially among women.

However, depression may be related to inequity in broader areas of marriage as well. Schafer and Keith (1980) predicted that (a) marriage partners who perceive inequity in the performance of marital roles (cook, housekeeper, provider, companion, and parent) will feel more distress than partners who perceive equity, and (b) marriage partners who perceive that the inequity is in their favor will feel less distress than those who perceive that the inequity is not in their favor. Depression was selected as the measure of psychological distress because it is regarded as a common condition of life. The respondents were from a nonclinic random sample of midwesterners, and the results supported the first hypothesis: Perceived inequity was related to higher levels of distress. Although the data were in the direction predicted by the second hypothesis, they were not statistically significant. Once again, caution must be used in interpreting direction of effect. It is possible that depression may influence the perception of fairness in the performance of household roles, or it may be that depression follows prolonged inequity.

Vanfossen (1981) attempted to address the issue of direction of effect by asking respondents about the relative duration of depression versus problematic marital relationships. She found that marital characteristics were reported to be more enduring and long term than were emotional states.

From 1940 to the present, one of the most significant shifts in the labor force has been the increasing numbers of women, especially married women. Although most women work outside the home because of financial necessity, the majority also report that they would keep their jobs even if they were not financially constrained to do so (e.g., Campbell et al., 1976). As Gove and Peterson (1980) point out, virtually all married women are job-holders in the sense that they are homemakers. Women who also work outside the home, thus, hold two jobs. One might speculate that role overload would lead to lower levels of marital quality for wives and for husbands as well, via diluted expressive and instrumental support from the overworked wives. Burke and Weir (1976) report that husbands of working wives do, in fact, experience less support from their wives, are less physically healthy than husbands of homemakers, and are at a competitive disadvantage in the workforce because of it. However, a subsequent study by Boothe (1979), with several methodological improvements, failed to find husbands of working women to be any less healthy or less satisfied than were husbands of housewives. *Attitudes* toward the wife working do, however, retain predictive power. Gerken (1979) found that the desire of the husband and wife for her to work outside the home or not was a much more powerful predictor of the relationship between marital satisfaction and the wife's employment status than either family life-cycle category or family income. Gove and Peterson (1980) report similar findings regarding the importance of preferences for outside work in an unpublished doctoral dissertation by Brocki (1979).

Vanfossen (1981) reports additional information that is relevant to reciprocity, supportiveness, and marital distress. In a random sample of employed husbands, nonemployed wives, and employed wives in Chicago, more husbands than wives reported having appreciative, affectionate, and reciprocating spouses. But each category of respondents responded to different aspects of reciprocity in marriage. Husbands were more likely to be depressed if their wives were perceived as unaffectionate and unaffirming, especially if the husband's work relationships were unsatisfactory. Nonemployed wives who were particularly depressed reported unaffirming spouses. Furthermore, spouses' evaluations of these nonemployed wives further increased the wives' dissatisfaction with the housekeeping role. Employed wives who were depressed were likely to perceive their husbands as unaffirming and inequitable, especially if there was disagreement over the husband's help with domestic duties. These data suggest that reciprocity and support may be most critical in those areas of life that each partner finds both most problematic and most central to feelings of self-worth: one's occupation.

A FAMILY LIFE-CYCLE PERSPECTIVE

Many studies document a slight curvilinear relationship between family life-cycle category and marital quality, with the child-dependent years being the period with lowest reported score (e.g., Anderson, Russell, & Schumm, 1983; Burr, 1970; Rollins & Feldman, 1970; Spanier & Lewis, 1980). Most of these studies are cross-sectional in design and, therefore, are subject to a variety of interpretations. They provide no assurance that couples in early stages at the time of data collection will necessarily, as a group, experience a dip in perceived marital quality at midstages, to recover in the final stages of the marital life cycle. However, a few short-term longitudinal studies suggest that a dip does, indeed, occur as children join the marital dyad (e.g., Feldman, 1971; Ryder, 1973). While the bulk of evidence does support a curvilinear pattern, Rollins and Cannon (1974) and Anderson et al. (1983) caution that only about 8% of the variance in reported levels of marital satisfaction is accounted for by family life-cycle category. Menaghan (1983) suggests that our current way of marking family life-cycle categories is not sensitive enough to reveal patterns that may, indeed, exist.

Rollins and Cannon (1974) and Rollins and Galligan (1978) suggest that additional variance in marital satisfaction may be explained by role expectations, role accumulation, role strain, and perception of role enactment. They suggest that marital quality may be maximized throughout the family life cycle by altering role expectations and monitoring the accumulation of roles and resulting role strain. Two recent studies suggest that role accumulation and role strain may, indeed, be especially significant variables. Cleary and Mechanic (1983) report that among a representative midwestern sample, having minor children in the household was especially stressful for em-ployed married women and countered the otherwise beneficial effects of employment on the psychological well-being of these women. The effects of children in the household on personal distress were stronger among working women with lower family incomes.

Schumm and Bugaighis (1986) reanalyzed the Anderson et al. (1983) data and found a similar pattern for the marital satisfaction of low-income mothers of preschool children who were employed full time. In fact, much of the observed decline in marital satisfaction during the middle stages of the family life cycle in the larger sample was explained by this specific group of low-income mothers. Rather than indicating a mild problem for *all* wives, the family life-cycle data actually reflected a very severe source of distress for this small group of wives. This sample included wives only, so it is not known if a similar pattern exists for husbands. Typically, women continue to perform large proportions of household tasks despite full-time em-ployment (e.g., Boulding, 1979). It is possible that the combination of full-time work, preschool children, and limited finances is especially stressful for wives and that data from husbands would not show the same pattern. Nevertheless, the Schumm and Bugaighis (1986) data offer intriguing support for the Rollins and Galligan (1978) model.

Miller (1976) tested a multivariate model of marital satisfaction. He included the following variables in his model: amount of antic-ipatory socialization (for last role transition), ease of last family role transition, length of marriage, number of children, amount of com-panionship, social class, and child spacing. The two most predictive variables were companionship ($r = .354$) and ease of last role transi-tion ($r = .204$). Interestingly, amount of anticipatory socialization was *inversely* related to ease of role transition. Although this was not hypothesized, Miller speculates that it was the most anxious couples who sought out the most preparation and that it was their level of anxiety, and not the preparation, that was predictive of difficulty with transitions. Number of children influenced marital quality via its negative association with companionship activities ($r = -.156$), while social class positively influenced companionship activities ($r = .265$). It would be interesting to know if companionship activities would moderate the effects of wives working full time and having preschool children in the home, as reported by Schumm and Bugaighis (1986).

Recent work by Steffensmeier (1982) is useful in identifying variables that moderate the effects of adding a child to the marital dyad. She used three dependent variables (parental gratifications, parental responsibilities and restrictions, and marital intimacy and stability). Role clarity was significantly and positively related to marital intimacy and stability and to parental gratifications, whereas it was significantly and negatively related to parental responsibilities and restrictions. Thus, new parents who were relatively clear about what they expected of themselves and of their partners as parents were able to ease stress during the transition and enhance benefits. These findings appear to lend empirical support to Rollins and Galligan (1978) who argue that role expectations may be more significant predictors of marital quality than family life-cycle stages. Adding children does not necessarily decrease marital quality if role expectations are clear and reasonable.

SUMMARY

Although some of the variables cited above cannot be influenced in therapy (e.g., stage of family life cycle), others can be influenced. Clarifying roles and teaching negotiating skills are among the most easily influenced in therapy. Role clarity appears to be *especially* important as children are added to the marriage and in marriages where both partners work outside the home. As new roles are taken on or are more fully activated, taking time to be clear about how these new roles are to be enacted and previously occupied roles are to be adjusted should be beneficial. This includes being clear about standards for "level of performance."

For instance, a certain level of household clutter may be defined as acceptable as the role of parent or breadwinner is added to a spouse's role complex. Less easy to influence, but still possible for the skilled therapist, are calming emotional reactivity and negative reciprocity, balancing equity, and encouraging growth into a commitment orientation. Hypotheses generated from the exchange perspective have generally been well-supported. However, research from the family life-cycle perspective has increased its explanatory power by shifting from a focus on life-cycle stage to a focus on how transitions are prepared for, including what spouses expect from one another (role clarity). This variable may be increasingly important as spouses are faced with heavy role responsibilities both inside and outside the family.

IMPLICATIONS FOR CLINICIANS

Research findings frequently are difficult to translate into suggestions for intervention. Clinicians work with individual couples, not large population means, and what is true of the larger population may not be true for a specific client couple. There is no substitute for good clinical judgment. However, there are some findings that may offer guidance to the practicing mental health professional. The following suggestions receive some degree of empirical support from the literature just reviewed:

1. Encourage the use of "negotiation" and "optimistic comparison" in confronting marital problem solving (Ilfeld, 1980; Menaghan, 1982; Pearlin & Schooler, 1978).
2. Calm emotional reactivity, especially to negative spouse behaviors (e.g., Levenson & Gottman, 1983; Margolin, 1981). Changing cognitions or the "meaning" attributed to behavior may be useful in accomplishing this (Dhir & Markman, 1984; Floyd & Markman, 1983).
3. Encourage companionate activities (e.g., Miller, 1976).
4. Assist couples in "balancing" levels of self-disclosure, decision-making power, and other relationship "inputs" and "outputs" (e.g., Balswick & Halverson, 1983; Davidson, 1984; Hoover & Fitzgerald, 1981; Merikangas et al., 1979). *However,* once trust in an equitable pattern has been established, encourage a shift to a nonexchange orientation (Murstein & MacDonald, 1983; Sabatelli & Cecil-Pigo, 1985).
5. Help couples clarify role expectations, especially during periods of increasing family demands, such as the transition to parenthood (e.g., Rollins & Galligan, 1978; Steffensmeier, 1982). In particular, help partners clarify preferences and negotiate an agreement around the issue of the wife's employment. These preferences appear to be more significant than the actual fact of the wife working or not working (e.g., Brocki, 1979; Geerken, 1979). Finally, it is important that couples support one another in the productive work roles they choose (e.g., Vanfossen, 1981).

Couple Therapy with One Person or Two 2

INSOO K. BERG

Before getting down to clinical issues in this chapter, a brief overview of various schools of thought and their translation into practice may be useful because it is hard for the beginning clinician to sort out the many and various theoretical frames and techniques. Growing out of a psychoanalytic tradition that dominated the practice of individual treatment, the marital and family therapy field was initially influenced heavily by psychoanalytic thinking (e.g., Stierlin, 1977). Marital conflict was thought to be caused by mutual projection of unacceptable, unconscious impulses.

Starting with the investigation of the schizophrenias, Bowen (1960), Wynne (1958), Ackerman (1970), and others applied concepts derived from psychoanalytic thinking and from systems thinking to the family unit. Terms such as "undifferentiated ego mass," "mutual projection system," "pseudomutuality," "rubber fence," "pseudohostility," and so on were used to explain families' "stuck" situations.

Subscribing to and continuing the historical orientation of the psychoanalytic view, a more recent adaptation is found in practice models that emphasize the multigenerational nature of family conflicts (e.g., Boszormenyi-Nagy, 1973). Close scrutiny is given to what each spouse brings to the marriage from his or her family of origin. In this tradition the family "genogram" is a popular assessment tool. Assessment seems to rely more on linear than systemic thinking.

Contemporaneous with the work of the pioneers on the East Coast (Bowen, Wynne, Ackerman, and others), on the West Coast Jackson, Weakland, Haley, and others, having been greatly affected by the biological and anthropological work of Gregory Bateson, investigated schizophrenia from a cybernetic, systems viewpoint and formulated hypotheses bearing on "sick" families' disturbed communication patterns (Bateson et al., 1956). Terms such as "double-bind theory," "paradoxical communication," and so on came out of their work. Although nonhistorical in their investigative approach, the West Coast group presented a linear, albeit multicausal, view of problems in relationships. Their early treatment efforts followed the path of correcting distorted communication patterns and the use of "counter-paradox" (Watzlawick et al., 1967).

Their later work focused on problem pattern interruption from a more systemic perspective (Watzlawick et al., 1974). Haley (1963) has been an effective spokesperson for the application of this group's hypotheses to the treatment of marital relationships. He viewed couple relationships as parallel, complementary, or symmetrical, and treatment was focused on changing patterns that were escalating into "more of the same." Clearly, treatment was directed toward changing the current interaction patterns rather than on conflicts derived from family history.

A substantial number of therapists have continued within a tradition of focusing on communication, and among these Satir (1983, 1985) has become especially well known and influential with succeeding generations of therapists. Satir focuses on esteem, awareness, and open communication and tries to increase each of these to improve couple and family functioning and thus enhance personal growth.

Another school has developed out of social learning theory and behaviorism. Jacobson (1979), Stuart (1980), Patterson et al. (1975), and others emphasize teaching sets of skills perceived to be lacking in each spouse, such as communication, negotiation, and the use of positive reinforcements. Behavioral treatments concentrate on skill development, taught in step-by-step fashion. They emphasize systematic assessment schemas and treatments leading to behavioral change. There is a considerable body of research data available in this area of practice.

THERAPY WITH ONE PARTNER

One of the many hotly debated issues in marital therapy is whether the treatment of one spouse is as effective as conjoint therapy and whether both partners must willingly be present in therapy sessions to produce change. The consensus in the field seems to be that more research on the efficacy of various models for treating marital dysfunction is long overdue, and at present there can be no conclusion as to which theoretical frame or technique is more effective (Baucom & Hoffman, 1986; Gurman et al., 1986). While waiting for more definitive findings, clinicians must work with the reality of the everyday clinical world and with the tools currently available.

As Wells and Gianetti point out (1986), the widespread acceptance of conjoint therapy as the exclusive tool for marital therapy runs the risk of refusing service to a client whose spouse is either unavailable or unwilling to seek help. Therefore, much of the therapist's energy is spent in trying to induce the absent spouse to enter treatment, or, more frequently, the burden of convincing the spouse is left with the initial client, most often the wife. Invariably, we hear that these potential clients were refused service by some agency or clinic because the spouse was unwilling to participate or she was unsuccessful in persuading him to participate.

The author contends that is possible, more frequently than previously thought, to produce changes in the interactional patterns of the couple by working with the one person who is willing to come in (de Shazer & Berg, 1985). This chapter presents the theoretical principles for producing changes in these situations, illustrated with clinical case examples. This chapter provides a map for putting together the information gathered in the first sessions and discusses in detail some of the assessment questions that may help therapists organize clinical material into a coherent outline from which to proceed. Finally, the discussion to include conjoint therapy is expanded. The therapy model discussed in this chapter is based on the work of the Brief Family Therapy Center, the model developed by de Shazer and his colleagues (de Shazer, 1982, 1985; de Shazer et al., 1986), which views human problems as embedded in the interaction between people rather than in individual pathology. This model provides clinical tools for implementing the research findings and recommendations for clinicians outlined by Russell in the previous chapter.

Initial Contacts

The majority of initial contacts for couple therapy with one person are made by women, who frequently indicate that their spouses are unwilling to come in and are adamantly opposed to talking to "strangers," or that their husbands deny that what is problematic for her is problematic for him. (For convenience here I will use the female pronoun for the client.) For example, Mrs. W was referred by her psychiatrist who, after a year of treatment for depression, had given up. Although Mr. W had participated in therapy initially, he now refused all therapy, saying that he felt "ganged up on" by his wife and the previous therapist.

The presenting problem as Mrs. W saw it was her husband's "unreasonable outbursts" of anger followed by remorse and attempts at making up. Thinking that there was no hope for improvement in the relationship, she sought help with the goal of "just learning to live with him." Following detailed investigation of the interactional pattern, we encouraged Mrs. W to experiment with responses different from her previous attempts, such as being attentive to him before he became upset and setting aside some private time together without the children. We also attributed a positive meaning to his insistence on going out with the boys twice a week as his way of taking care of himself, instead of seeing it as an uncaring and selfish behavior. Mrs. W came to realize how much she could influence her husband's behavior toward her by not criticizing and attacking his "selfishness," which were her previous problem-solving attempts. She also came to realize that she felt more in control of the relationship when not trying to control him. When she began to encourage his outside interests, while maintaining her own interests, she became much more attractive to Mr. W, who began staying home more, thus changing the interaction pattern.

Assessment

The following questions help organize therapy sessions and offer direction to the therapist on how to proceed:

1. Whose problem is it? Who is most upset by the problem?
2. What is the presenting problem?
3. How does the client explain the problem?
4. When does the problem not occur? What works?
5. What has been attempted that does not work?
6. What is the sign of initial change? What are the signs that therapy has succeeded and may be terminated?
7. Does the couple have positive regard for each other?

These questions apply equally well to therapy sessions when both partners are present. Each question and how it applies is explained next.

Whose Problem Is It? Who Is Most Upset by the Problem?

It cannot be assumed that the person who sits in your office is necessarily the person most upset or most anxious to take steps to solve the problem. Assessment of the client's investment in change is an important step in any therapeutic endeavor. Although your client may view "the problem" as the direct result of the absent spouse's behavior, careful questioning may reveal that the absent spouse does not regard it as a problem, or at least not as serious a problem as does the client in your office.

If your client is using therapy only to threaten separation, without really meaning it, or is looking for the therapist to side with her, you may not have a real "client." "A client" is someone who conveys to you verbally and nonverbally that she is desperate for change. "It can't go on anymore," "I am at the end of my rope," or "something must be done" along with appropriate affect are frequently heard clues. Sometimes "the client" may be the referral source or the community, if they are more upset about the problem than the person in your office.

A close examination of what are described as the most frustrating cases in consultation or supervision frequently reveals that the therapist has become his or her own client: That is, the therapist is more upset about and more invested in changing the problematic symptoms or the problem than is the person with the symptom or problem. When the sense of urgency or the investment for change is not present, it is only natural that the "client" in your office may not be as motivated as you think she should be.

Some clients who come to sessions under duress—for example, following a threat of divorce, separation, or "refusal of sex,"—may not appear to be motivated to change; nevertheless, they may become willing to do something constructive if the therapist handles the session skillfully. In such situations a careful negotiation of a treatment contract must be done early and in such a way that coming to the sessions and making changes will be viewed as fulfilling the client's own goals and not merely someone else's.

For example, when Mr. S was sent by his wife to therapy to have his "temper problem" treated, he was only interested in satisfying his wife's demand so that she would agree to reconcile. Although Mr. S was more interested in having his wife return to him rather than in learning to control his temper, he was helped to see that the means to his goal *was* to control his temper. He agreed that controlling his temper was advantageous to him and began to do so.

One task of assessment is to establish whether the person in your office is invested in changing anything and is therefore a client. When the therapist establishes that she has a client, the following will help organize the clinical material.

What Is the Presenting Problem?

Whatever the client presents as a problem must be accepted as indeed her or his focus of concern. The tendency among many clinicians is to look for "deeper" or "real" problems, which can lead the therapist and client astray. For example, a common mistake is to assume that a parent-child problem is necessarily related to marital dissatisfaction and therefore to offer or sometimes even insist on marital therapy when the parents are asking for help with the child. This is likely to cause the family to leave treatment prematurely.

In dealing with one part of the couple system, it is important to get the client's perception of her spouse's view of the problem in addition to her own. Questions such as the following are very helpful in assessing conflict between the client and the absent spouse: "If your husband were here, what would he say is the problem between the two of you?" "Would your wife agree that her poor housekeeping habit is a problem for her?" "How would your husband describe the difficulty between the two of you?" "If he were here, what do you think your husband would say must be changed between the two of you?" This question can be followed with "Do you agree with him?" Such questions also encourage the client to differentiate her view of the problem from her spouse's view and help her begin to realize that there are differing points of view on many things and that the therapist assumes that differences are a normal and expected part of life.

When clients present a long list of problems instead of one simple, clearly identified problem, asking a straightforward question such as "What is the most pressing problem we should tackle first?" or "Which of these problems would it make the most sense to solve first?" helps the client organize her thinking. Clients are often so overwhelmed by the enormity of their problems that they have difficulty setting priorities.

How Does the Client Explain the Problem?

Answers to this question reveal how the client conceptualizes the problem and tells the therapist how to approach the client. For example, a client may say that her spouse "comes from a bad family" and she believes secretly that he is "damaged" for life. It may be more helpful for the therapist to accept this position and work toward the therapy goal within this context than it would be to struggle with her openly or indirectly to change her belief. Another client may conceptualize the problem quite differently, for example, they are having problems because they are "both stubborn." Your approach with this client will be consistent with a situation involving two very stubborn people. Even if you intervene in a similar way in both situations, your explanation for the intervention in each case may be quite different. It is true, of course, that many successful interventions involve attempts to help clients change the way they think about a partner or about their relationship. The point is that therapists should tread lightly and not attempt to force change.

It is common for a client to say that "if only my husband were different, my problem would be solved" and therefore invest much of her energy in trying to stop his problematic behavior. It is also common for therapists to try to force the client to own up to her part of the problem, which only compounds the problem. In such instances, the wife sees the husband's refusal to change as "resistance" to improving the marriage while the therapist sees the wife's refusal to own up to her part of the problem as "resistance" to therapy (de Shazer, 1984). Therefore, you may have a parallel situation of a wife investing energy trying to change the husband while the therapist invests an equal amount of energy trying to change the wife, with both quite frustrated.

When Does the Problem Not Occur?

In every couple relationship, there are periods when the partners are reasonably comfortable with each other and getting along well. Most clients forget this at the point when they are upset enough to seek professional help. To them it appears that they are "fighting all the time" or "he is angry all the time." However, we know that most relationships have ups and downs and a positive earlier history, a period when things went reasonably well. Discovering these better times and the successful interaction patterns that characterize these times helps clients maintain some perspective on the nature of their relationship and helps them use the resources that they already have. Detailed questions regarding successful interaction patterns such as when they both managed to control their "spat" and prevented it from turning into a "brawl" can be very helpful.

Useful questions are the following: "What did you do to keep the argument from turning into a fight?" "What was he doing when you did that?" "What did it take to help him cool down?" "What did he do to stop himself from blowing up?" "What would he say you did to stop the fight from getting out of hand?" These questions provide the therapist with useful information about the interaction patterns and provide important clues as to what the couple can do again to solve problems. In addition, the client feels that the therapist is supportive of the couple's successes, and the problem may begin to seem less overwhelming.

If the couple had successful problem-solving experiences in an earlier part of their relationship, it would be helpful to have them recall those skills for use in solving current problems. If they have even occasional successes now, it is helpful to explore these so that the client can discover the successful patterns along with unsuccessful ones. Clients are relieved to discover that they have solved some problems on their own, and they become hopeful that they can do it again!

John and Rose requested therapy when their arguments reached a point that they were questioning the wisdom of their impending marriage. It soon became apparent that their arguments occurred mainly on weekends, and during the week they were getting along very well. Once the pattern of "getting along" was established in some detail, it was easy to duplicate the same pattern on weekends. The differences between the weekday and weekend patterns was that both tended to drink more than they would have liked on weekends. They also discovered that when John walked out of arguments, both calmed down more. Because drinking less and leaving the scene were the elements that made a difference, the couple readily agreed to experiment with new patterns for the weekend. By focusing on patterns that were working for this couple, therapy took only three sessions.

What Has Been Attempted That Does Not Work?

Patterns that maintain problematic symptoms frequently include attempted solutions (Fisch et al., 1982; Watzlawick et al., 1974), for example, attempting to force agreement by arguing. The result is that one loses sight of the more important goal of getting on well together, and the attempted solution becomes part of the problem pattern. A detailed account of what the client has tried to do to solve problems not only acknowledges her efforts and good intentions but also points out to both therapist and client what *not* to do. Because arguing to reach agreement has been tried and has not worked, it only seems reasonable that arguing should be ruled out as a possible solution.

Again, to gain the absent spouse's perception of the attempted solutions, useful questions are "What would your husband say that you have tried to do to solve problems?" or "If he were here, what do you think he would say that you both have tried to do to solve this problem?" These help the client become more objective about the attempted solutions and set the stage for the client's willingness to try other solutions.

What Is the Initial Sign of Change?

When negotiating the treatment contract, the more concrete and specific the agreed-upon signs of improvement, the better. Vague statements such as "I will just know things are better," "He will feel better about himself," "We will communicate better," or "We will love each other more" should not ordinarily be accepted as goals. Instead, ask questions like the following: "When you communicate better, what would the two of you be doing different than you are doing now?" "When he feels better about himself, what do you think he would be doing different that he is not doing now?" "How do you think he will know that you are feeling better about yourself?" "What would you be doing differently when you get along better?" "What would he notice you doing differently about his habit of ignoring you?" All are useful questions in seeking to obtain statements of concrete, specific, and achievable goal(s).

Notice that these questions should seek beginning indicators, not a completed package. This is deliberately designed to establish a minimal sign of improvement that can then be amplified later.

In seeking to obtain a statement of concrete and specific treatment goals, a common mistake therapists make is to push too hard for clarity of goal with clients who are implacably vague. A pattern can easily develop where the more the therapist pushes for clarity and specificity, the more vague the client becomes. In such situations perhaps the therapist should try to match the client's vagueness with equally vague statements about the nature of the problem and suggestions for solutions.

Does the Couple Have Positive Regard for Each Other?

This is a difficult question to answer because initially the client can be so angry at the absent spouse that it is easy to miss the signs of their emotional bond and their genuine caring for each other. When couples care about each other, they are more likely to take action to improve their relationship; thus, this is an important question to keep in mind in this assessment stage. Frequently, a client's intense emotional reactions to the event such as "one more fight" or "once too many times" that precipitated seeking help can mask her positive regard for him as well as mask his willingness to change. If suggestions for change are presented in a way that is appealing to him, he may be much more cooperative with her than suspected initially.

Questions such as the following reveal the client's assessment of her own and the spouse's investment in the relationship and often provide good clinical clues as to what it is that keeps this couple in the marriage: "Why have you not left the marriage?" "What would he say is the reason he is staying?" "What do you think might be the reason he is staying?" "Do you think he loves you, in his own way?" "If I were to ask him, would he say that you love him?"

Asking questions such as "Why do you think he has not left the marriage?" or "What do you think he would say about why you are staying?" gives an added dimension to the assessment of their emotional ties based on their perception of each other. Answers such as "Because of the children," "We can't afford it," "It is against my religion," "I would miss him terribly," or "He is a good father" may give the therapist some clues as to what the client perceives as the reason she and the spouse are staying together. If the reason for staying is purely economic or religious, you may end up with a minimal goal such as making their life together a little less conflicted rather than a goal of achieving intimacy. Alternatively, the client may move toward terminating the relationship after examining what is holding it together.

Building a Plan for Action

Now that you have gathered information, the next step is to put together a workable plan of action for therapist and client. The following are some concrete, step-by-step suggestions to get you started.

Identifying the Repetitive Patterns

Detailed, step-by-step descriptions of the problematic interaction pattern between the couple can be the beginning steps to building a plan for what to do. Such patterns are often described by clients as "spinning our wheels." It is essential that the therapist include attempted solutions to this pattern. How does the therapist get this information? By asking detailed questions around the pattern, as suggested in the "Assessment" section of this chapter. Questions such as who does what, when, where, and in what sequence provide a picture of the pattern.

Examples of questions that elicit information on sequences are as follows: "What does he do that gives you the idea that he is withdrawing?" "How can you tell he is about to withdraw?" "What do you do when you notice his beginning to withdraw?" "What does he do when you remind him he is withdrawing?" "What do you do then?" "What does he do then?" "What happens next?" "How does it stop?" "What have you tried to stop this pattern?" "How would he say he tries to stop the argument?" "How often would you say this happens?"

As you determine the sequences of the problematic patterns, keep in mind that such detailed information provides clues about how to intervene and disrupt the pattern, allowing a new and different pattern to emerge. Changing one part of the sequence of the pattern may produce a quite different overall pattern in their interaction.

Where and How to Intervene

First, focus on what works. Before the therapist proceeds with plans for intervention, it is essential to ask the client about the times when she managed to solve the problems by herself as indicated in Question 4 in the "Assessment" section. "What were you doing when you successfully dealt with the situation?" "How did you circumvent the usual pattern and change it?" "What worked to defuse the usual friction point that would normally escalate into a blow-up?" "How did that work?" "How did he respond to what you did then?" "What did he do differently as a result?" These questions about *exceptions* to the problematic patterns may reveal the solutions that the client has tried and that worked. The therapist then can help the client to expand on solutions already in her repertoire. It is much easier for the client to recall and use these solutions than to create something new and unfamiliar. The therapist's task may be simply to reinforce, highlight, and monitor the client's successes and get her to repeat these when she is faced with similar problematic situations. Clients usually tend not to see these successes as strengths and dismiss them as insignificant. They look instead for big solutions for "big" problems when a simple solution is already available.

Second, when an exception cannot be found, the target of intervention may be frustrating attempted solutions. For example, "her nagging," as the husband sees it, or "his withdrawing," as the wife sees it, may be viewed as their attempts at solving his "withdrawing" and her "nagging." Therefore, the therapist may decide to interrupt this pattern of nagging and withdrawing, or withdrawing and nagging, by suggesting something else to do, such as giving him a hug whenever she feels like nagging or giving her a kiss whenever he feels like withdrawing. You can imagine what a different chain of events such a small behavior can create.

The therapist must start with thinking about what would be the most sensible thing to do, something that involves the least amount of effort. The goal is to find the simplest way to reduce the conflict while significantly altering the problematic pattern. Because of the recursive nature of interactional patterns, one small element introduced into the ongoing pattern may alter its nature, thus changing crucial interaction.

Pattern interruption can be accomplished by

Making the exception the rule
Changing the location of the pattern
Changing who is involved in the pattern
Changing the sequence of the pattern
Adding a new element or step to the pattern
Increasing or decreasing the duration of the sequence
Introducing random elements to the pattern
Changing the meaning of the behavior.

Does the Intervention Fit the Client?

However clever and ingenious the intervention, if it does not fit the client's way of life or the way she views herself, she is not likely to follow through with the therapist's suggestions. It is the therapist's task to be congruent with the client's way of seeing the world and to fit the intervention to the client as much as possible.

A common concern for therapists is what to do when the client does not follow recommendations. Instead of looking at this as "resistance," a more useful way is to take an experimental approach and consider it as the client's way of letting the therapist know that the recommendation may have been incongruent with her view. When some clients alter or modify the suggestions made by the therapist, the therapist should take this as an indication that suggestions should be offered that leave room for modification.

All interventions should lead to the same point: achieving the goal originally stated by the client. This goal should be reviewed every session. Sometimes saying out loud "When do you think we should stop meeting like this?" is a safe, humorous way to remind the client that you are keeping track of progress.

Some very outspoken clients, particularly those who are coming because of the pressure to do so from their spouse, may be quite open with unflattering opinions about the suggestions or assigned tasks. This can be looked upon as his or her openness, honesty, and a positive trait rather than a difficulty. For example, a successful businessman was brought in for therapy by his wife who thought he needed to be more openly affectionate with her. Following a session in which he was directed to keep track of when he felt more affectionate than usual, he called back and said that was "the dumbest thing" he ever heard because he always felt affectionate toward his wife. The therapist agreed that she should have known this about him and expressed appreciation for the open and honest way he let her know about how to work with him. He eventually became much more cooperative with the therapist and his wife.

How to Find Out If Things Are Getting Better

When the client returns for the next session, it is important to follow up on the tasks and the progress made. Instead of waiting to be told that things are wonderful, the therapist needs to pursue information about the differences in the client's life since the last session. "So, what have you noticed happening this past week that you would like to have continue to happen?" and "If your husband were here, what would he say was different this past week?" are examples of a therapist-initiated discussion of change. Most clients, being accustomed to look for big changes such as the spouse transforming into a perfect person overnight, may overlook small but significant changes. A persistent, investigative stance taken by the therapist may uncover many important changes that the client did not see.

When a change is discussed, it is important to follow through with questions about whether this is new behavior or behavior the clients have experienced before. The purpose is to help clients become aware of their existing problem-solving abilities, which either they had forgotten they had or have not used for some time.

What to Do When Things Get Better

The therapeutic task at this point is to encourage and reinforce the client's solution to the problems in such a way as to give her a sense of competence and control over her life, not to keep the client in treatment until she resolves all possible and potential problems (which could be a long time).

Whether her solutions involve completely new behaviors or things she knew how to do before, any behaviors that bring successful results must be reinforced. It is important to help your client reinforce her spouse's desirable behavior in order to maintain their emerging positive interaction patterns. At the same time, a gentle reminder that "life is full of ups and downs" or that changes occur in "two steps forward and one step back" helps the client keep her expectations about change realistic.

"What might be the warning sign to you that things may start to slide back?" "What might be going on between the two of you for your husband to notice that things are getting tense again?" "What would be the early sign to you that you and your husband must get back on the right track?" "How would you recognize that your husband thinks that you are starting to bring up the past?" These questions help remind the client to look for early signs of trouble and take steps to correct them.

CASE EXAMPLE

Session One

Linda, 30 years old and divorced 5 years after one-and-one-half years of marriage, owns the house she lives in, is self-supporting, and has been involved with 27-year-old Jake for the past 4 years, during two of which they lived together. Even though she "begged" him to come with her for therapy, mixed with threats of having him move out if he refused, he did refuse, saying he had control over his drinking. Besides, he did not want to be blamed for their difficulties.

Linda's main question was whether to stay or leave the relationship. The question arose anew because Jake didn't come home until very late and had been drinking, even though he had only recently had his driver's license reinstated (after 3 months of revocation because of drunk driving). The pattern involved her becoming upset with his drinking, monitoring when and how much he drank, trying to "control" his drinking, checking up on him by calling the bar where he "hung out," and so on. Jake reportedly refused to enter a treatment program, saying his drinking was not a problem.

When they get along, Linda thinks about getting married and having children and worries about her "biological clock running out," but when he drinks she sees no hope for the relationship. The therapist agreed on the goal of her making a decision about the relationship, whether to leave or stay, independent of what Jake wants. After a short intrasession consultation, the team gave her the following message:

> We are impressed that you decided to take action about the relationship by seeking help for yourself now instead of waiting for Jake to

be ready, which could be a long time. We think that for the time being your confusion about the relationship may be preventing you from making a premature decision that you may regret later. Even though it is clear that you want to make the relationship work, it takes two people to make it work, and you cannot do it alone. Because Jake seems to be more comfortable with the way things are than you, you may have to be the one to make a decision. In the meantime, while you are waiting to make the right decision, we would like you to keep track of what goes well between the two of you that you want to have continue.

Session Two

A week later Linda returned saying that they had a very good week and that Jake even came home early some evenings on his own without her reminding him. She listed a number of positive things they did together, such as visiting their families and looking for a Christmas tree together, things they did in their earlier years. The team said the following:

> We are impressed that you both got into this good phase because it is easier to take advantage of this positive phase than to start a new one. To keep it going, we suggest the following: Whenever Jake behaves himself, such as when he comes home early and not drunk, act as if this is normal, but the next day we want you to do something nice for him, something he will consider as your being good to him. While you are doing it, do not make any comments connecting his good behavior with the reward. If he asks if you are rewarding him, deny it. We want you to keep track of his reactions.
>
> If he were to come home drunk, we suggest that you pretend nothing happened. Giving him a cold shoulder or not talking to him has not worked in the past, so call your therapist instead.

The suggestion of a phone call here was designed to detour Linda's usual behavior of reacting in anger, which in turn triggered their usual pattern of angry accusations of uncaring, a cold truce, followed by remorse and promises to do better. There was one phone call during the next 3 weeks. Because it took her a while to reach the therapist, by the time they talked Linda had calmed down enough to weigh various alternatives. Linda reported that she chose to visit her sister and made sure that she was not home when Jake returned home drunk. Her doing something different to interrupt their pattern sequence led to further change.

Session Three

Three weeks later Linda returned, reporting that she had been thinking a lot about their interaction patterns such as her demanding and overreacting behavior. She and the therapist discussed how she had managed to defuse a near-disastrous episode and how she had promoted a peaceful 3 weeks. Linda reported that Jake had even volunteered to come to the session, although he backed out at the last minute. Fortunately, she was able to resist the temptation to pressure him. Further, she recognized this departure from their usual interactions. The team said the following:

> We think that you and Jake are on the right track because you two are doing many good things, which makes it easier to stay on the right track. The combination of the two of you doing something different makes it easier to stay on track. We think that one way to test your ability to trust his desire to come home on his own is to insist that he go out and stay out until a certain time. Then you will know that he is coming home on his own, not because you pressured him. Another thing you could do is to go out without telling him where you are going.

This message was designed to enlarge on the emerging positive pattern while giving Linda the option of acting independently, thus giving her a sense of control instead of waiting for Jake, which made her react to Jake in anger.

Session Four

Two weeks later things went well except for one episode when Jake decided to get drunk on the last day of his drunk driving class and missed out on a family function. This episode heightened her desire to make a decision about whether to leave or stay in the relationship, even though she managed to control her urge to give him an ultimatum to "shape up or ship out." She was afraid that he would take her up on her threat and walk out on her, which deep down she did not want.

The team complimented Linda both on her ability to keep things going well and on maintaining control. In the past, numerous ultimata about his misbehavior had not been successful. Typically, she would react impulsively to his drinking and then back out instead of executing a carefully thought-out plan.

Session Five

One month later Linda returned, very depressed about the relationship, which she saw as just "sitting on one spot and not going anywhere." Most of the time Jake had his drinking under control, but nevertheless she felt depressed about their lack of direction. She had come to the conclusion that "the problem is mine." Even though she often became so angry at Jake for "killing himself with his drinking," the question of whether to leave became more clearly her decision, independent of what Jake did. She realized that as things improved between them, each setback was more depressing to her. The message from the team was:

> We agree that the decision must be made on your own, independent of what Jake does, but we can also see how scary it is for you to think about being alone. To help you think about what it would be like, we suggest the following: Each morning toss a coin and if you get a head, all day long act as if you made a decision to leave regardless of what Jake does. When you get a tail, act all day as if you made a decision to stay no matter what Jake's behavior is. We suggest that you do this without telling Jake what you are up to, but watch his reactions.

Most people blame their ambivalence and inability to make a decision on another person and thus end up feeling helpless and out of control. A typical reaction, as with Linda, is to attempt to control the other's behavior, which usually results in conflict. The random coin-tossing task was designed to show Linda that she can act independently of what Jake does and that she can influence his behavior.

Session Six

Linda returned, saying that she "hit rock bottom" and had decided that there was no hope. Jake had been drunk for a solid week. Even though this had happened before, his having started on cocaine made her decide to give him the final word to move out. When pressed about what was different this time because she had "been there" before, Linda felt that for the first time she had become afraid of Jake's potential for physical abuse. The message from the team was:

> We agree that Jake is not likely to change. People like Jake change only when they "hit rock bottom," but our experience is that most people never head straight down, they go through a gradual up-and-

down process. No matter what happens to Jake, you are the only person who can take charge of your life, and waiting for him to make up his mind will only prolong your waiting. We are concerned that you may decide to wait to make a decision on the way to the hospital with broken bones or on the way to the morgue. It is easier to deal with guilt alone than to deal with guilt and a broken neck. It seems to us that you have been confused about looking for challenges in a relationship rather than challenges in life. You have an important decision to make in the coming weeks.

The therapist highlighted the dangerous situation Linda was putting herself in and emphasized the need to take care of herself.

Session Seven

One week later Jake moved out, and for the first time made a commitment to enter an alcohol-treatment program and was placed on the waiting list. Linda was doing well while waiting to join Jake in the treatment program. She was much less scared of being alone than she had expected. There had been a couple of contacts during which things had been very tense. Linda spent the session wondering about whether she had a tendency to choose men who have problems because her ex-husband was "addicted" to hunting and fishing. The therapist ended the session in agreement that she now had a choice of what kind of relationship she wanted.

Session Eight

Three weeks later Jake and Linda had begun a treatment program together, and he had been sober for 4 weeks. Linda bought a brand new car of her own for the first time. They went out to dinner a couple of times and had a pleasant time. Linda realized that they both must change their lifestyle if Jake were to maintain his sobriety. She was much more hopeful about the relationship than ever before but made it clear to Jake that she was not ready to have him move back home. The therapist warned her about the possibility of relapse in Jake's sobriety and discussed how she might handle it.

Session Nine

Two months later Linda returned for a follow-up session, reporting that things were continuing to improve in their relationship and that Jake was back to taking on big projects such as remodeling the house in his spare time (which he seemed to enjoy). When the therapist discussed when she would know that she was ready to have Jake move back home, Linda outlined some specific changes such as a new network of friends, more good times together without drinking, and new and different interests that would indicate changes to Jake as well as to herself. We further discussed her relationship to her parents, who are both deceased. She was maintaining her Al-Anon contacts. The therapist decided to terminate treatment. The time span for this case was 7 months.

At 6-month follow-up, Linda and Jake were continuing to do well, and Linda sent two of her co-workers with similar problems to see the therapist. At 1-year follow-up, she reported continuing to do well, they were discussing marriage and thinking of having a baby.

THERAPY WITH BOTH PARTNERS PRESENT

The "Therapy With One Partner" section of this chapter emphasized intervention with the couple system by working with one partner. The same principles described previously are applicable when working with both partners present. Of course, the preferred approach would be to meet with both partners from the beginning of treatment because the therapist can assess their motivation for change quickly and can generate more ideas for intervention. When both partners can be helped to do "something different," for example, there are twice as many opportunities for disrupting the problematic patterns. Therefore, a task of "keeping track of what you want to have continued between the two of you" leads both partners to become mindful of what the other person is looking for and encourages a quicker pattern change because both are doing something new.

The useful questions described earlier, when asked in the presence of the spouse, have a powerful impact on the couple because this is a new way of thinking about problems and solutions. Because people rarely think to ask these questions of themselves or of each other, most couples are attentive to their partner's answers to those questions. (It helps the therapist to maintain neutrality by asking similar questions of each spouse.)

Principles of assessment and intervention described earlier are applicable when both partners are present. However, some aspects of treatment need special consideration when both partners are coming for treatment.

Neutrality

Maintaining neutrality when both partners are in the session is often difficult, especially when the couple mirrors the therapist's own issues or conflicts. Therapists become much more vulnerable to taking sides when one partner obviously is "stubborn," "so unreasonable," "talks too much," "is so unrealistic about life," and so on. If such views of the client persist in the therapist's mind, this is a danger signal that the therapist may be losing objectivity.

Couples almost always present their conflicts in linear, causal terms. However, a systemic orientation to couple problems helps a therapist remember that there is no clear cause-and-effect relationship in human interactions. It is difficult to delineate who or what "caused" certain problems or whose "fault" it is that a couple disagrees.

When Communication Is a Problem

The most frequent factor that seems to cause couples to seek treatment is their perception that they disagree often on a myriad of issues such as in-laws, money, children, sex, and who is more responsible for what tasks. They are likely to attribute these differences to a communication problem.

When a client complains about a "communication problem," he or she usually means that the spouse will not agree to his or her point of view. Differences of opinion are perceived as "a problem" and even "pathological" at times, so naturally the solution to such a definition of the problem is to persuade the spouse to agree to a change of opinion. The common pattern then develops in which the more one partner tries to persuade with logic and reasoning, the more the other insists on his or her view as the correct one.

Instead of getting caught up in which is the "correct" or "right" point of view, the therapist needs to see both as valid. For example, Mr. L was convinced that his wife's lenient way of dealing with their 13-year-old Brian was contributing to his difficulty at school and disrespect toward his mother. Mrs. L, on the other hand, was convinced that her husband's rigid and authoritarian approach to Brian was causing him to rebel against authority. Therefore, she felt compelled to be lenient toward Brian to let him know that he was loved.

This seemingly irreconcilable difference was framed as their way of caring about Brian, and it was suggested that Brian needed both approaches: firmness and gentleness. The intervention was directed to helping them recognize and accept their different views as a strength rather than a problem. The therapeutic task then became to help them put their strength to use in a positive way. Thus, the couple was told to keep track of what they noticed about the other person's way of dealing with Brian that worked. They were to take turns and handle Brian in the way each thought useful. When Mr. L handled Brian in the way he thought appropriate, Mrs. L was to keep track of what her husband did that worked with Brian. And when Mrs. L handled Brian in the way she thought appropriate, Mr. L was to keep track of what his wife did that worked. The couple returned to the next session with a more positive view of each other's approach because they now saw that both approaches could work with Brian to some degree.

Conflicting Goals

As long as there is evidence that the couple cares about each other and wants to make the relationship work, what may appear to be conflicting goals, such as his wanting her to be assertive with him and her wanting him to be sensitive with her, can be viewed as two aspects of the same issue. That is, both partners want to improve their relationship. The only disagreement is how to do it. As long as the couple agrees on the outcome of the therapy, such as wanting to stay together or improvement on some aspect of their marriage, disagreement over immediate objectives usually poses no serious difficulty.

As in the case of Mr. and Mrs. L, such seemingly irreconcilable differences as romantic/unromantic, too clean/too sloppy, or too aloof/too close, for example, can be reframed as their attempts to improve the marriage.

A very troublesome situation for therapists is when the couple has opposite goals, such as her wanting to leave the marriage while he is desperate to "hang on." It may be advisable to see the partners separately in order to help them assess the situation for themselves and establish separate treatment goals. This may lead to divorce therapy, which is discussed in Chapter 4.

The Issue of Affairs

A middle-aged couple, both successful professionals in their own fields and who had raised three children, sought help around the crisis that followed the accidental discovery of the husband's affair.

The husband promptly ended the affair because it became clear to him that his wife and his marriage were more important to him than he had thought. Following this discovery, the couple had talked almost nonstop for 6 weeks before seeking help, examining every aspect of their 27-year marriage and discussing the future. Both partners agreed that they had become closer than ever, had better sex than before, and spent more time together than they had in many years. However, the wife was "obsessed" with curiosity about the other woman and with a fear of not being able to trust her husband again.

The therapist reframed their crisis as an opportunity to reexamine their relationship and make a renewed commitment to each other because they were at the developmental stage of "becoming a couple again" after many years of devoting their energy to raising children and establishing their respective careers. The wife's preoccupation with the affair and mistrust of her husband was normalized as appropriate at this time because any premature decision to trust him again might cause them to stop working on their relationship.

Unless the spouse either refuses to stop the affair or is clearly preparing to leave the marriage, it is usually helpful to view the affair as a clumsy attempt to solve problems of the relationship rather than to view it as a manifestation of pathology.

A more difficult dilemma is posed when the therapist is put in the position of knowing about an affair of which the other spouse is unaware. Agreeing to keep the secret with one spouse would make it difficult to maintain neutrality, whereas not doing so would violate the confidentiality of the professional relationship. In such situations the client's request for service and treatment goals may guide what steps to take. If the spouse having an affair is leaving the marriage, disclosure of the affair may not be as compelling as it would be if he or she is both planning to stay in the marriage and also planning to continue the affair. If the affair has ended and he or she is committed to making the marriage work, disclosure of the secret may not be relevant.

Rick and Ann requested marital therapy because of Ann's bouts of depression, which she attributed to her unsatisfactory job. They both agreed that this had affected their relationship to such a point that they had become distant, tense, and unhappy with their lives together. One area of agreement was their 3-year-old child. What complicated the problem was that both were new to the community and felt socially isolated; in addition, they were working in jobs beneath their abilities and inconsistent with their education levels.

During one individual session, Rick disclosed that he had been having an affair with Ann's younger sister for a year and a half and that he had no intention of disclosing the affair, ending it, or ending the marriage. He felt that he was quite capable of maintaining both relationships without jeopardizing the marriage and, in fact, had always made it clear to Ann that he would not commit to a monogamous relationship. The therapist was caught in the difficult dilemma of attempting the impossible task of helping the couple achieve intimacy within a context that did not lend itself to intimacy. The therapist's options were to align with Rick to keep his secret, refuse to keep the secret and clash with Rick, or terminate therapy. An individual session with Ann indicated that, indeed, she had no inkling of the affair and wanted to stay with Rick. Her depression appeared related to this vague sense of inadequacy and inability to figure out what was wrong.

Having consulted with colleagues about this dilemma, the therapist met with Rick alone and firmly told him that under the current situation she refused to continue to treat the couple because she felt placed in an untenable situation. The condition for continuing therapy was for him to either end the affair or tell Ann about it. Following a mild protest, Rick decided to end the affair and even seemed relieved. The treatment moved along well and ended on a positive note.

OUTCOME RESEARCH

Very little controlled outcome research on marital therapy, with random assignment of subjects, has been completed, and there is practically none focusing on strategic or structural modes of practice. Most of the studies completed that use random assignment and controls focus on some form of behavioral marital therapy (BMT).

From their review of controlled outcome studies employing random assignments, Baucom and Hoffman (1986) found that 10 of 13 BMT investigations indicated significant improvement in marital adjustment relative to couples on a waiting list.

Despite some evidence for the success of BMT approaches, however, the reviewers concluded that (a) evidence is lacking for the superiority of behavioral marital therapy (BMT) over nonspecific and "attention" control groups in prompting increases in marital adjustment and happiness and that (b) with certain exceptions few significant differences have been found between BMT and certain other approaches—that is, a systems approach, a group interaction approach, cognitive restructuring plus BMT, and communication training emphasizing emotional expressiveness and listening skills.

The exceptions noted were (a) a study that found BMT and conjoint-group BMT superior to conjoint-group communication therapy in altering presenting problems, communication, and marital adjustment (Hahlweg et al., 1981); (b) a study that found BMT more effective than an interaction group in increasing positive communication and self-reports of marital adjustment (O'Farrell et al., 1983); and (c) a study that found an experiential approach using Gestalt and client-centered techniques superior to BMT in increasing marital adjustment (Johnson & Greenberg, 1984).

Turning to controlled outcome studies of communication therapy (CT), Baucom and Hoffman found five studies comparing CT to waiting-list conditions (Ely et al., 1973; Epstein & Jackson, 1978; Girodo et al., 1980; Hahlweg et al., 1984; Turkewitz & O'Leary, 1981). Summarizing their review of these studies, Baucom and Hoffman noted that CT appeared to result in improved communication but produced little overall effect on marital adjustment as compared to a no-treatment condition.

Baucom and Hoffman located five studies comparing systems, insight-oriented, and cognitive behavioral approaches to various control conditions (Baucom & Lester, 1982; Boelens et al., 1980; Crowe, 1978; Epstein & Jackson, 1978; O'Farrell et al., 1983). The systems approach was combined with a BMT-treatment condition in comparing results to a waiting-list condition, and the two approaches together were superior to the waiting-list condition in increasing marital adjustment. A group-analytic approach was found to be not significantly different from a supportive control group in improving marital adjustment. Studies of two interaction approaches revealed no significant improvements in marital adjustment compared with couples on a waiting list. Cognitive restructuring followed by BMT was found to be significantly more effective than a waiting-list condition in increasing marital adjustment.

Baucom and Hoffman conclude from their review that "if the unique characteristics and needs of the couple are not considered, then no theoretical approach has demonstrated superiority" (p. 609). They caution, however, that "the current research findings do not indicate that when a particular couple requests marital therapy the treatment approach does not matter" (p. 609). It is clear from this review and others (e.g., Gurman et al., 1986) that studies are needed that reveal which approaches are most effective with which couples.

In their review of a more extensive body of outcome research, including uncontrolled studies, Gurman et al. (1986) appear to reach conclusions similar to those of Baucom and Hoffman. They find that the evidence is established for the effectiveness of behavioral therapies and that there is evidence for the probable effectiveness of psychodynamic-eclectic approaches, especially, for the latter, when "attention to out-of-awareness experience and feelings is paired with active therapist efforts to reframe and modify overt behavior and to translate the connection between inner experience and overt behavior, as in the Johnson and Greenberg (1985a, 1985b) studies" (p. 584). They rate other approaches as either "untested" (most approaches) or "effectiveness uncertain" (p. 595).

The solution-focused model presented at length in this chapter must at the present time be placed in the "untested" category as regards success in helping specifically with marital discord, although periodic follow-up calls to clients (across all categories of problems) have found that in over 70% of cases clients reported services received were helpful, that is, the problem was resolved or significant improvement made and no further help was sought or needed 3 to 8 months after termination (de Shazer et al., 1986).

CONCLUSION

This chapter on the treatment of couple problems presented a model for working with one partner when the other partner refuses treatment for various reasons, followed by application of the same model to working with both partners, along with some common clinical dilemmas that arise when treating couples. Because of the recursive nature of any relationship, it is possible to introduce a new element into the couple system by working with whomever is invested and motivated enough to make changes in the relationship, thus changing the nature of the couple system.

3

Children of Divorce:

THE DILEMMA OF A DECADE

JUDITH S. WALLERSTEIN

INCIDENCE AND SOCIAL IMPACTS OF DIVORCE

The experience of growing up in the United States has changed within the past decade. The startling prediction made in the middle 1970s (Bane, 1976) that 30% to 40% of children born in the 1970s would experience their parents' divorce has been overtaken by reality. Current trends translate into even more startling expectations. It is now estimated that 45% of all children born in 1983 will experience their parents' divorce, 35% will experience a remarriage, and 20% will experience a second divorce (A. J. Norton, Assistant Chief, Population Bureau, United States Bureau of the Census, personal communication, 1983). In 1981 approximately 22.5 million young people, or 36% of all children under 18, were living in a family other than the traditional two-parent family. This group included 11.4 million children living with their mothers only; 1.2 million living with their fathers only; 6.4 million living with one biological parent and one stepparent; and the remainder living with adoptive parents, grandparents, or in foster homes. For black children, living with two parents is already less common than living with one parent (Zill, 1983).

Although the incidence of divorce has increased across all age groups, the most dramatic rise has occurred among young adults (Norton, 1980). As a result, children in divorcing families are younger than in previous years and include more preschool children. In 1981 31% of the country's children aged 5 or younger lived with their mothers only (United States Bureau of the Census, 1982b). A recent study of California couples divorcing between the years 1966 and

AUTHOR'S NOTE: The Center for the Family in Transition, of which the author is the Executive Director, is supported by a grant from the San Francisco Foundation. The Zellerback Family Fund supported the author's research in the California Children of Divorce Project, one of the sources for this chapter. A slightly different version of this paper has been published in *Psychiatry Update: The American Psychiatric Association Annual Review, Vol. III.* L. Grinspoon (Ed.), pp. 144–158, 1984.

1977 found that marital dissolution was associated with the presence in the family of a child age 2 or under (Rankin & Maneker, 1983). There is also evidence that very young children are predominant among those whose custody and visitation is in contest. Pearson reported on a tally of children involved in mediated cases in four widely separated court systems: 44% of the children in dispute were 5 years old or younger (Principal Investigator of the Divorce Mediation Research Project, Denver, Colorado, personal communication, 1982).

Although many children weather the stress of marital discord and family breakup without psychopathological sequelae, a significant number falter along the way. Children of divorce are significantly overrepresented in outpatient psychiatric, family agency, and private practice populations compared with children in the general population (Gardner, 1976; Kalter, 1977; Tessman, 1977; Tooley, 1976). The best predictors of mental health referrals for school-aged children are parental divorce or parental loss as a result of death (Felner, Stolberg, & Cowen, 1975). A national survey of adolescents whose parents had separated and divorced by the time the children were seven years old found that 30% of these children had received psychiatric or psychological therapy by the time they reached adolescence compared with 10% of adolescents in intact families (Zill, 1983).

A longitudinal study in northern California followed 131 children who were age 3 to 18 at the decisive separation. At the 5-year mark, the investigators found that more than one-third were suffering with moderate to severe depression (Wallerstein & Kelly, 1980a). These findings are especially striking because the children were drawn from a nonclinical population and were accepted into the study only if they had never been identified before the divorce as needing psychological treatment and only if they were performing at age-appropriate levels in school. Therefore, the deterioration observed in these children's adjustment occurred largely following the family breakup.

Finally, several studies suggest that children of divorce show lower achievement and experience greater difficulty in learning than their classmates from two-parent families. One national survey reported a higher incidence of disrupted learning, erratic attendance, higher dropout rates, increased tardiness, and deteriorated social behavior among youngsters from single-parent families (Brown, 1980). Another survey revealed that 15% of teenagers living with divorced mothers had been expelled or suspended from school at some time between elementary school and high school, whereas only 3% of teenagers from low-conflict, intact families had sustained a similar experience (Zill, 1983). Also relevant to the children's experience is the fact that divorced adults use inpatient and outpatient mental health services at a significantly higher rate than adults in intact marriages (Bloom, White, & Asher, 1979).

Divorce differs from many other stressful childhood experiences in that its immediate impact is not confined to children in the divorcing family or even to those in the immediate social or psychological vicinity. Teachers in widely separated communities report that after a family quarrel children from intact families come to school asking anxiously, "Will my parents divorce?" The high proportion of young adults who are postponing marriage today may well reflect anxieties associated with the accelerated breakup of marital relationships (Cherlin, 1981). The long-range consequences of the widespread pattern of conjugal succession (Furstenberg, 1982) for society and for future forms of the family are, of course, unknown. Some researchers have cautiously reported "a real, although small, amount of intergenerational transmission of marital instability" (Pope & Mueller, 1979, p. 109). Other recent research has revealed an unexpectedly powerful commitment to ideals of fidelity and lifelong monogamy among children of divorce as they enter young adulthood many years after the family crisis (Wallerstein, 1978).

The many divorced families in our midst and the burdens imposed on parent and child are familiar aspects of the social scene and have become part of our national consciousness. Surely it is no accident that the widely acclaimed 1982 film *E.T.* depicts both the central character, Elliott, a sober and sensitive child, and his alter ego, E.T., a funny-looking extraterrestrial child with super coping skills, as lonely children who are cut off from home base and who must fend for themselves in a world where adults are unsympathetic and sometimes hostile and dangerous. Also no accident, the film notes almost casually that Elliott's father has run off to Mexico with another woman while his unhappy mother careens her way through work, child care, and household chores with little time or capacity left for pleasure in her children. As the author has noted elsewhere, *E.T.* captures and offers almost *en passant* some essential truths about today's family (Wallerstein, 1982). In a great many American homes today the overburdened and unhappy single parents can provide only limited nurturance to their children, and a great many children, especially young children, feel cut off and lonely, estranged from parents whose behavior they find incomprehensible or frightening.

Still another aspect of divorce distinguishes it from other stresses of childhood: Divorce is inextricably intertwined with family law and family policy. Marital dissolution occurs within a public forum in which the conflicting rights and complementary roles and responsibilities of men, women, and children are basic issues. At stake is the capacity of the family following divorce to carry out its child-rearing functions adequately. Accordingly, a lively debate has focused on how to safeguard the child's interests subsequent to marital rupture.

Much of the recent debate within the political arena and the courts has been passionate and shrill, infused with the private angers and public indignation of men and women who are engaged in struggles with each other over real or imagined wrongs, over power, and over money. The various parties have generally agreed with the principle that the complex issues should be decided carefully with full regard to the available knowledge, the grave issues at stake, and the best interests of the child. However, the specific policies that have emerged have too often reflected political expediencies and compromises. Major policy changes are often too readily adopted, radically altering the lives of thousands of children, without a searching examination of the issues, without adequate knowledge, and without building in methods for evaluating the consequences of these changes. When this occurs, significant numbers of children can be placed at even greater risk, and the system, the law, or both may end up adding substantially to children's suffering.

Although policy makers, legislators, and judges have increasingly sought support from the findings of behavioral science and guidance from the mental health profession, the accumulation of psychological knowledge has not kept up with the rapid pace of family law. Knowledge is fragmentary and insufficient to address the many changes proposed for family policy. Despite the wide acknowledgment given to the interface of law and mental health, the major task of building cooperation and mutual understanding lies ahead. The subtleties of psychological thinking and the shadings of individual differences that are so critical to the clinical process translate poorly into the arenas of courts and legislatures. Moreover, the several years of follow-up required to assess the impacts of changed circumstances or family arrangements are ill-suited to the pressured agendas of the political and judicial process.

THE NATURE OF DIVORCE

We have within the past decade begun to acquire solid knowledge in many critical areas: the nature of the divorcing process, the responses of children and adolescents by age and sex, the immediate and long-lasting impacts of divorce on children and adults and on parent–child relationships, factors in good and poor outcomes in the short- and long-term perspective, custody and visitation, the role of the father and the role of the visiting parent, and the staying power of anger and the dangers of continued interparental conflict to the child. We also have begun to develop a range of intervention methods and strategies aimed specifically at this population. Many methodological issues remain, however, related to sample sizes, sampling techniques, the need for more extensive cross-sectional and longitudinal studies, the need for appropriate comparison groups, and the need to study divorce within diverse social and cultural contexts and to examine different custodial and visitation arrangements. There also remains the major issue of translating the broad goals of primary and secondary prevention into intervention theory and program. In neither research nor treatment has it been easy to maintain in focus the many complex issues that converge in the divorcing family. The unfortunate tendency, as Richards (1982) has suggested in a recent overview of the field, is to collapse all of the varieties of divorce into a single category as if divorce were a single event occurring at a precise moment in time.

Perhaps even more important than recognizing these issues is to acknowledge that the examination of divorce leads us into an uncharted terrain in our understanding of child development, of parent–child relationships, and of the complex interrelationships of the child and both parents, whether they live together or separately. What is striking overall is that the entire pattern of conscious and unconscious psychological needs, wishes, and expectations that parents and children bring to each other is so profoundly altered under the impact of marital rupture and its many ripple effects. Yet neither developmental nor clinical theory has incorporated the new observations that have come out of the work with separation, divorce, and remarriage.

The Process of Divorce

Divorce is a long, drawn-out process of radically changing family relationships that has several stages, beginning with the marital rupture and its immediate aftermath, continuing over several years of disequilibrium, and finally coming to rest with the stabilization of a new postdivorce or remarried family unit. A complex chain of changes, many of them unanticipated and unforeseeable, are set into motion by the marital rupture and are likely to occupy a significant portion of the child or adolescent's growing years. As the author and her colleague have reported elsewhere, women in the California Children of Divorce study required three to three-and-one-half years following the decisive separation before they achieved a sense of order and predictability in their lives (Wallerstein & Kelly, 1980a). This figure probably underestimates the actual time trajectory of the child's experience of divorce. A prospective study reported that parent–child relationships began to deteriorate many years prior to the divorce decision and that the adjustment of many children in these families began to fail long before the decisive separation (Morrison, 1982). This view of the divorcing process as long lasting accords with the perspective of a group of young people who reported at a 10-year follow-up that their entire childhood or adolescence had been dominated by the family crisis and its extended aftermath (Wallerstein, 1978).

Stages in the Process

The three broad, successive stages in the divorcing process, while they overlap, are nevertheless clinically distinguishable. *The acute phase* is precipitated by the decisive separation and the decision to divorce. This stage is often marked by steeply escalating conflict between the adults, physical violence, severe distress, depression accompanied by suicidal ideation, and a range of behaviors reflecting a spilling of aggressive and sexual impulses. The adults frequently react with severe ego regression and not unusually behave at odds with their more customary demeanor. Sharp disagreement in the wish to end the marriage is very common, and the narcissistic injury to the person who feels rejected sets the stage for rage, sexual jealousy, and depression. Children are generally not shielded from this parental conflict or distress. Confronted by a marked discrepancy in images of their parents, children do not have the assurance that the bizzare or depressed behaviors and moods will subside. As a result, they are likely to be terrified by the very figures they usually rely on for nurturance and protection.

As the acute phase comes to a close, usually within the first 2 years of the divorce decision, the marital partners gradually disengage from each other and pick up the new tasks of reestablishing their separate lives. *The transitional phase* is characterized by ventures into new, more committed relationships; new work, school, and friendship groups; and sometimes new settings, new lifestyles, and new geographical locations. This phase is marked by alternating success and failure, encouragement and discouragement, and it may also last for several years. Children observe and participate in the many changes of this period. They share the trials and errors and the fluctuations in mood. For several years life may be unstable, and home may be unsettled.

Finally, *the postdivorce phase* ensues with the establishment of a fairly stable single-parent or remarried household. Eventually three out of four divorced women and four out of five divorced men reenter wedlock (Cherlin, 1981). Unfortunately, though, remarriage does not bring immediate tranquility into the lives of the family members. The early years of the remarriage are often encumbered by ghostly presences from the earlier failed marriages and by the actual presences of children and visiting parents from the prior marriage or marriages. Several studies suggest widespread upset among children and adolescents following remarriage (Crohn, Brown, Walker, & Beir, 1981; Goldstein, 1974; Kalter, 1977). A large-scale investigation that is still in process reports long-lasting friction around visitation (Jacobson, 1983).

Changes in Parent–Child Relationships

Diminished Capacity to Parent

Parents experience a diminished capacity to parent their children during the acute phase of the divorcing process and often during the transitional phase as well (Wallerstein & Kelly, 1980a). This phenomenon is widespread and can be considered an expectable, divorce-specific change in parent–child relationships. At its simplest level this diminished parenting capacity appears in the household disorder that prevails in the aftermath of divorce, in the rising tempers of custodial parent and child, in reduced competence and a greater sense of helplessness in the custodial parent, and in lower expectations of the child for appropriate social behavior (Hetherington, Cox, & Cox, 1978; 1982). Diminished parenting also entails a sharp decline in emotional sensitivity and support for the child; decreased pleasure in the parent–child relationship; decreased attentiveness to the child's needs and wishes; less talk, play, and interaction with the child; and a steep escalation in inappropriate expression of anger. One not uncommon component of the parent–child relationship coincident with the marital breakup is the adult's conscious or unconscious wish to abandon the child and thus to erase the unhappy marriage in its entirety. Child neglect can be a serious hazard.

Parental Dependence on the Child

In counterpoint to the temporary emotional withdrawal from the child, the parent may develop a dependent, sometimes passionate, attachment to the child or adolescent, beginning with the breakup and lasting throughout the lonely postseparation years (Wallerstein, 1985). Parents are likely to lean on the child and turn to the child for help, placing the child in a wide range of roles such as confidante, advisor, mentor, sibling, parent, caretaker, lover, concubine, extended conscience or ego control, ally within the marital conflict, or pivotal supportive presence in staving off depression or even suicide. This expectation that children should not only take much greater responsibility for themselves but also should provide psychological and social support for the distressed parent is sufficiently widespread to be considered a divorce-specific response along with that of diminished parenting. Such relationships frequently develop with an only child or with a very young, even a preschool, child. Not accidentally, issues of custody and visitation often arise with regard to the younger children. While such disputes, of course, reflect the generally unresolved anger of the marriage and the divorce, they may also reflect the intense emotional need of one or both parents for the young child's constant presence (Wallerstein, 1985).

Parents may also lean more appropriately on the older child or adolescent. Many youngsters become proud helpers, confidantes, and allies in facing the difficult postdivorce period (Weiss, 1979b). Other youngsters draw away from close involvement out of their fears of engulfment, and they move precipitously out of the family orbit, sometimes before they are developmentally ready.

The Visiting Relationship

The visiting relationship has no real counterpart in the intact family. Insufficient recognition has been given to the difficulty involved with transplanting a parent–child relationship that has developed within the rich soil of family life into the relatively impoverished, strange, and limited ground of the visit. A great many close parent–child relationships fail to take root outside of the family, but many parent–child relationships that were failing within the unhappy marriage take on new life within the narrow constraints of the visit (Wallerstein & Kelly, 1980b). Although the tensions stirred by the visits are likely in many, if not most, families to be very intense, these tensions tend to diminish over time. The extent of the father's visiting depends more on his feelings about the divorce, on the children's ages and responsiveness, and on his and their capacity to overcome the inherent difficulties in the visiting relationship than on the presence of children within the remarriage or on his own psychological stability (Kelly, 1981; Kelly & Wallerstein, 1976; Wallerstein & Huntington, 1982). In a national survey of children between the ages of 11 and 16 from divorced families, close to half the children had had no contact with their outside parent, customarily the father, during the 5 preceding years (Furstenberg, 1982). There is encouraging evidence that a brief intervention immediately after the decisive separation can turn this around and significantly reduce the incidence of disrupted contact between father and child. For example, less than 10% of the children in the California Children of Divorce project had not had any contact with their fathers at the 5-year mark (Wallerstein & Kelly, 1980a).

The emotional importance to children of their relationships with both parents does not become any less following divorce. Although the mother's caretaking and psychological roles become increasingly central in families where the mother has custody, there is no evidence that the father's psychological significance declines correspondingly. The children's yearning for the father is poignantly evident following divorce, and the visiting relationship remains centrally important to children and their well-being long after the parents' separation, divorce, or remarriage. The self-image of a child reared in a two-parent family prior to a divorce appears tied to both biological parents, regardless of the parent's subsequent physical presence within the family (Kelly, 1981; Wallerstein & Kelly, 1980a).

CHILDREN'S REACTIONS TO DIVORCE

Initial Responses

Children and adolescents experience separation and its aftermath as the most stressful period of their lives. The family rupture evokes an acute sense of shock, intense anxiety, and profound sorrow. Many children are relatively content and even well-parented in families where one or both parents are unhappy. Few youngsters experience any relief with the divorce decision, and those who do are usually older and have witnessed physical violence or open conflict between their parents. The child's early responses are governed neither by an understanding of issues leading to the divorce nor by the fact that divorce has a high incidence in the community. To the child, divorce signifies the collapse of the structure that provides support and protection. The child reacts as to the cutting of his or her lifeline.

The initial suffering of children and adolescents in response to a marital separation is compounded by realistic fears and fantasies about catastrophies that the divorce will bring in its wake. Children suffer with a pervasive sense of vulnerability because they feel that the protective and nurturant function of the family has given way. They grieve over the loss of the noncustodial parent, over the loss of the intact family, and often over the multiple losses of neighborhood, friends, and school. Children also worry about their distressed parents. They are concerned about who will take care of the parent who has left and whether the custodial parent will be able to manage alone. They experience intense anger toward one or both parents whom they hold responsible for disrupting the family. Some of their anger is reactive and defends them against their own feelings of powerlessness, their concern about being lost in the shuffle, and their fear that their needs will be disregarded as the parents give priority to their own wishes and needs. Some children, especially young children, suffer with guilt over fantasied misdeeds that they feel may have contributed to the family quarrels and led to the divorce. Others feel that it is their responsibility to mend the broken marriage (Wallerstein & Kelly, 1980a).

The responses of the child also must be considered within the social context of the divorce and in particular within the loneliness and social isolation that so many children experience. Children face the tensions and sorrows of divorce with little help from anybody else. Fewer than 10% of the children in the California Children of Divorce study had any help at the time of the crisis from adults outside the family although many people, including neighbors, pediatricians, ministers, rabbis, and family friends, knew the family and the children (Wallerstein & Kelly, 1980a). Thus, another striking feature of divorce as a childhood stress is that it occurs in the absence of or falling away of customary support.

Developmental Factors

Developmental factors are critical to the responses of children and adolescents at the time of the marital rupture. Despite significant individual differences in the child, in the family, and in parent–child relations, the child's age and developmental stage appear to be the most important factors governing the initial response. The child's dominant needs, his or her capacity to perceive and understand family events, the central psychological preoccupation and conflict, the available repertoire of defense and coping strategies, and the dominant patterning of relationships and expectations all reflect the child's age and developmental stage.

A major finding in divorce research has been the common patterns of response within different age groups (Wallerstein & Kelly, 1980a). The age groups that share significant commonalities in perceptions, responses, underlying fantasies, and behaviors are the preschool ages 3 to 5, early school age or early latency ages 5½ to 8, later school age or latency ages 8 to 11, and, finally, adolescent ages 12 to 18 (Kelly & Wallerstein, 1977; Wallerstein, 1977; Wallerstein & Kelly, 1974; 1975; 1980a). These responses, falling as they do into age-related groupings, may reflect children's responses to acute stress generally, not only their responses to marital rupture.

Observations about preschool children derived from longitudinal studies in two widely different regions, namely, Virginia and northern California, are remarkably similar in their findings (Hetherington, 1979; Hetherington et al., 1978; 1982; Wallerstein & Kelly, 1975, 1980a). Preschool children are likely to show regression following one parent's departure from the household, and the regression usually occurs in the most recent developmental achievement of the child. Intensified fears are frequent and are evoked by routine separations from the custodial parent during the day and at bedtime. Sleep disturbances are also frequent, with preoccupying fantasies of many of the little children being fear of abandonment by both parents. Yearning for the departed parent is intense. Young children are likely to become irritable and demanding and to behave aggressively with parents, with younger siblings, and with peers.

Children in the 5- to 8-year old group are likely to show open grieving and are preoccupied with feelings of concern and longing for the departed parent. Many share the terrifying fantasy of replacement. "Will my daddy get a new dog, a new mommy, a new little boy?" were the comments of several boys in this age group. Little girls wove elaborate Madame Butterfly fantasies, asserting that the departed father would some day return to them, that he loved them "the best." Many of the children in this age group could not believe that the divorce would endure. About half suffered a precipitous decline in their school work (Kelly & Wallerstein, 1979).

In the 9- to 12-year-old group the central response often seems to be intense anger at one or both parents for causing the divorce. In addition, these children suffer with grief over the loss of the intact family and with anxiety, loneliness, and the humiliating sense of their own powerlessness. Youngsters in this age group often see one parent as the "good" parent and the other as "bad," and they appear especially vulnerable to the blandishments of one or the other parent to engage in marital battles. Children in later latency also have a high potential for assuming a helpful and empathic role in the care of a needy parent. School performances and peer relationships suffered a decline in approximately one-half of these children (Wallerstein & Kelly, 1974).

Adolescents are very vulnerable to their parents' divorce. The precipitation of acute depression, accompanied by suicidal preoccupation and acting out, is frequent enough to be alarming. Anger can be intense. Several instances have been reported of direct violent attacks on custodial parents by young adolescents who had not previously shown such behavior (Springer & Wallerstein, 1983). Preoccupied with issues of morality, adolescents may judge the parents' conduct during the marriage and the divorce, and they may identify with one parent and do battle against the other. Many become anxious about their own future entry into adulthood, concerned that they may experience marital failure like their parents (Wallerstein & Kelly, 1974). By way of contrast, however, researchers have also called attention to the adolescent's impressive capacity to grow in maturity and independence as they respond to the family crisis and the parents' need for help (Weiss, 1979a).

Sex Differences

In the preschool and latency ages boys are reported to be more vulnerable than are girls to the acute stress of the marital rupture as well as to the more chronic stresses of the transitional phase. Major differences between preschool boys and girls in a wide range of cognitive, social, and developmental measures have been reported (Hetherington et al., 1982). Although divorce did not appear to disrupt traditional sex-role typing for girls, 2 years after the divorce boys were scoring lower on male preference and higher on female preference on the sex-role preference tests. The boys were also spending more time playing with girls and with younger children. They showed an affective narrowness and a constriction in fantasy and social play and were more socially isolated than were their female peers.

Sex differences also emerged in the California Children of Divorce study. Although boys and girls did not differ in their overall psychological adjustment at the time of the marital breakup, by 18 months later the boys' psychological adjustment had deteriorated markedly, whereas that of the girls had greatly improved, making for a significant gap between the two groups (Wallerstein & Kelly, 1980a). Other evidence further suggests that marital turmoil has a greater impact on boys than it does on girls both in divorced families and in intact, discordant families (Block, Block, & Morrison, 1981; Emery & O'Leary, 1982; Rutter, 1970).

How much of this differential effect between the sexes is mediated by the mother having custody is unknown. The Texas custody research project compared a small group of latency-aged children in the custody of the same-sex parent with a matched group in the custody of the opposite-sex parent and with a matched group of children in intact families. Again, the result suggested that the sex of the custodial parent has a direct bearing on the child's social adjustment. Children in the custody of the same-sex parent showed more maturity, greater sociability, more independence, and less demanding behavior than did children in the custody of the opposite-sex parent (Santrock & Warshak, 1979; Warshak & Santrock, 1983).

Finally, a confounding set of observations are reported from the 10-year follow-up study of the California Children of Divorce project. Findings here suggest that girls from divorced families may have a more stormy adolescence and a more conflict-ridden entry into young adulthood than do their male counterparts. A significant number of the young women were caught up in a web of short-lived sexual relationships, and they described themselves as fearful of commitment, anticipating infidelity and betrayal (Wallerstein, 1978). It may be that boys, especially young boys, have a more difficult time immediately following the divorce but that girls find adolescence a particularly hazardous time. An important research agenda resides in the questions of whether and how and at what ages the development of boys and girls is mediated by custodial and visitation arrangements.

Long-Range Outcomes

The child's initial response to divorce should be distinguished from his or her long-range development and psychological adjustment. No single theme appears among all of those children who enhance, consolidate, or continue their good development after the divorce crisis has finally ended. Nor is there a single theme that appears among all of those who deteriorate either moderately or markedly. Instead, the author and her colleague (Wallerstein & Kelly, 1980a) have found a set of complex configurations in which the relevant components appear to include (a) the extent to which the parent has been able to resolve and put aside conflict and anger and to make use of the relief from conflict provided by the divorce (Emery, 1982; Jacobson, 1978a, b, c); (b) the course of the custodial parent's handling of the child and the resumption or improvement of parenting within the home (Hess & Camara, 1979); (c) the extent to which the child does not feel rejected by the noncustodial or visiting parent and the extent to which this relationship has continued regularly and kept pace with the child's growth; (d) the extent to which the divorce has helped to attenuate or dilute a psychopathological parent–child relationship; (e) the range of personality assets and deficits that the child brought to the divorce, including both the child's history in the predivorce family and his or her capacities in the present, particularly intelligence, the capacity for fantasy, social maturity, and the ability to turn to peers and adults; (f) the availability to the child of a supportive human network (Tessman, 1977); (g) the absence in the child of continued anger and depression; and (h) the sex and age of the child.

The central hazards that divorce poses to children's psychological health and development are the diminished or disrupted parenting and the interparental conflict that so often follow and that can become consolidated within the postdivorce family. When parents undertake divorce thoughtfully after careful consideration of alternatives; when they have anticipated the psychological, social, and economic consequences for all involved; when they have provided comfort and appropriate understanding to the children; and when they have arranged to maintain good parent–child relationships, then the children are not likely to suffer developmental interference or enduring psychological distress. Alternatively, if the divorce is undertaken primarily to humiliate, anger, or grieve a partner; if anger and unhappiness dominate the postdivorce relationship; if the children are poorly supported or informed, coopted as allies, fought over, or viewed as extensions of the adults; if the child's relationship with one or both parents is impoverished and disrupted; and if the child feels rejected, then the most likely outcome for the children is developmental interference, depression, or both (Wallerstein & Kelly, 1980a).

Another way to conceptualize outcome in divorce is to consider whether the child him- or herself has been able to master successfully the tasks posed by the divorce. Although the child's long-range adjustment is significantly related to many factors in the postdivorce family, his or her own capacity and efforts at mastery are also significant in the ultimate outcome. To maintain psychic integrity and development, the child engages in mastery efforts that can be seen as a series of six coping tasks, beginning with the time of the marital rupture and culminating with the close of adolescence. These tasks represent a substantial addition to the usual tasks of growing up (Wallerstein, 1983).

DISPUTED CUSTODY AND VISITATION

Aptly described as "children of Armageddon" (Watson, 1969), the most stressed children of divorce are those who are the objects of continuing acrimonious legal battles between their divorcing parents. Approximately 10% of divorcing families with children go on to full-scale legal battles, and one-third return to court for modification of the original orders (Freed & Foster, 1974). Most families make custody and visitation arrangements without recourse to the courts. Even these private arrangements occur under the shadow of the law, and in contested cases they are very much influenced by the court's decision making (Mnookin & Kornhauser, 1979).

While those adults who engage in continuous conflict over their children have been insufficiently studied, some evidence suggests a clustering of severe psychiatric disorder among them (Tall & Johnston, 1982). The causes of continued legal contests between divorcing spouses are complex and multidetermined. A history of repeated unmourned losses in one or both adults is not uncommon and may go hand in hand with a pathological dependence on the constant presence of the child to ward off depression. In addition, the severe narcissistic injury of the divorce may trigger a rage against the divorcing spouse that continues via the conflict over the children, undimmed by the passage of years and binding the partners to each other.

The experiences of the past decade have cast increasing doubt on the appropriateness of the court as a forum for the resolution of these issues. Not only is it acknowledged that the adversarial system is poorly suited to resolving family conflict, but it is also recognized that the adversarial system adds significantly to the already overwhelming stress of the children and adults.

Mediation

Mediation has taken hold quickly as an intervention for divorcing families in dispute (Coogler, 1978; Haynes, 1981). Some programmatic issues are unresolved, however, such as (a) whether mediation falls within the domain of the attorney, the mental health professional, or both, working separately or in tandem, and (b) what should be required in the way of licensing, professional standards, and training. A more important issue is whether mediation will live up to its early promise. An important concern is that the mediator's role may leave the child's interests without adequate protection. The mediation process makes the assumption that the child's interests will be protected by the parents, but this may prove to be unwarranted, considering the impaired judgment of parents who are in intense conflict (Huntington, 1982).

In January 1981 California enacted mandatory mediation for divorcing families who are disputing custody, visitation, or both. Because California has been a leader in family law, other states are likely to follow suit in the near future. Mandatory mediation has to date achieved a high settlement rate, ranging from 55% to 85% of the disputing families in the different counties. Preliminary reports from a study of mediation in four court systems (Hartford, Denver, Minneapolis, and Los Angeles) indicate that families who use mediation are pleased with the process and the outcome but that a significant number reject mediation (Pearson, Thoennes, & Vanderkooi, 1982).

Another reflection of the trend away from the adversarial system has been mental health professionals' increasing conviction that mental health experts should serve the court in its decision-making process rather than act as a partisan for one party to the dispute (Derdeyn, 1975, 1976, 1978; Solow & Adams, 1977). The growing conviction among practitioners is that "the adversarial system is ill suited to deal optimally with custody conflicts, causes psychopathology in parents who resort to it to settle custody conflicts, is psychically detrimental to children, and is therefore antithetical to good psychiatric practice" (Gardner, 1982, p. 11). The Group for the Advancement of Psychiatry (1980) recognized the impact of the entire family's interrelationships during the postdivorce years and argued that the whole family be examined before a custody or visitation decision.

Custody

The changing roles of men and women are mirrored in the courts and in legislation regarding custody and visitation. Our society has moved away from the expectation that single-parent custody, combined with reasonable visitation with the noncustodial parent, is the expectable legacy of divorce. Early in this decade the courts relied extensively on the concept of "the psychological parent" (Goldstein, Freud, & Solnit, 1973), assuming that except under unusual circumstances or for older children the mother would fulfill this role. Recent attention has focused on the contribution of the father as parent and as potential primary parent (Jacobs, 1982; Santrock & Warshak, 1979; Warshak & Santrock, 1983). Actually, custodial arrangements have changed little throughout the nation over the past 10 years, and approximately 90% of children of divorce remain in their mother's custody (United States Bureau of the Census, 1982b). At the same time, however, approximately one-half of the states have enacted legislation that permits joint custody. The push in some states, notably California, is toward joint custody as the presumptive preference for all divorcing families, including families in dispute. Community attitudes and social policy are in flux.

Many custodial arrangements fall under the rubric of joint custody. These include joint legal custody, in which the child resides with one parent but both parents share decision making in areas yet unclarified, and joint physical custody, in which the child may divide his or her time in varying combinations between each parent's home.

Joint physical custody selected by both parents can be regarded as a new family form or structure. Under the appropriate circumstances it may have advantages for the divorcing family, especially perhaps in the transition from divorce to remarriage. Some research suggests that children in latency can benefit greatly from joint physical custody when the arrangement is accompanied by cooperation between parents, by strong, steadfast commitment to the parenting role, and by genuine love and respect for the children (Steinman, 1981). In a comprehensive review of the literature on joint custody, Clingembeel and Reppucci (1982) propose a detailed research agenda that would encompass, along with the characteristics of child, parent, and community, the expectable changes in the family life cycle, notably remarriage, and the changing developmental needs of child and parent.

Because parents in most places are free to select joint physical or legal custody for their children without recourse to the courts, subject only to fairly routine court approval, the sticking point has been whether the law should award joint custody in the face of one parent's strong opposition. Except for one admittedly very limited tally of court returns of such families (Ilfeld, Ilfield, & Alexander,

1982), no research findings bear directly on this issue. By and large, experts in psychiatry and law have opposed joint physical custody unless the parents agree fully on the arrangement (Benedek & Benedek, 1979; Gardner, 1982; Goldzband, 1980).

FUTURE DIRECTIONS

Despite the accumulating reports of the difficulties that many chidren in divorced families experience, society has on the whole been reluctant to regard children of divorce as a special group at risk. Notwithstanding the magnitude of the population affected and the widespread implications for public policy and law, community attention has been very limited; research has been poorly supported; and appropriate social, psychological, economic, or preventive measures have hardly begun to develop. Recently the alarm has been sounded in the national press about the tragically unprotected and foreshortened childhoods of children of divorce and their subsequent difficulties in reaching maturity (Winn, 1983). Perhaps this reflects a long-overdue awakening of community concern.

The agenda for research on marital breakdown, separation, divorce, and remarriage and the roads that families travel between each of these way stations is long and has been cited repeatedly in this chapter. The knowledge that we have acquired is considerable but the knowledge that we still lack is critical. More knowledge is essential in order to provide responsible advice to parents; to consult effectively with the wide range of other professionals whose daily work brings them in contact with these families; to design and mount education, treatment, or prevention programs; and to provide guidelines for informed social policy.

The research priority should be to examine the many issues on the interface of marital breakdown and social policy because the social hazards of uninformed legislative and judicial decisions are grave. Priority in the development of interventions should be given to special high-risk groups. These groups include adolescents and children living in families where divorce represents the first step in the deterioration or disintegration of the family and children who are experiencing a second divorce. Very young children are also at high risk, they represent an entirely unexamined group, and they are likely at the time of the marital breakdown to experience disruption of their relationship with both parents at the same time. A final high-risk group includes those children in postdivorce families where the custodial and visitation arrangements are fragile and where the divorcing process itself fails to reach closure or resolution.

Although children of divorce have been identified as a major group for preventive intervention, few programs have been developed (Philips, 1983). A major obstacle to designing and implementing preventive programs is the paucity of appropriate intervention theory and clinical knowledge. The vast body of theory and clinical wisdom accumulated over the decades of practicing psychotherapy still has no counterpart in preventive intervention. The dominant paradigm of crisis theory and crisis intervention, based on the early work of Lindemann (1944) and Caplan (1955), may be more applicable to acute stress and bereavement than to the chain of events in marital breakdown and the extended time trajectory of the divorce process. What are critically needed are prevention programs aimed specifically at divorcing families and based on the considerable knowledge we already have regarding the stages in the divorcing process, the predictable changes in parent–child relationships, and the configurations of factors associated with good and poor outcomes.

Finally, we must recognize that almost all divorce research and interventions have dealt with predominantly white, middle-class children in communities where the two-parent nuclear family is the dominant family structure. The usefulness of our observations could therefore be limited to these communities. On the other hand, more extensive research could show that the responses to major life experiences of loss, death, and divorce are rooted in developmental factors that span broad social, economic, racial, and ethnic differences.

4
Treating Issues Related to Divorce and Separation

DOUGLAS H. SPRENKLE

As noted in Chapter 3, literature related to the treatment of divorce and separation has not kept pace with the outpouring of empirical and theoretical analyses of these phenomena. In fact, the interventions to be described in this chapter have gained public as well as professional respectibility only recently. Many interventionists have apparently associated divorce with pathology and have believed that divorce therapy is somehow "anti-family" or "anti-marriage" (Sprenkle, 1985). As Brown (1976, p. 159), a pioneer in divorce intervention, wrote:

> Historically, the marriage centers wanted no part of divorce. Success meant keeping couples together, not helping them end their marriage. Those who saw a need for divorce counseling and tried to interest the established marriage and family agencies received a chilly response until very recently. Therefore, as with many new ideas, the innovative work in developing divorce services was done outside the mainstream, usually in small, private organizations which focused on one or more aspects of divorce.

The new form of family intervention to be described in this chapter—divorce therapy—has developed not only in response to the large increase in the number of divorces but also because of an increased awareness that divorcing people need help uncoupling (Olson, Russell, & Sprenkle, 1980). It is striking, however, that although overview articles or book chapters on divorce therapy began appearing in the literature (Brown, 1976; Kaslow, 1981; Storm, Sprenkle, & Williamson, 1985) and books have been written about certain special topics such as mediation (Coogler, 1978; Haynes, 1981; Irving, 1980) and treating postdivorce families (Hansen, 1982; Sager et al., 1983; Visher & Visher, 1979), by 1986 only several general texts on divorce therapy had been published (Rice & Rice, 1986; Sprenkle, 1985).

DEFINING DIVORCE THERAPY

Viewed as ideal types, marital therapy could be described as relationship treatment that focuses on maintaining, enhancing, and strengthening the marital bond. Conversely, divorce therapy could be described as relationship treatment that focuses on decreasing the function of the marital bond with the eventual goal of dissolving it (Brown, 1976).

Such a clear-cut dichotomy, however, often is not found in clinical practice. Marital and divorce therapy are not so much distinct entities as they are segments along a continuum that cannot easily be demarcated. Persons who present themselves for marital therapy frequently have desires and/or behave in ways that suggest they want to terminate their marital relationship. Similarly, divorce therapy clients are often ambiguous about uncoupling. Hence, establishing and redefining therapeutic contracts is often a major aspect of this work (Sprenkle & Piercy, 1986).

This writer has found it useful to consider three interrelated continua in doing this contractual work (Figure 4.1).

The first continuum centers on the *commitment* to the relationship. The second relates to the *focus* of the therapy sessions themselves. Do in-session behaviors focus on strengthening the marital bond or terminating the marital bond? The final continuum relates to the *motivation* to use therapy to facilitate the commitment and focus described in the first two continua.

Contracting is even more complex in that the husband, the wife, and the therapist may be at very different points on each of these continua. In its purest form divorce therapy would be contracted for when the husband and wife are both committed (or at least resigned)

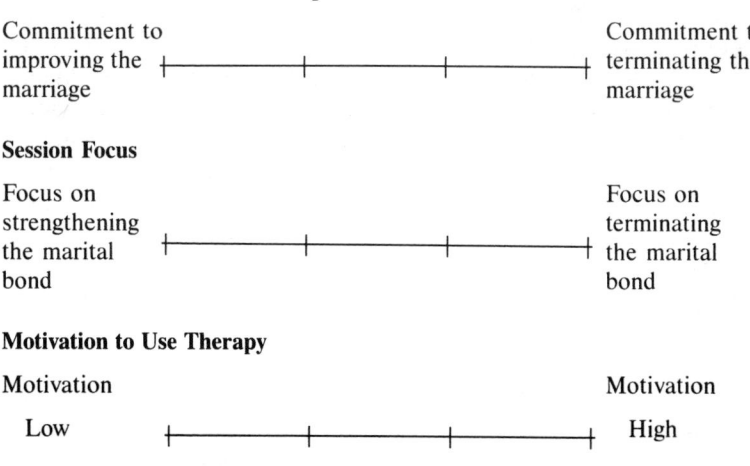

Commitment to the Relationship

Commitment to improving the marriage |————————+————————+————————| Commitment to terminating the marriage

Session Focus

Focus on strengthening the marital bond |————————+————————+————————| Focus on terminating the marital bond

Motivation to Use Therapy

Motivation Low |————————+————————+————————| Motivation High

Figure 4.1 Three continua useful in defining divorce therapy.

to ending the relationship and the therapist accepts this commitment as the basis for his or her own commitment to the couple. The husband, wife, and therapist would all engage in behaviors in the session consistent with this commitment. Finally, the husband, the wife, and the therapist would all be highly motivated to use therapy for this purpose.

Frequently, however, even when couples present themselves for "divorce therapy," one or both partners (and even sometimes the therapist!) are not committed to working toward ending the relationship. The session focus frequently drifts away from behaviors related to terminating the marital bond. Then, too, even when someone truly wants a divorce, he or she frequently is not motivated to work on this process in therapy. Perhaps he or she wants the therapist to "take this person off my hands." Alternatively, when some clients discover that the therapist cannot save the marriage (their real intention), they will abruptly terminate therapy.

These ambiguities are not necessarily bad and are discussed in more detail below in the section on "Therapy Around Divorce Decision Making." The point here is to stress that the distinction between divorce therapy and marital therapy is seldom tidy. As therapy progresses and circumstances change, the therapist frequently must, in keeping with the continua in Figure 4.1, (a) clarify the commitment of the clients as well as to him- or herself, (b) monitor the congruence of session focus and commitment and take appropriate action, and (c) recognize the level of motivation and try to enhance it when appropriate.

Case Example

Jim and Susan contacted the author to mediate their divorce settlement. Although both indicated that the decision to divorce was irrevocable and that their main goal was to avoid the deleterious effects of the adversary legal process, it became increasingly clear that Susan was not committed to ending the relationship. She repeatedly failed to complete assigned tasks, such as preparing lists of marital assets, and complained about the "mechanical" nature of the mediating process. Clearly, Sue's in-session behavior was inconsistent with her originally stated goal. Privately (and, hopefully, sensitively) this author clarifed with Sue that her commitment was really to convince Jim of the mistake he was making. Conjointly the therapist shared with the couple that they appeared to have different contracts for therapy and that one of three options was possible. They could move ahead with divorce mediation (not acceptable to Sue) or refocus on preserving the marriage (not acceptable to Jim). Alternatively, we could proceed with a "marital evaluation" that would suspend the ultimate outcome. Fortunately, both parties were amenable to this approach.

After four sessions examining the viability of their relationship, Sue was more willing to "let go," and the divorce mediation proceeded satisfactorily for awhile. Later, however, Jim became disenchanted with Sue's child support requests and became convinced that he could "do better" in court; hence, his motivation to utilize therapy to facilitate ending the marriage diminished. To enhance his motivation, I showed him support tables used by the local judge and suggested that Sue's requests were reasonable—if not generous—to him. His motivation was enhanced, and the mediation was completed satisfactorily.

A Broader Definition

This author favors a broad definition of divorce therapy that goes beyond simply focusing on dissolving the marital bond. He conceptualizes divorce therapy as helping couples and families through the stages of (a) predivorce decision making, (b) divorce restructuring, and, (c) postdivorce recovery.

In Stage 1, the author helps couples look at divorce as one alternative to relationship difficulties and helps them to appraise the consequences of such a major decision. The therapist also encourages nondestructive communication about the decision so that family members are better prepared for the major changes that will follow. In Stage 2, the therapist helps family members make the social, emotional, legal, financial, and parental arrangements necessary for the transition from marriage to the postmarriage family. In Stage 3, the therapist facilitates the growth of divorced persons as autonomous individuals with stable lifestyles and helps them develop social relationships independent of the former love relationship. Continuing difficulties related to parent–child relationships, sibling relationships, and custody/visitation issues often occupy therapists during this postdivorce stage. Preparation for remarriage and facilitating the remarriage process can also be included here, or remarriage can be considered a fourth stage, because the majority of divorcing families will experience the remarriage of one or both partners (Sprenkle, 1985). However, because treating families around remarriage issues is dealt with in a separate chapter in this volume, it is not discussed further here.

It is important to note that these stages are more heuristic than literally descriptive of all divorces, because divorces vary widely and issues cycle and recycle among the various stages. Some individuals, for example, have no time or even the option to think about the decision to divorce because they are abruptly abandoned (Sprenkle & Cyrus, 1983). Other persons, far into the second stage, reevaluate their decision and reconcile. Nonetheless, these stages are generally accurate and serve as useful benchmarks for the divorce process and for categorizing interventions. The reader should note that many authors have posited other stage theories of divorce, which may be heuristic for therapists. Useful tables that compare the various models are found in Price-Bonham and Balswick (1980) and Salts (1979).

THE GOALS OF DIVORCE THERAPY

Before proceeding to interventions, it is important to reflect on the goals toward which intervention should be working. This author agrees with Feldman ". . . that in many ways the most important initial task of family therapy is goal setting" (1976, p. 111). Goal setting is perhaps especially important for therapeutic work with divorced and divorcing clients because divorce therapy requires understanding the divorce adjustment process more than it demands unique therapeutic skills (Kaslow, 1981; Sprenkle, 1985).

The goals delineated in this section are based on a study of a random sample (N = 400) of clinical members of the American Association for Marriage and Family Therapy as reported in Sutton and Sprenkle (1985). The study sought to establish criteria for the constructive, *long-term* adjustment to divorce because the authors recognize that divorce is not easily growthful, creative, or freedom producing. Judith Wallerstein, in the previous chapter, stresses the length of the adjustment process, and Robert Weiss has offered the often-quoted statistic that it typically requires 2 to 4 years to achieve a constructive resolution of divorce-related changes and stress (Weiss, 1975). However, time alone is not sufficient for achieving positive outcomes, and some divorced persons never adjust constructively. Divorce can have a range of long-term outcomes, positive as well as negative. Therefore, it is helpful to note that the mediating and ultimate criteria that research and theory suggest are most salutary (Sutton & Sprenkle, 1985).

Before noting the criteria themselves, readers should recognize the following caveats. First, these criteria are not comprehensive nor exhaustive. It is not possible to cover all types of divorces. For example, second or third divorces following complex stepfamily forms may require unique criteria. Researchers have only recently begun to distinguish among different kinds of divorce (Sprenkle & Cyrus, 1983). They have recognized it is a myth that "a divorce is a divorce is a divorce" (Baker, 1981).

Second, it is much easier to delineate these criteria than to actually help divorcing persons achieve them. It is probably impossible for any one person to actually attain all of these goals, either quickly or completely. The criteria are for long-term adjustment, and it is assumed that progress is typically slow, if not plodding. Furthermore, the "graph" of divorce recovery is typically jagged rather than straight, and divorcing persons' forward steps are often matched by retreats. Hence, although these goals can guide the therapists' work, they do not delineate the typical process of adjustment (Sprenkle & Cyrus, 1983); Sutton & Sprenkle, 1985).

Dimension One: Acceptance of the End of the Marriage

The cornerstone of long-term adjustment is accepting that one is not, and will no longer be, married to one's ex-spouse (Fisher, 1981). One must develop an identity that is tied neither to one's former marital status nor one's ex-spouse (Kitson & Raschke, 1981). This process is made very difficult by the bonding that often develops between spouses. Weiss (1975) has written about the "persistence of attachment" between spouses that persists even after the "erosion of love." However, Ahrons (1980a) has stressed the difference between "normal" attachment to the ex-spouse and "pathological" attachment.

Dimension Two: Functional Postdivorce Relationship with the Ex-Spouse

This goal entails making "peace" with the ex-spouse, hopefully both within one's self and between one's self and one's former mate. Sprenkle and Cyrus (1983, p. 68) write:

> Eventually the divorcee must learn that nastiness only begets nastiness and that acting in aggressive (active or passive) and hostile ways only hurts one's self. Part of "becoming free" of the other person is the capacity not to engage in tit-for-tat retribution. The ultimate expression of this freedom is the capacity to forgive the other for his contribution to the demise of the marriage.

Ahrons (1980b) found that the most successful divorcing parents were those who were capable of separating parental and spousal roles, while the least well-adjusted were those who continued to act out marital conflicts though the children.

Dimension Three: Emotional Adjustment

Although divorce inevitably entails negative emotional consequences, it is important that divorcing persons not get stuck in long-term self-blame, guilt, or anger. This author recognizes, however, that in the short term, certain negative emotions may have constructive value. For example, anger may galvanize energy and help clients to get through the trauma of separation.

Dimension Four: Cognitive Adjustment (Development of Realistic Understanding)

Divorcing persons need to understand their own contributions to the dysfunctional behavior that led to the failure of the marriage. Only if one accepts personal responsibility is one empowered to be able to do something about it. It is valuable when each partner is aware of the ways in which the marital failure is related to struggles in his or her family of origin (Napier & Whitaker, 1978). It is also valuable for each partner to learn about his or her reasons for choice of mate so that one is less likely to repeat the same mistake (Kressel & Deutsch, 1977).

Dimension Five: Social Support and Adjustment

Kitson and Raschke (1981) define social support as formal and informal contacts with individuals and groups who provide emotional or material resources. Finding sources of support, other than one's ex-partner, is highly related to low stress and better adjustment (Kitson & Raschke, 1981). However, the paradox of adjusting to divorce through social participation is that divorcing persons also need to live as single persons and to deny the temptation to escape divorce-related stress through developing another intimate relationship (Fisher, 1981).

Dimension Six: Parental Adjustment

A number of studies have demonstrated that a co-parenting relationship free of conflict and hostility is positively related to children's adjustment (Ahrons, 1980a; Goetting, 1980; Heatherington, Cox, & Cox, 1981; Wallerstein & Kelly, 1980a). Therefore, it is important for ex-spouses to communicate directly and not through their children.

Parents should not compete for their children's affection and, as Wallerstein notes in the previous chapter, should not be overly emotionally dependent on their children. Parents should come to feel more competent and comfortable in postdivorce parenting roles.

Dimension Seven: Children's Adjustment

Jacobson (1978a, b, c) has stressed the importance of parents discussing the reasons for the separation or divorce with their children in age-appropriate ways. Parents should help dispel any beliefs by the children that they caused the divorce. It is crucial that children believe that both parents still love them even if the parents no longer love each other; they must also believe that loving either parent will not jeopardize their place in the affections of the other. Children should be encouraged to express their painful emotions in age-appropriate ways and should not nourish fantasies about parents reconciling. It is constructive for children to have regular contact with the noncustodial parent, provided this is not a dysfunctional relationship (Wallerstein & Kelly, 1980a). Contact with both sets of grandparents and relatives (again barring unusual circumstances) is also constructive (Ahrons, 1983). Children who are adjusting well to divorce should be doing satisfactory work in school, be reasonably active in social and recreational activities, and have satisfactory peer relationships (Sutton & Sprenkle, 1985).

Dimension Eight: Use of Opportunities for Learning and Personal Growth

Although divorce is typically painful and traumatic, it often "shakes up the system" in ways that might not happen otherwise and hence forces people to clarify values and revise priorities. An important therapeutic goal is to help the individual develop feelings of competency and mastery as a single person. The author frequently reminds clients that "in divorce, you always get custody of yourself" (Sutton & Sprenkle, 1985). Establishing a new identity for oneself, setting new goals, or developing a new set of roles or activities can also be salutary.

Dimension Nine: Process and Outcome of the Legal Settlement

Because the legal process frequently exacerbates the pain of divorce, divorces are most constructive if they are not contested or at least if neither partner feels embittered by the adversary process. Divorcing persons need to walk a fine line between taking care of themselves and being assertive about their rights and not using the legal process as a punitive measure (Irving, 1980; Sprenkle & Cyrus, 1983). The literature also suggests that individuals who are active participants in the settlement process and who are not overly influenced by guilt and resentment become better adjusted. It is more constructive when divorcing persons believe they neither gave nor took too much and are satisfied with the terms of custody and visitation (Sutton & Sprenkle, 1985).

Dimension Ten: General Life Adjustment and Physical Well-Being

Separated and divorced persons have been shown to have more physical and mental health problems than married persons (Bloom, Asher, & White, 1978). These include the abuse of alcohol and drugs, physical health problems, disturbed sleep patterns, poor eating habits, poor hygiene and grooming, the inability to make appropriate decisions, diminished job performance, memory difficulties, and financial stress. Because these problems may have preceded the divorce and contributed to its cause, they do not necessarily indicate the quality of postdivorce adjustment. However, experiencing difficulties with life adjustment and physical well-being may make achieving a constructive divorce more difficult, and resolving these concerns can be an appropriate goal in therapy (Sutton & Sprenkle, 1985).

GENERAL GUIDELINES FOR INTERVENING

There is certainly no one way to do divorce therapy. In fact, Gurman and Kniskern (1981, p. 694) have written ". . . there is little that is strategically or technically unique to divorce therapy itself." As this author has reviewed the literature, proponents of most of the major marital and family therapy theories have described divorce intervention from this perspective. What is unique about divorce therapy is its goals and content. Gurman and Kniskern (1981, p. 694) also note that ". . . specialized knowledge of the common patterns in the divorce process does seem central to clinical work in this area."

The following general guidelines are offered for professionals commencing work in this area. First, it is crucial that one understands both the nature of the divorce process and the criteria for constructive divorce (such as those just outlined).

Second, effective divorce therapy tends to have a strong didactic component. People going through divorce and experiencing its typical symptomology frequently think they are "going crazy," and it is important that the therapist be able to teach the client about the divorce recovery process and what is likely to happen in the ensuing months. The therapist also must encourage clients to engage in those specific behaviors that research has shown to be beneficial. For example, clients frequently must be encouraged to get socially involved, to develop creative uses of their time, to develop basic life skills, and so on. The professional must also be familiar with a specific body of knowledge on practical matters such as household management, law, and finances.

Third, the therapist also must maintain a balance between support and confrontation. Initially, intervention must be highly supportive and relationship skills such as warmth, empathy, and unconditional positive regard cannot be underestimated. Divorcing people often feel deeply wounded, and the short-term goal is not so much "healing" as it is "sustaining." On the other hand, clients eventually must be confronted with the fact that they are at least partially responsible for where they are at this point and are totally responsible for where they go from here. In short, the therapist cannot afford to reinforce a "helpless victim" mentality. It is crucial that the professional help divorcing persons gain a sense of power and control over their own destiny. Only to the extent that they realize that they had something to do with their current predicament can they also choose to do something about their future (Sprenkle & Cyrus, 1983).

THERAPY AROUND DIVORCE DECISION MAKING (STAGE I)

The existing literature on divorce therapy offers the least help in this area. As noted previously, therapy at this time can be frustrating because of potentially different agendas of husband, wife, and therapist. For this reason it is often profitable to contract for "marital evaluation" as an alternative to either "divorce therapy" or "marriage therapy."

As Salts (1985) has pointed out, the couple can be helped to see that "divorce" itself is not their problem. Divorce is only one alternative solution to an unhappy marriage. Therefore, the goal of the evaluation contract is to ascertain whether the couple's needs can be met *within* the marriage (not necessarily *by* the marriage).

Salts (1985) then goes on to identify an effective decision-making process during this time of marital evaluation:

1. Identification and definition of the needs and problems of the individuals and couple

2. The development of alternative solutions to meet these needs and to solve the problems
3. Consideration of the potential outcome to each alternative solution
4. Choice of the best and most fair solutions
5. Implementation of the choices
6. Evaluation of the outcomes
7. Further identification of needs and problems if the evaluation is not satisfactory

Frankly, once the therapy has been framed as "marital evaluation" and the focus is on whether the couple's needs can be met within the marriage, a good deal of what the therapist does can be patterned after his or her typical marital therapy. The crucial difference is that this frame "joins" and is more respectful of the partner who is highly ambivalent about remaining in the marriage or who believes it is "hopeless." Pushing "marital" therapy on these reluctant partners will almost surely engender resistance and sabotage the therapist's work.

This author has found the framework for asking circular questions described by Fleuridas, Nelson, and Rosenthal (1986) to be an excellent way to proceed. The purpose of these questions is to ascertain from each member of the family his or her opinions and experiences of the couple's major concerns, the sequences of interaction related to these concerns, and differences in their relationship over time. The goals of these questions are (a) to provide the couple and the therapist with a systemic frame that can (b) enable the therapist to generate hypotheses and design interventions to disrupt dysfunctional cycles and that can (c) challenge myths or beliefs that are detrimental to the relationship. While the first two call for a structural-strategic emphasis, the third leads this writer to do considerable family-of-origin work.

When clients remain highly ambivalent, several techniques offered by Nathan Turner (1980, 1985) may be useful. Turner has drawn upon the social-psychological decision-making theories of Janis and Mann (1977) to make some sense out of the often bizarre decisional behavior of persons undergoing divorce—frequently marked by seeming irrationality, extraordinary ambivalence, regressive behaviors, decisional reversals, or impulsive behavior.

The *grid balance sheet* described by Turner (1985) and adapted from the work of Janis (1983, p. 171) is a "left-brain" approach. Clients are given a handout that has two columns called "positive anticipations" and "negative anticipations." A grid is formed using the following "rows": "tangible gains and losses for self"; "tangible gains and losses for others"; "self-approval or disapproval"; and "social approval or disapproval." A separate sheet is made out for each major alternative, such as "Remaining Married" or "Trial Separation." This method forces the client to investigate carefully all alternatives and systematically consider the major gains and risks.

A more "right-brain" approach is the *outcome psychodrama*. The client experiencing decisional conflict concerning divorce is asked to assume one side of the ambivalence—for example, "Let us say you have decided to get a divorce." As Turner (1985, pp. 35–36) describes the procedure:

> The therapist leads the person through all of the consequences of that decision. "You are now telling your husband/children. What are you saying? How does that feel?" The client is led further. "You are now in the court. What are feeling as you look over at your partner across the room? As you leave the courtroom as a newly single person? The sequence progresses. "It is now six months after the divorce. What are you doing? What do you feel? How much support are you receiving?"
>
> The process is then repeated, taking the other polarity. You have decided to stay in your marriage. You are telling your husband of the decision. "What are you saying? How does that feel?"
>
> By giving the client the freedom to fantasize about the consequences of both outcomes, there is the opportunity to clarify thoughts and feelings and to assess the emotional readiness for a given decision.

Ambivalent clients therefore are given the opportunity "to picture" or fantasize themselves acting out each decision, being aware of their feelings as they do so. Through this focused fantasy they are encouraged to get in touch with affect, cognitions, and behaviors related both to choosing divorce and to staying married (Sprenkle, 1985).

A related technique is suggested by Imber-Black (1986). Building on the work of the Milan group, she has couples enact a ritual where on the "odd days" of the week they act "as if" they have made the decision to stay together; on the "even days" they proceed "as if" they had made the decision to divorce. One day per week is "free." The couple is encouraged to live out the various sides of their ambivalence, and this often moves them off dead center.

This author generally favors conjoint treatment during the stage of divorce decision making. Certainly the old practice of working individually with one spouse to the exclusion of the other at this time is often "an intervention in favor of divorce" (Whitaker & Miller, 1971, p. 254). The children or parents of one or both spouses may be included in therapy at this time depending on the nature of the relationship issues and theoretical orientation of the therapist. Nonetheless, because the final decision regarding divorce is a couple issue rather than a family issue, the major emphasis should be on conjoint therapy with a low emphasis on both individual and family therapy (Storm & Sprenkle, 1982). Once an irrevocable decision to divorce has been made, however, it is important to work with the couple around the important issue of informing the children. Depending on circumstances, the children may or may not be present.

Another advantage of conjoint work is that it offers the therapist the opportunity to do what Kressel and Deutsch (1977) call "orchestrating the motivation to divorce" in the resistant spouse. If it is clear that the marriage cannot be restored, the therapist may need to inform the resistant party that "there is only one thing worse than a divorce you don't want—and that is being married to someone who doesn't want to be married to you."

Sometimes the process of challenging destructive or unrealistic expectations or beliefs about marriage, disrupting dysfunctional behavioral sequences and finding better ones, reframing relational patterns, and creating new realities leads both partners to opt to stay in the marriage. In such cases, there can be a new contract for "marital therapy" that is satisfactory to all parties. If this does not occur and both spouses become resigned to ending the marriage or the therapist orchestrates the motive to divorce in the reluctant spouse, then a contract can be established for "divorce" therapy.

When the latter happens, this author attempts to achieve several often difficult tasks (which, even if successful, may carry over into the subsequent two stages of divorce therapy):

1. Each partner is encouraged to articulate his or her own contributions to the failure of the marriage.
2. Each is asked to express to the other an appreciation of what was good or positive in their shared life together.
3. Each spouse is encouraged to express forgiveness to the other for his or her contribution to the family hurt.

Realistically, these are difficult tasks, and often it is not possible to achieve them. Positive movement, however, significantly contributes to successful outcomes in the subsequent two stages of divorce therapy. Couples also can be encouraged to devise a ritual as a means of saying "good-bye" to their relationship. There is considerable opportunity for therapist and client creativity here. Generally, it is best to offer clients only general guidelines and let them work out the details of a ritual that will be meaningful for them (Imber-Black, 1986). Kaslow (1981) also offers helpful suggestions on the role of rituals in divorce work.

THERAPY FOR RESTRUCTURING (STAGE II)

Salts (1985) has indicated that if a couple's decision to divorce was facilitated by a therapist who created a mutually acceptable decision and, hence, toned down the intense emotions surrounding divorce, then the couple is more likely to restructure successfully. If the therapist was not involved with the couple during the decision-making phase, then reviewing this process with them may be important for assessing the feelings each one has about the decision. The purpose of this intervention is not to change the decision to divorce but to provide the opportunity for the couple to reaffirm that the decision is the best one for them or to move the unwilling spouse to the point of acceptance (Salts, 1985).

The restructuring process entails the legal, emotional, financial, social, and parental arrangements necessary to make the shift from marriage to singlehood (Storm & Sprenkle, 1982). As Wallerstein indicated in the previous chapter, this is a time of inordinate stress because of the multitude of changes that often occur—moving, lowered standard of living, shifting parental arrangements, changing social networks, and so forth. The degree of difficulty in this stage depends, in part, on the process used to arrive at the decision to divorce. If one spouse feels callously "dumped" and is desperately "holding on," restructuring will be more difficult (Sprenkle, 1985).

Ideally, conjoint couple therapy with family therapy to deal with children's issues is preferable. It is interesting that conjoint work has been controversial here. In a study of the views of psychotherapists regarding divorce interventions, Kressel and Deutsch (1977, p. 300) reported that "disinclination to see couples jointly after the divorce decision is correlated with the view that the therapist has no role to play in the mediation of divorce settlements." This writer strongly disagrees with this view and believes that the therapist *can* play a significant role in the mediation of divorce settlements. A conjoint approach can be used not only to mediate custody, visitation, and financial arrangements but also can facilitate the timing of separation and can be used to facilitate the continuation of tasks delineated at the end of the section on divorce decision-making therapy.

In addition, a conjoint approach provides a setting to continue dealing with the inevitable unresolved feelings that accompany divorce. If emotions of anger, disappointment, and hurt are not dealt with, they are often disguised in ongoing custody and visitation disputes. Individual therapy would only be the treatment of choice if there were a brief marriage, no children, and no concerns about the settlement and the couple already had an understanding of their relationship dynamics and their own contribution to the demise of the marriage. Of course, frequently people who have been "left" will initially seek help around the time of physical separation, and even the most engaging therapist will have difficulty getting the other spouse to participate (Salts, 1985).

Including children at least sometime during this stage is typically crucial. Often children are neglected emotionally during this period because, as Wallerstein has noted, parents are overwhelmed by their own needs. Because there is compelling research evidence that children's postdivorce adjustment is directly related to the parents' own adjustment (Wallerstein & Kelly, 1980a), therapists may gain leverage in encouraging partners to continue working on their own emotional issues by informing them of the benefits the children will reap (Kaslow, 1984; Salts, 1985). Fortunately, there are a variety of resources for the professional who wishes to learn more about working with the children of divorce (Cantor & Drake, 1984; Gardner, 1976; Hetherington et al., 1981; Kurdek, 1983; Nichols, 1984, 1985; Stuart & Abt, 1981; and Wallerstein & Kelly, 1980a). There are also some good resources therapists can share with parents to help their children (Francke, 1983; Newman, 1981; Oakland, 1984). Finally, there are several excellent books written for children themselves (Gardner 1971, 1978, 1982; Rofes, 1982).

The time around the physical separation is typically the most stressful time for children of all ages. The therapeutic challenge is to help the children deal with their feelings of loss as the separation occurs while working with the parents to minimize parental conflict and encourage cooperation in parenting (Nichols, 1985).

In sessions that include the children, this writer works toward the goals specified previously in this chapter ("Dimension Seven: Children's Adjustment"). Children are given the opportunity to express their feelings, to work through their grief, and to feel "parented."

While all else seems to be crumbling, it is exceedingly important to maintain a psychological sense of family (Nichols, 1985). This can be accomplished by helping the parents demonstrate continued and consistent love. It can also be helpful to involve grandparents or mobilize other portions of the children's social support network.

In private time with the parents, still focused on child issues, this writer uses whatever leverage can be employed to stress that they should compartmentalize their marital conflict from their ongoing role as parents. The temptation to triangulate the children is normalized, but the deleterious consequences of such action is driven home in whatever way the clients will accept. The goals described above (Dimension Six: Parental Adjustment") guide this writer's intervention. Couples are encouraged to provide as much continuity for the children as possible and to make it very clear that parenting is forever, even if marrying is not. Ex-spouses are encouraged to communicate directly with each other and not through their children and certainly not to "pump" the children for information about the other's activities. With highly inflammatory clients, the author has occasionally used the paradoxical directive, "If you wanted to be harmful to your children, how, specifically, would you go about doing it?"

The form of intervention most directly related to restructuring is divorce mediation (see also the previous chapter by Judith Wallerstein). Although mediation has been widely practiced in other aspects of life (e.g., labor disputes), it has only recently been applied to divorce (Cohen, 1985). Divorce mediation arose as a reaction against the destructive effects of the adversary legal system and was also facilitated by the widespread acceptance of no-fault divorce.

It is important to stress that mediation does not replace the legal system but attempts to circumvent its more negative aspects. When this writer initiates mediation with a couple, he emphasizes that he can help them to prepare a "statement of intentions" about the terms of their dissolution, but an attorney or attorneys will be necessary to translate this statement into acceptable legal language.

The mediation process is typically present-centered and time-limited and focuses on the goals of reaching an agreement around such crucial issues as custody, visitation, and finances. A full discussion of the mediation process is beyond the scope of this chapter. Fortunately, therapists desiring to learn more about mediation have a variety of books to consult (Coogler, 1978; Haynes, 1981; Irving, 1980; Saposnek, 1983; Shapiro & Kaplan, 1983).

There is considerable debate as to the proper scope and direction of mediation (Cohen, 1985). Many court-related mediating services have focused exclusively on the mediation of custody and visitation issues and have avoided mediating financial matters. Other mediators feel strongly that mediators should avoid dealing with psychological issues unless they can be dealt with very briefly and have an immediate bearing on the goal of reaching a settlement. Subscribers to this point of view are often mediators who begin meeting with couples only after a decision to mediate has been made following an irrevocable decision to divorce. The current author's mediation practice, however, is comprised mainly of couples with whom he has worked during the decision-making phase and with whom he has also assisted through the acute separation portion of restructuring. More than once this author has mediated a settlement only to find that the process led to a recommitment to maintain the marriage.

Case Example

Ralph, an executive of a large company, became embroiled in a torrid affair with a younger co-worker. Throughout the decision-making phase he maintained that his behavior was "caused" by his wife's frequent rejection, her inability to share activities that he liked, such as golf, and her refusal to meet his sexual needs. Although he said he "thought through everything carefully" (perhaps a clue that he wasn't so committed to divorce), he insisted that divorce was nearly certain and that, in any event, the settlement must be mediated. In addition to this author, he consulted with a tax advisor about the intricacies of settling his complicated estate. After the mediation was completed and after his wife had demonstrated a nonpunitive approach and sincere interest in his welfare, he reconsidered. We contracted for marital therapy and it was successfully completed. Four years later the couple reports "never having been happier."

Perhaps this case would have had a different outcome had the author not been sensitive to the psychological and interactional dynamics that were operating. The mediation seemed to serve as a kind of closure ritual on the "old" marriage and made it possible for a "new" relationship to be born. In short, there is a place for a form of mediation/therapy that some professionals might find uncomfortable. It seems clear that issues related to money, property, visitation, and child support are often inextricably intertwined with the marital drama and therefore cannot be readily separated.

THERAPY FOR POSTDIVORCE RECOVERY (STAGE III)

Following restructuring the therapist can begin to focus more on "individual" issues such as coping with loneliness, regaining self-confidence, and rebuilding social relations (Storm & Sprenkle, 1982).

Unless there are continuing problems with parent–child relationships and custody/visitation issues or unless remarriage issues are the focus, the individual is the unit of treatment during this stage (Storm & Sprenkle, 1982).

This writer envisages the goals of divorce therapy at this stage as threefold. First, the therapist should facilitate the remaining grief work the client must do to "let go" of the marriage. In his popular book for the lay person, Fisher (1981) offers a number of useful methods for dealing with emotional "leftovers" such as deliberately mourning over family pictures and then eventually setting them aside. Fisher's book describes a series of "rebuilding blocks" upon which the divorcing person must ascend on the way to recovery, and each chapter offers a useful self-quiz that serves as a milemarker along the way. This author typically uses Fisher's book as an aid on the road to recovery.

Second, the client should be helped to revise self-destructive meanings attributed to the divorce. This author has previously identified (Sprenkle & Cyrus, 1983) an unholy triad of interpretations that act as roadblocks for divorcing persons. These are "unworthiness," "meaninglessness," and "helplessness." Johnson (1977) demonstrates how rational-emotive methods can be used to attack these destructive beliefs. This writer finds even more refreshing the recent work of Brown (1985) who uses a structural-strategic approach to create "new realities" for the newly divorced. Brown builds upon clients' own language and perspective and gently reframes it to engender more hope. For example, if the client complains, "I can't concentrate at all," the therapist might query, "Did you drive yourself over today?" If the client responds affirmatively, the therapist might say, "So you are able to concentrate some, but not to the degree to which you would like" (Brown, 1985, p. 104).

Third, the therapist should help the client maximize resources so as to develop alternatives to the now-defunct relationship. The second and third goals are interdependent because, as the client learns to develop his or her resources, this makes it easier for the client to attribute less destructive meaning to the divorce. Conversely, to the extent that the client quits making debilitating interpretations of the divorce, he or she will be more free to develop resources (Sprenkle & Cyrus, 1983).

One needs to tap into resources that have either been under-utilized or outside the client's awareness, such as friends, family, children, community, work, and, most importantly, one's self. The author helps the client to identify his or her resources and strengthen those that seem most amenable to amplification. Obviously, this varies from client to client. There is considerable empirical evidence that a support group of friends and social participation is helpful to divorce adjustment. Similarly, a job for which one is adequately compensated has been demonstrated to be highly related to adjustment (Kitson & Raschke, 1981). Often men and women differ in the extent to which these resources need to be cultivated. Typically, men need less help developing their vocational resources and more help in the friendship and social areas, whereas the reverse is often true of women (Johnson, 1977; Sprenkle & Cyrus, 1983).

Developing the "self" as a resource is the most challenging and crucial task of the therapist. This typically includes:

1. *The development of certain basic life skills.* Men, for example, often need to learn to cook and sew, whereas women may need help with fiscal management and basic maintenance and repairs. (There are, of course, many exceptions to these stereotypical needs.)
2. *Time-management skills.* Clients frequently need to learn how to use their time in ways that maximize creativity. Frequently, clients can learn to come to terms with loneliness following a program of "loneliness tolerance training" (Johnson, 1977) where they are progressively introduced to longer periods of time alone.
3. *Assessing inner strengths.* Clients need help learning how to access personal sources of strength and competence that have been useful in the past. For example, Kirsten and Robertiello (1978) describe a method of helping a client to distinguish between his or her "Big You" and "Little You." The latter is the part of one's personality that represents his or her emotional and belief system as a frightened, small child. Often the divorcing person feels overwhelmed, incompetent, frightened, and demanding, as a child in a state of panic might. The "Big You" represents that part of oneself that feels competent, confident, and capable of dealing with stress. Using the "empty chair" technique, this author frequently helps clients utilize their Big You (strong part) as a resource to parent their Little You (weak part).

OTHER METHODS OF DIVORCE THERAPY

This section briefly describes other methods of divorce therapy not used by the author but worthy of attention.

In the decision-making stage, structured separation is sometimes utilized for couples who do not appear to be benefiting from marriage counseling but are doubtful that divorce is the best alternative. Granvold (1983) is an excellent source describing different models of structured separation. Most require a written contract that specifies ground rules which include time limits (typically between 6 weeks to 3 months). Separation is structured in such a way as to maintain a balance between "absence makes the heart fonder" and "out of sight, out of mind" (Granvold, 1983, p. 407). All these models mandate that couples attend therapy, typically once a week, and the therapist attempts to create a more rational environment for decision making (Sprenkle, 1985). This author is cautious about structured separation because follow-up studies suggest a high rate of marital termination (Green, Lee, & Lustig, 1973; Toomin, 1972). It is certainly important to match the technique to the needs of the couple, and Granvold (1983) does offer some guidelines to assess the suitability of the technique.

In the restructuring phase several authors have argued for the value of interdisciplinary teams composed of attorneys and therapists (Bernstein, 1977; Kaslow & Steinberg, 1981). They argue that therapists cannot keep up with the complex issues related to property, pension, taxes, support, and so forth, and that attorneys are not well trained to deal with the complex emotional issues surrounding divorce.

Because mediated divorces more often result in joint custody, therapists should be aware of Volgy and Everett's (1985) five criteria that may be used to determine if couples are adaptative enough to make joint custody work. These authors stress that joint custody, like mediation, should not been seen as a panacea and that therapists cannot be oblivious to contraindications to these approaches (Sprenkle, 1985).

For the recovery stage a great deal has been written about group and educational approaches. A variety of such programs and their goals are reviewed in Storm et al. (1985). Typically, groups are less expensive than individual therapy. The group experience also tends to normalize divorce and generates support and acceptance. Formats include short didactic educational emphases, skills training, group therapy, or combinations of these modalities (Storm et al., 1985).

The single-parent phase following divorce is often especially difficult, and Weiss (1979b) offers a text that is valuable both for the single parent as well as for the mental health professional. Isaacs (1982) and Weltner (1982) offer structural family therapy models for dysfunctional single parents. Eno (1985) demonstrates how sibling relationships are affected by divorce and how they can be used therapeutically to abet divorce adjustment in children.

RESEARCH EVALUATION OF DIVORCE THERAPY

Sprenkle and Storm (1983) offer a very thorough review of the empirical research on divorce therapy, and readers desiring more detail should consult this resource. Basically, they report that the only methodologically solid research has been done in the area of mediation of child custody and visitation conflicts.

In direct comparisons between mediation and traditional adversary methods, mediation produced (a) considerably higher rates of pretrial stipulations or agreements than did control groups, (b) a significantly higher level of satisfaction with mediated agreements than those imposed by the courts, (c) dramatic reduction in the amount of litigation following a final order, (d) an increase in joint custody arrangements, and (e) a decrease in public expenses such as custody studies and court costs. One study (Pearson & Thoennes, 1982), however, suggests that attorney fees may not be reduced by mediation.

Controlled research of conciliation court counseling demonstrated a significantly greater number of reconciliations in experimental as opposed to no-treatment control groups, but only short-term results are reported.

Sprenkle and Storm (1983) conclude that the field of divorce intervention is still woefully underdeveloped empirically. Aside from the conclusion that the mediation of custody and visitation disputes is preferable to the traditional adversary process, there is not a strong data base to conclude that any other form of divorce intervention is superior to no-treatment. There is no controlled research whatsoever about what is probably the most widely practiced form of divorce therapy—namely, individuals or couples who go to a therapist for help in getting through the trauma of divorce. Therefore, the most basic controlled research in the process and outcome of divorce has yet to be done (Sprenkle & Storm, 1983).

None of the studies of divorce therapy has investigated effects of treatment on the children of divorce. Children have not been included as participants in the therapeutic experience, and such investigations are crucial for public policy as well as for clinical reasons (Gurman, Kniskern, & Pinsof, 1986).

There appears to be no research on interventions related to single-parent families or to remarriage despite the excellent theoretical books in these areas.

Divorce mediation research must be broadened to include examining the mediation of child support and property settlements.

Finally, it is important that investigators compare various forms of treatment with each other. No one, for example, has examined the results of individual versus conjoint versus family treatment for divorcing people. Although on theoretical grounds, Storm and Sprenkle (1982) argued that specific units of treatment (individual, conjoint, family, and group) are most appropriate for persons in various stages of the dissolution process, there has been no research to verify this speculation (Sprenkle & Piercy, 1986).

CONCLUSION

The field of divorce intervention clearly remains in its infancy. We know much more about the phenomenon of divorce than we know about how to intervene effectively. Given the fact that only a minority of marriages being contracted will survive "till death do us part," it behooves family professionals to devote their creative time and energy to this significant, if highly challenging, field.

Troubled Relationships Between Parents and Children

5

CATHERINE S. CHILMAN

This chapter deals with knowledge and theory regarding troubled relationships between parents and children, focusing on families in which there are children aged 18 or less. It is limited to certain dimensions of these problematic relations so as not to overlap with other related chapters in this book series, such as those that focus on family violence and child neglect (Volume 4); divorce and remarriage (Volume 4; problems of single parent families (Volume 5); mental illness (Volume 4); chemical dependency (Volume 4); crime and delinquency (Volume 5); and illness, handicaps, and learning disabilities (Volume 2).

The emphasis here is more general; it is on two major kinds of difficult child behaviors that are apt to reflect and/or affect disturbances in parent–child relationships. These major behavior patterns are: (a) highly aggressive, rebellious, hostile behavior; or (b) very shy, withdrawn, inhibited behavior. Ledingham, Schwartzman, and Serbin (1984) write that these are two fundamental types that emerge repeatedly from studies of deviant behavior.

Note that labeling both kinds of behavior as problematic is specific to mainstream United States culture. In other cultures either type might be viewed as normative and desirable. However, our concern here is with parents and children in the United States where the dominant culture values such behaviors as autonomy, self-reliance, competence, assertiveness (but not uncontrolled aggression), educational and occupational achievement, conformity to mainstream social group norms, and the like.

SOME PROBLEMS WITH THE RESEARCH

There are a multitude of variables within and outside families that affect parent–child relationships over a period of time. Many of these factors have not been adequately studied. Although it has been more common to view parent characteristics and behaviors as causing developmental outcomes for children, there is increasing evidence that the characteristics of children also have a marked effect on their parents (see, for example, Clarke-Stewart, 1977; Hetherington, 1984; Rutter, 1979).

Further considerations are in order. Most of the research projects that describe various kinds of parent behaviors actually have only studied mothers. Although fathers are now receiving research attention, there is still very little recognition that within a family maternal and paternal behaviors are apt to be quite different because marital partners are often highly dissimilar in personality traits and bring different life experiences and, therefore behaviors to parenting. These dissimilarities may well cause conflict between parents as to what behaviors are appropriate, and this conflict often has negative effects on their children. On the other hand, these dissimilarities may have positive aspects in that they may complement and balance each other. How well or how poorly this works out depends a great deal on the nature of the marriage relationship as well as on many other factors in the entire situation.

In general, almost none of the research reviewed for this chapter sufficiently recognized the important contributions of the internal and external dynamics of family systems to parent–child relationships. Although there is a growing body of theory in the family systems field, this theory is yet to be adequately applied to most formal research regarding parenting and child development. Admittedly, such research would be extremely difficult because of the huge number of variables involved. However, much more effort in this direction is strongly indicated.

Studies of internal family dynamics must take into account interactions within the family from children to parents, parents to children, children to each other, and parents to each other, with every interaction (both overt and covert) affecting all other interactions. Other internal family reactions must be studied. These include interactions with other members of the kin network, whether they are living in the home, whether they are geographically near or far, and whether they are still alive or deceased (Carter & McGoldrick, 1980).

Studies of parent–child relationships and their outcomes also require recognition of families as open systems strongly influenced by a host of factors in the larger environment. For instance, Bronfenbrenner et al. (1984), among others, have pioneered this approach, using the term "family ecology" and conceptualizing families as open systems interacting with a host of other systems in the larger society, such as schools, businesses, industries, government programs, community services, and the like. (See also Elder, 1984;

Hartup, 1978; Lamb, 1978; Lerner & Spanier, 1983). Adverse factors in the many facets of the larger environment can have undesirable effects on family members and hence entire family systems.

Adverse reactions in families, in turn, are apt to have negative effects on varying facets of the larger environment (such as places of employment and schools). Thus, circular feedback loops may be created, often with escalating problematic effects with respect to both families and the outer environments. Conversely, circular feedback loops can have benign effects, depending on the nature of families and their members as well as the various facets of the larger environment.

How children eventually "turn out" as adults partly depends on their original constitutional endowments, their interactions within their family systems, the characteristics of family members (especially parents), and their experiences within the many parts of the larger environment. It also depends on individual and family development and change over the life span in the context of environments that are apt to be changing also.

Ideally, and difficult as it may be, the many complexities sketched above must be included in research designs if we are to have a more complete understanding of the many variables that affect parent–child relationships and the development of children from infancy through the adult years. Both research and intervention models must take these multiple interacting factors into account. However, because the vast majority of research projects have taken a more simplistic approach, the summary of findings that follows is, of necessity, fraught with important limitations which are essential for readers to bear in mind. Note, further, that as in all research findings apply to *group* tendencies; they may or may not apply well to specific individuals.

GENERAL RESEARCH FINDINGS

A summary of research results strongly suggests that parental acceptance, warmth, and support tend to be positively associated with favorable emotional, social, and cognitive characteristics of children and that extreme restrictiveness, authoritarian, and hostile punitiveness are apt to be negatively associated with a child's positive self-concept and emotional and social development.

Patterson, Littman, and Bricker (1967) found that highly aggressive children, compared to more normal ones, have often grown up in families in which members have stimulated and perpetuated each other's aggressive behavior. All members of these families showed aggression, both the parents and the siblings. Also, compared to other parents, these mothers and fathers were inconsistent in discipline; for instance, they made many threats but did not back them up with action.

Walters and Stinett (1971) as well as Mussen, Conger, and Kagan (1979) report that shy, withdrawn youngsters are often low in self-esteem. They tend to have parents who lack self-confidence; are unstable, inflexible, and lacking in self-reliance; and are in a poor marital relationship. Low-self-confidence parents, moreover, tend to see their children as burdens, to treat them harshly, to give them little guidance, to often be inconsistent in behavior, to be authoritarian, and to lack open communication with their children (Coopersmith, 1967; Sears, 1970). Armentrout and Bunger (1972) write that mothers who are excessively controlling of their children tend to have youngsters who are dependent and immature, and Schaffer (1972) found that such mothers tended to interfere with the child's formation of realistic goals and mature peer relationships.

Prosocial behavior, with low aggression, is often associated with having parents who are warm, loving, responsible, and ready to serve as role models. In general, the development of prosocial behavior is associated with direct training by parents as well as with opportunities for identification with mothers and fathers who are both nurturant and democratic in behavior and attitudes (Mussen, et al., 1979).

Baumrind (1973) learned that preschool children who manifested the most positive behaviors (self-reliance, self-control, competence, and an explorative nature) tended to have parents who were especially loving, consistent, secure, and firm in discipline. These parents tended to give reasons for their decisions and to be highly communicative with their youngsters. Baumrind also reports that parents whose children exhibited little self-control and self-reliance tended to be insecure about their ability to influence their children and to be low in their own sense of well-being. In following the development of these children into their adolescence, Baumrind (1973) found a continuation of these trends with teenagers of loving, consistently firm parents being more apt than other adolescents to be clear about their own value systems and increasingly capable of self-determination.

Overly permissive mothers tend to have children who lack self-control and who are impulsive and hostile. Poor maternal discipline has been found more frequently among children who are overly assertive and easily frustrated. Moreover, permissive mothers may be seen by their children as being fundamentally rejecting and hostile; this perception by the children may lead to further maternal rejection (Field & Widmayer, 1982).

Elster and Lamb (1986, pp. 178–179) summarize research on positive parental behaviors, including those of fathers, as well as mothers. They write:

> Over the last few decades, many theorists have come to believe that a pattern of parental behavior involving warm, sensitive responsiveness to children's needs or signals coupled with a rational, inductive disciplinary style in later years facilitates secure, trustful infant–parent attachments, a self-confident and assertive style of interaction with peers, an internalized conscience, cognitive competence, and an enthusiatically resourceful approach to challenging tasks. Although researchers have generally studied the effects of "sensitive," "optimal," or "authoritative" maternal behavior, the few studies of fathers that have been completed confirm that a similar pattern of effects is also obtained with them.
>
> Originally, theorists assumed that the ability to provide sensitive parental care was an intrinsic characteristic of the parent, with individual differences in sensitivity constituting an enduring characteristic or trait. It has become increasingly clear, however, that although some enduring personality characteristics may be correlated with sensitivity, parental competence may vary substantially depending on the parent's circumstances and the child's characteristics.

Another group of studies has indicated that poor relationships between parents and children are strongly associated with delinquency among adolescents. Many delinquents were found by researchers to have parents who were lax and erratic or overly strict and punitive in disciplinary techniques. Mutually hostile relations, lack of family cohesiveness, parental indifference, low aspirations for sons and daughters, and hostility toward the school characterized many of these parents.

A large amount of research from the early 1930s through the 1980s indicates that boys more than girls appear to be adversely affected by problems in parenting on the part of both mothers and fathers. For example, on the average, boys are more adversely affected than are girls by family conflict in both one- and two-parent families (Cadoret

& Cain, 1980; Emery & O'Leary, 1982). When family conflict occurs, boys are more prone to respond with less control than girls. Poor control, particularly when it takes the combination of aggressiveness, non-compliance, and demandingness found in stressed boys, may be particularly likely to turn off compassionate responses in others (Hetherington, 1984).

Various streams of research, including some of the studies quoted above, have shown that parenting effectiveness and satisfactions tend to be closely associated with feelings of self-confidence and a sense of personal competence (Campbell, 1980; Pearlin & Schooler, 1982). Other research provides evidence that feelings of worthlessness and depression are associated with problems in parenting such as lack of sufficient attention to a child's needs, inconsistency of discipline, and high impulsivity (Coletta, 1983; Conger et al., in press; Field, 1984; Weissman, Paykel, & Klerman, 1972). Conversely, a number of recent studies have revealed the positive association between high ego strength, favorable self-regard, and the personal flexibility of parents with their responsivity, nurturance, and warmth toward their children (Benn, 1985; Heinicke, 1985; Stevens, 1986).

Fairly similar results were obtained in a number of studies of life satisfactions carried out during the 1970s. They revealed that the great majority of adults in this country reported themselves to be mostly happy and satisfied with their lives, with their families being the central feature in their happiness (Campbell, 1980; Campbell, Converse, & Rodgers, 1976; Chilman, 1979, 1980; Hoffman, Thornton, & Manis, 1978; Veroff, Douvan, & Kulka, 1981).

About 18% of the mothers and fathers in a midwest study expressed dissatisfaction with their parenting roles (Chilman 1979, 1980). When parents with high satisfaction scores were compared to those with low ones, in this middle-class sample it was found that the two groups differed in a number of ways, with dissatisfied parents more apt than satisfied ones to say they felt incompetent as parents. They also tended to rate their marriages as unsatisfying and to view their childhood relationships with their own parents as having been unhappy.

This research also inquired about the parents' satisfactions with many factors in the outer environment: jobs, income, child care facilities, schools, recreation, friends, and health and other community services. It was learned that no aspect of the environment differentiated the satisfied parents from the dissatisfied ones. It was also learned that the numbers and ages of children within the family did not make a difference to parent satisfactions. In short, the psychological characteristics of the parents themselves and their experiences within their families of origin seemed to be central to parents' satisfaction with motherhood or fatherhood.

The importance of the experience of parents in their own early development has been recently underscored by Elder, Caspi, and Downey (1986). These researchers drew on the Oakland and Berkeley growth longitudinal studies of more than 100 men and 100 women. They found that there was a significant (albeit rather small) correlation between hostile, conflicted marital and parent–child relationship patterns from generation to generation for a total of four generations. For example, growing up in a home in which parents' behavior was unstable, where marital conflict was frequent, and in which parental care was seen as unloving, dominant, and hostile had pervasive effects on their youngsters who, when they became adults, tended to become involved in unhappy marriages and generally cold, inconsistent parent–child relationships. This tendency had a more than chance probability of being repeated in following generations unless positive, corrective interventions occurred such as forming strong marriages with competent, affectionate, supportive spouses, receiving effective therapy, or enjoying highly satisfying educational or occupational success.

Although fairly similar results were found in nationwide studies during the 1970s, the Chilman findings, noted above, may particularly apply to the kind of middle-class sample she studied—a population with little experience of serious job, income, housing, and similar problems. For example, a number of studies document the strains imposed on blue-collar men who often feel that they are locked into dead-end employment with little job security (Elder, 1974; Schorr & Moen, 1979). These strains often cause them to be either uncommunicative and withdrawn or irritable and authoritarian in their family relationships (Pietrowski, 1979). Then, too, studies by Kohn and Schooler (1983) reveal that employees who have low-level jobs with little freedom for initiative or opportunities for power are apt to be autocratic as fathers and stress conformity in their child-rearing behaviors (see also Volume 1, Chapter 1).

As noted earlier, few research projects have focused on the total interaction of families. In contrast, numerous clinical observations have been made by child and family therapists regarding the maladaptive relationships of family members who have children with severe emotional disturbances or such illnesses as autism or schizophrenia.

A thorough discussion of the problems of psychotic children and adolescents is beyond the scope of this chapter. Suffice it to say here that much of the research and theory building regarding family dynamics originated with clinical studies of families with mentally disturbed members. In searching for the probable causes for these disturbances, investigators frequently placed the blame on parents with a now-familiar thesis emerging that difficulties were usually caused by overly dominant mothers and weak, passive fathers.

More recently this thesis has been seen as simplistic. It appears that genetic factors play a large part in the onset of schizophrenia for some patients, although the role of genetics is unclear for others. Goldstein (1978) comments that there are probably a number of kinds of schizophrenia with different precipitating factors for differing types (in general, onset rarely occurs before age 15). He presents evidence from his own research and that of others to the effect that a combination of communication deviance (lack of commitment to ideas or precepts, unclear communication of ideas, disruptive speech) plus a negative affective style (criticism, guilt inducement, and intrusiveness) were more typical of parents with a schizophrenic child than parents of nonschizophrenic offspring. Goldstein points out further that while parental style along these dimensions seems important, children may well differ in their vulnerability to difficult parent behaviors. Moreover, the disturbed behavior of a psychotic daughter or son may well elicit many of the behavioral difficulties observed in parents.

Effects of Child's Age on Parent–Child Relationships

A fairly large body of social and psychological research explores the effects of the child's age on parent–child relationships. Because both children and parents are apt to have somewhat different characteristics at different stages of their development, their effect on each other is apt to vary as both move through the life course. The most extensive studies have focused on the effects of pregnancy and the first birth. Relatively little attention has been paid to the impact of the middle years of childhood (ages 6 to 12). Somewhat more emphasis has been placed on parent–child relationships during adolescence with a particular focus on adolescent problem behaviors such as teen pregnancy and parenting, drug use, and delinquency (see Volumes 4 and 5).

The brief overview of pertinent age-related research given here particularly emphasizes associated problematic parent–child relationships because this is the focus of this chapter. A more general coverage of the topic would far exceed the limits of this total volume.

Pregnancy Effects

Although there is less agreement among researchers than formerly that the pregnancy experience has a strong, permanent effect on both parent and child, there is still recognition that a negative pregnancy and childbirth experience often adversely affects parent–child relations, at least in the first few months of the baby's life. Osofsky and Osofsky (1984) report on their own related research and that of others. Through their case studies they found that many pregnant women experience fears and worries about themselves and their coming babies. They are concerned about work and home patterns and how their adult relationships will be affected by their new status. Sharing these concerns with husbands and others was found to be helpful.

Lamb (1978) indicates that pregnancy often triggers dramatic changes in all the family relationships and may lead to changes in maternal behavior, including changes toward older children in terms of decreasing warmth, intimacy, and child-rearing effectiveness. Marital relationships are also probably affected during this period but, unfortunately, little research attention has been given to this topic. Zeits and Prince (1982) provide an important reminder that pregnancy is also characterized by a host of profound physiological changes that are apt to have pervasive physical and psychological effects, both on the mother and on the members of her family.

Entwisle and Doering (1981), in another intensive series of case studies, found that prior preparation helps couples better cope with pregnancy, labor, and delivery. Social support from family, community, and friends is also important.

Shereshefsky and Yarrow (1973) did a series of case studies of middle-class families during pregnancy and delivery. They learned that personality factors, especially a woman's relation to her own mother, were strongly related to the woman's ability to cope with pregnancy. (See also Chodorow, 1978.) In virtually all of these investigations the importance of a positive marital relationship was also noted. For instance, Shereshefsky and Yarrow (1973) learned that families burdened with more stresses initially and those already involved in serious marital disharmony at the time of pregnancy tended to experience more stress than others in their sample.

Very few investigators have adequately looked at the coping and developmental processes of American fathers during pregnancy. Conclusions from the few available studies strongly suggest that most husbands go through considerable emotional upheaval during their wives' pregnancies (the reactions of unmarried couples have not been studied). Life circumstances, preexisting levels of emotional development, family and community supports, the strength of the marital relationship, and opportunities to discuss their feelings all affect the adjustment of husbands to the pregnancy.

The Impact of the Birth of the First Child

Many research projects have been undertaken to prove or disprove the thesis that the birth of the first child creates a crisis for parents. Conflicting results have been obtained (Dyer, 1963; Feldman, 1971; Hobbs, 1963; LeMasters, 1957; Ryder, 1974). For many parents, probably the majority, the stresses that generally arise in the transition to parenthood (such as physical and financial strains, reduced freedom, change in status, shift in focus from a twosome to a triangle) are offset by the deep psychological, social, and physical gratifications that the new baby is apt to bring.

Belsky (1984) found in an intensive year-long study of the impact of an infant's birth on first-time, white, middle-class parents that the transition to parenthood had negative effects only on some of the mothers and some of the fathers in their perceptions of their marital satisfactions. This was most likely to occur for women when their expectations of what motherhood would be like were rosier than they later perceived it to be. Belsky also found that, in general, couples reported that their sense of marriage as a romance and friendship decreased but their sense of marital partnership increased during the last trimester of pregnancy and after the baby's birth. Moreover, their interaction style tended to change from a largely emotional to a more instrumental one.

Recent investigations of father involvement in infant care have generated an important shift in the conceptualization of parent–child relationships. These investigations found that the involvement of the father in child care had a positive effect on the mother–child relationship (Pederson et al., 1981) and that the quality of the marital relationship heavily affected the nature and degree of paternal involvement with the child. Thus, far more attention than formerly has been given in recent years by researchers to the impact of family system relationships (at least marital relationships) on parent–child interaction (Lamb, 1981). It is interesting to note that some researchers have found that for women the roles of parent and spouse appear to be more independent than they are for men who seem to be either highly involved in the family (via interaction with spouse) or not very involved. It also appears that child-oriented communication from mother to father seems to foster father involvement.

A number of studies are quoted by Pederson and colleagues (1981) to show that a high quality of marital relationship plus psychological support in infant care given by each parent to the other was highly predictive of a smooth transition to parenthood. These qualities also helped to override the negative effects of having an ill or difficult child.

As mentioned earlier, studies have shown that individual characteristics of infants have strong effects on parent–child and husband–wife relationships. For instance, prematurity of a child and the related anxieties plus demands for intensive infant care put severe stress on marriages, with divorces occurring more often following this event than in the case of full-term infants.

Field and Widmayer (1982) write that disturbed interactions between mothers and children often first appear during infancy. For example, a passive, unresponsive infant may stimulate a mother to become either hyperactive, anxious, and controlling or uninvolved and depressed, depending, in part, on the mother's personality. Inappropriate behaviors of mothers, stimulated by the characteristics of their infants, tend to have an unfortunate circular effect, with infants developing disturbed responses that in turn stimulate undesirable maternal behaviors such as either over-control or neglect. Maternal over-control tends to elicit dependent, passive, withdrawn behavior on the part of children. On the other hand, maternal passivity and inattention tends to inhibit a child's cognitive, language, and social development (Field & Widmayer, 1982).

Although there is much argument in the literature about the meaning and importance of infant–parent attachment, a general conclusion emerges to the effect that attachment processes are weakened when mothers are cold, rejecting, inattentive, or inconsistent in their presences and absences. Weak attachment between parent and child undermines the youngster's cognitive, social, and emotional development. She or he tends to have little trust in the self or other people and slight ability to withstand short periods of separation from parents (Ainsworth et al., 1978).

Mother-infant attachment theories have been altered by the growing interest of researchers in the role of fathers in child rearing. Here again, most of the research has focused on infancy. Such specialists in the field as Parke (1979), Lamb (1978), and Clarke-Stewart (1977) have found that fathers tend to interact with their babies and young children in a more playful and rough-and-tumble fashion than do mothers, with the latter being both more instrumental and verbal in their care-taking behaviors.

Recent studies have also examined the effects of substitute day care on young children because in a growing number of cases both parents (or the single parent) are employed outside the home. In general, findings so far lead to the tentative conclusion that infants and young children are not adversely affected by substitute care if that care is of high quality (a rather large if) and if the parents are consistently available to the child for frequent, intensive, nurturant interactions (another large if). (See also Volume 1. Chapters 1 and 2).

Mussen and colleagues (1979) write that behavioral and personality characteristics of very young children are not necessarily permanent. For example, if children show problem behaviors at less than 2 years of age, these difficulties may no longer be observable by age 5 if the child does not have a constitutional defect and if the conditions that produced the characteristics are favorably altered in the next 3 or 4 years.

Much of the psychological research about parent–child relationships and child behaviors has been traditionally carried out in laboratory settings. This has tended to produce artificial results and to overlook the realities of everyday family life. For instance, aside from the Hoffman and Manis (1978) nationwide studies, little appears in the research regarding both the pleasures and pains of living with babies and toddlers. As this author's studies of parent satisfactions and dissatisfactions show, although the majority of parents say they find child-rearing very enjoyable and important, it is also much harder work than other jobs they are experiencing or have experienced (Chilman, 1979, 1980).

Parenting Preschool Children

The sheer physical labor of rearing young children is quite astonishing, especially in a period with little household help and few ready sources of support from the neighborhood. This is especially true when there are two or more closely spaced young children in the family and particularly so for single-parent and low-income families. The psychological stresses of living with the dependency, self-centeredness, narcissism, and impulsivity of young children are also seldom recognized by the researchers. Then, too, the push of toddlers for self-determination, exploration, and mastery puts severe demands on the protective vigilance of the parent or substitute caretaker.

Although the majority of American parents report this period of a child's life as being very rewarding in terms of love for the child and the enjoyment of watching him or her develop, they also find it to be extremely demanding of their time, energy, and patience (Chilman, 1979, 1980; Hoffman & Manis, 1978; Veroff, Douvan, & Kulka, 1981). Moreover, Hoffman and Manis (1978) found in a national study that more highly educated mothers were particularly apt to express dissatisfaction with this stage, presumably because they had a wide variety of aspirations and goals and were especially frustrated by the many demands of their young children.

Hetherington (1984) notes that far too little attention has been paid by psychologists to the impact of children on the marital relationship as well as the impact of that relationship on the children. Conflict between spouses is apt to have particularly negative effects on young children, especially if they are boys and/or temperamentally vulnerable youngsters. These vulnerable children tend to react with behavior problems to spousal conflicts and this, in turn, tends to direct displaced parental anger on to them (Block et al., 1981; Emery & O'Leary, 1982); Hetherington, 1984; Rutter, 1983).

Children at Midstage

Children's psychological problems appear to be more prevalent at some ages than are others. For instance, referrals to child guidance clinics tend to peak at ages 4 to 7, 9 to 11, and 14 to 16. Mussen and colleagues (1979) speculate that these appear to be ages of transition when shifts in physiological and cognitive growth plus pressures imposed by parents and the larger society put particular stresses on youngsters. Prior to puberty boys tend to have a far higher incidence of problem behaviors than do girls. These problems include learning difficulties, disruptive school behaviors, and high levels of aggression and destructiveness. Girls are more apt to be shy, fearful, anxious, and withdrawn.

Children at midstage (ages 6 to 12), emerging from the many vulnerabilities and dependencies of the earlier years, become young "commuters" from home to an ever-widening world. School, neighborhood peer groups, and youth organizations become more and more important as increasing cognitive, social, and physical abilities make most of these girls and boys more able to cope with the larger world.

Highly aggressive youngsters are apt to get into more trouble than they did earlier as their scope for action widens and as the larger society takes their acting-out behavior more and more seriously. Because school is the major serious business for this age group, learning and behavior problems in this setting become increasingly problematic as the child grows older and, as is often the case, learning problems become cumulative. Parents of such children are apt to grow more and more alarmed, and their mounting concerns may be translated into inappropriate behaviors that further strain parent–child relationships.

Although shy, fearful, anxious children at midstage are less apt to get into overt trouble than are their aggressive counterparts, they may well have learning problems at school and difficulties in the development of physical and social skills. Their problems often elicit negative parent behaviors, behaviors that are apt to vary depending on the personalities, values, and goals of the parents. For instance, some parents may exert pressure for improved performance, others may be overprotective, others may distance themselves from the child and see him or her as a "loser." (Of course, some parents may respond more appropriately to both their shy children and their expressive ones by increasing their acceptance, warmth, and support, attempting to understand the child's problem, but our focus here is chiefly on *disturbed* rather than on positive parent–child relationships.)

As noted earlier, although most of the research and writing in this field tends to view both the mother and father in the child's family as having similar attitudes, goals, and behaviors, this is actually far from the case in many families. Husband and wife reactions to a child's problems are apt to be quite dissimilar, with the result that each parent may be giving different messages to the child. Moreover, the different perceptions of the two parents, plus their anxieties when their children have problems, may well create (or escalate already existing) marital conflict and disruptive child–mother or child–father coalitions.

Further development of gender and sex identity is also an important aspect of the child's life at midstage. Although Freud and his colleagues saw this period as the "latency" stage in which, compared to earlier and later developmental stages, sexual issues were of little importance to children, later studies have questioned this assumption. It seems more likely that apparently "sexless" midstage children have chiefly learned to hide their sexual interests and behaviors from adults.

Although sexuality is generally recognized as being a central aspect of human life, very little systematic social and behavioral research with human subjects has addressed this topic with respect to the years before adolescence. In contrast, clinical literature has numerous references to the topic and, of course, the development of sexuality during infancy and early childhood has been a core element of psychoanalytic theory. A few studies have been carried out concerning gender role identity and sex education as provided (or rather, *not* provided) by parents—far less delicate subjects than childhood masturbation, sex "talk" and curiosity, exhibitionism, voyeurism, and attempts at coitus (Chilman, 1983).

Although systematic research evidence seems to be lacking, it appears likely that aggressive youngsters who have little impulse control would tend to "act out" their sexual interests more openly than less disturbed children. Because these youngsters usually suffer from already strained parent–child relationships, such behaviors would probably have a strong negative impact, given the usual sex taboos in our society.

In the case of children who are particularly inhibited, fearful, and anxious, sexual interests may be denied but then be expressed through secret fantasies, compulsions toward purity and cleanliness as a defense against (sexual) dirt, nightmares of being (sexually) attacked, and so on. Such defenses may make the child withdraw further from interpersonal contacts, including interaction with parents.

Of course, the impact of a child's sexuality on parents will vary according to the feelings, values, and beliefs each parent has about his or her own sexuality as well as that of the children. Among other things, the sexuality of daughters and sons is apt to have an impact on the marital relationship of parents, especially if they have unresolved sexual issues in that relationship.

Returning to the relatively safe topic of establishing gender identity, children are usually clear about whether they are girls or boys and about many of the sex-role behaviors expected of them by the time they are 3 or 4 years old. This comes about, for the most part, through the child's cognitive development, identification with the same sex parent, support of the youngster's gender behavior by both parents, and social learning from the family and the larger society (Hetherington, Cox, & Cox, 1979; Kohlberg, 1964; Money & Ehrhardt, 1972; Shepherd-Look, 1982).

Disturbances in gender identity may arise from those rare constitutional difficulties that result in problems in gender assignment at birth (Money & Ehrhardt, 1972); physical or psychological absence of the mother or father from the home; negative, rejecting relationships with parents; failures of mothers or fathers to accept *their* gender; confusion about new norms that favor complete similarity between the sexes; and the like.

Parent–Youth Relationships During Adolescence

Already strained parent–child relationships and associated behavioral problems are apt to become even more acute when children enter adolescence unless helpful intervening factors such as family treatment have occurred earlier. However, this does not imply that all or even the majority of adolescents go through a profoundly troubled, stormy period at this stage. Although adolescence has been frequently described as a period of turmoil and revolt against parents, studies by Douvan and Adelson (1966) and Offer and Offer (1969), among others, reveal that most adolescents pass through this period with only minor disturbances. However, children whose behavior has been difficult in the past, who have had poor relationships with their parents, or who have lived in strife-torn families may well show an increase in difficulties during the teen years in response to a host of interacting variables including enormous changes within their own bodies; the particular timing of their puberty, especially if it is earlier or later than the average of about age 12 for girls and 14 for boys; their stage of cognitive development; difficulties within the family system; pressures from parents, peers, and teachers; the characteristics of the surrounding society; and so on (Chilman, 1983; Coleman, J. C., 1980; Conger, 1973; Dragastin & Elder, 1975; Elkind, 1967; Marcia, 1980).

Issues of autonomy and independence from parents are apt to be particularly acute in early adolescence, whereas such issues as individual identity, a personal set of values, and the search for a (more or less) permanent mate often become more central in late adolescence

(Gordon, 1972). These varying issues at different stages put varying kinds of pressures on parents and the young people themselves. These pressures are often perceived as particularly acute because adolescents by virtue of their age, developmental stage, and size are able to get into far more serious trouble than younger children and society is far less forgiving of teenagers than of little girls and boys. Then, too, parents of adolescents are apt to be in a vulnerable transition stage themselves from young adulthood to middle age, and they may find living with teenagers particularly stressful.

Although it is generally assumed that membership in and conformity to peer groups is of central importance to all adolescents, research indicates that the influence of peers compared to that of parents is relatively minor when young people are over age 15; are high in self-esteem; and belong to families in which there is little conflict and in which parents have been affectionate, accepting, open in communication, clear, and firm about discipline as well as self-reliant themselves (Coleman, J. C., 1980; Conger, 1973; Jessor & Jessor, 1975). (See also the section in this chapter "General Research Findings.")

Various kinds of problems become more acute, or at least clearly recognized, during adolescence. Delinquency, school truancy, chemical dependencies, and early non-marital sex activity with a number of partners may be defined as belonging to the typology of aggressive, uncontrolled, acting out behaviors (see also Volume 5). On the other hand, depression and suicide may be classified as extremes of withdrawn behavior. However, depressed adolescents may mask their basic feelings of loss and hopelessness through a range of acting-out behaviors in a frantic search for relief from feelings of despair.

Sexuality is an important aspect of adolescent development that often strains parent–youth relationships. As discussed earlier, adolescents do not suddenly errupt into being sexual; rather, their feelings, behaviors, beliefs, and attitudes about themselves as young women or men slowly evolve from infancy through childhood and into the teen years. However, their sexuality becomes more obvious and pronounced as they move through puberty and as their parents and society perceive them as being able to reproduce, with all of the costs and rewards that this may entail. Parents tend to become especially concerned about the sexuality of their daughters, partly because it is girls who become pregnant and partly because of the double standard of sexual morality that often labels sexual activities of girls as deviant and dangerous but accepts the sexuality of boys as being inevitable and normal: a spectacular example of sexism in our culture.

How smooth or troublesome the development of adolescents' sexuality is to themselves and to their families depends on a host of factors, both internal and external to the family. The physical, social, and psychological development of the adolescent as a masculine or feminine person is a fundamental part of this stage. It is natural and necessary for teenagers to be highly concerned about their gender identity, physical and social adequacy as young women and men, and values and beliefs about all aspects of sexual behavior including issues of appropriate sex-role functioning and the expression of their increasingly strong sex drives (Chilman, 1983; Gagnon & Simon, 1973; Matteson, 1975; Vener & Stewart, 1974).

The proportion of adolescents who engage in nonmarital inter- course has increased markedly in recent years, just one aspect of the recent social and sexual revolution. For instance, in 1979 almost half of 17-year-old girls and boys in this country had become sexually experienced before marriage; this is in contrast to about 10% of girls and 20% of boys before the mid-1960s (Chilman, 1983).

Note that changes in sexual behavior do not mean that every adolescent is having intercourse. Also, despite public alarms, these behaviors do not mean that "all sexually active girls get pregnant." In 1980 this was the case for about 20% of those who had coitus in that year, and half of this group terminated their pregnancies through abortion. Then, too, most sexually active teenagers are not engaged in "promiscuous" sexual behavior. For instance, in 1979 the majority who were participating in coitus usually had only one partner and had intercourse only several times a month, if that often (Zelnik, Kantner, & Ford, 1982).

Major points were made at the start of this chapter to the effect that a complex of factors interact to affect the behaviors of children and adolescents, with the child-rearing behaviors of parents being only one of them. Analysis of large bodies of research regarding factors associated with adolescent nonmarital coitus and adolescent use of contraceptives illustrates this point. These factors are many and are both internal and external to the family and to adolescents as individuals. They include such variables as race; age at puberty; socioeconomic and marital status of the parents; period of time in which the young person grew up; stage of his or her physical and cognitive development as well as his or her educational aspirational level and employment history; religiosity of parents and teens; the young person's self-esteem and needs for affection and attention from others; child-rearing patterns of the parents, especially expressed affection and open communication, role modeling, and use of clear, consistent discipline; alienated and risk-taking attitudes of teens; behaviors and attitudes of siblings and friends; conflict between the teenager's family and his or her peer groups; and the availability of high-quality educational and health (including family planning) services. (See, for example, Chilman, 1983; Cvetkovich & Grote, 1975; Furstenberg, 1976; Jessor & Jessor, 1975; Presser, 1974; Zelnik, Kantner, & Ford, 1982). It is important, then, to recognize that relationships between parents and their adolescent youngsters are only one part of a complex of variables affecting the young person's sexual behavior (see also Volume 5, Chapter 5).

Characteristics of the young person's total family system also play a vital part in many aspects of his or her behavior, but to date clinical observations rather than research tend to highlight this point. However, Olson, McCubbin, & Associates (1983) carried out a welcome study of marital and family system factors associated with different levels of family adjustment. They found that the adolescent stage presented the highest level of stress and tension in the families they studied. Families with strong marital relationships in which parents felt confident about themselves as a couple and were satisfied with their couple communication and conflict-resolution skills as well as their overall quality of life were the most satisfied with this generally difficult period in the family life cycle. Good parent–adolescent communication was also a strength characteristic of those families which handled this stage with a minimum of stress.

SUMMARY

This chapter has examined research concerning strained relationships between parents and their children under the age of 18. It is limited in its coverage, avoiding related topics discussed elsewhere in this series: family violence and neglect, divorce and remarriage, single parenthood, mental illness of adults, chemical dependencies, crime and delinquency, and physical illness and handicaps.

Two major types of problematic child behaviors associated with strained parent–child relationships were discussed. These types are aggressive, acting-out behavior and shy, fearful, withdrawn behavior. Although child-rearing patterns are often seen as the cause of these behaviors, a much broader research and theory approach is needed that takes into account father–child as well as mother–child relationships plus the whole complex of family interactions including those of the extended kinship network and their effect on the development of children in that network. Moreover, it is also important to recognize the impact of environmental systems external to the family, the effects of the period of time in which family has lived together, and the physical and constitutional characteristics of individual family members. In brief, it is overly narrow to view children's development into adulthood as being solely or even chiefly a product of the relationships between them and their parents, important as these relationships may be.

Despite deficits in the research, numerous studies over the years have concluded that parental acceptance, warmth, and support along with firm, mild, consistent discipline appear to be central to a child's positive self-concept and favorable emotional and social development. Parental behaviors of these kinds tend to rest upon the parents' sense of competence in family roles as well as their feelings of general well-being and self-confidence. Moreover, satisfaction with one's marriage and a harmonious relationship with the spouse are conducive to the favorable parent behaviors cited above. Parental and marital satisfactions also appear to be tied to positive relationships within the family of origin. Also important are the temperamental, physical, and intellectual characteristics of the children themselves and the ways they interact with their parents at different stages in the family life cycle.

Although adolescence is not necessarily a period of turmoil, many critical factors may intersect at this time to intensify whatever parent–child relationship problems have tended to exist, and this period of transition is illustrative of others in the family development process. These factors include biological changes within the developing adolescent and transition stages within the family (including midstage for parents and retirement stage for grandparents), social norms of the larger society (such as the impact of the so-called sexual revolution of the 1960s), the state of the economy, the availability of jobs for both parents and youth, the presence of racism and sexism that may create barriers for racial minorities and women, and so on.

All these variables as well as others are apt to affect relationships between parents and children. To the extent that these factors have only moderately stressful components for family members and to the extent that these members have inner psychological and outer environmental resources to deal with stress, to that extent will fathers, mothers and their teenage children be more likely to deal effectively with these and other frequently difficult problems in family relationships over the lifespan.

The Treatment of Disturbed Parent–Child Relationships

6

EVE LIPCHIK

This chapter discusses the clinical treatment of disturbed parent–child relationships. The definitions of children (under 18) and of problematic child behavior associated with these disturbed relationships (as recognized by highly aggressive, rebellious, hostile or very shy, withdrawn, inhibited behavior) can be found in Chapter 5.

This chapter is written from an interactional point of view, and symptoms are thus seen as bits of troublesome interactional patterns *between* people rather psychopathology *within* individual family members or the family system. Therefore, disturbed parent–child relationships must always be thought of in terms of the child's behavior and the parents' response as well as the parents' behavior and the child's response. Also, it is not useful for treatment purposes to think of behavior simply as aggressive or withdrawn. These are general categories that do not permit easy recognition of concrete signs of difficulties and change. Therapists will find it essential to get more specific descriptions of child behaviors from families, such as disobedience, running away, excessive weepiness, refusal to attend school, eating or sleeping too little or too much, not doing homework, stealing, bedwetting, setting fires, and lying. They also need specific descriptions of parent behaviors such as yelling, criticizing, hitting, not spending enough time with the child, not praising accomplishments, and so on. Small, concrete changes for the better, when indentified, provide motivation to continue trying and perhaps take even larger risks toward solutions.

The behavior of children who have been diagnosed as or are said to be hyperactive, or hyperkinetic, is also included as problematic child behavior associated with disturbed parent–child relationships. Because the symptoms (restlessness, short attention span, impulsiveness, low frustration tolerance) are not unique to hyperactivity and because the literature indicates that to date there is no reliable method for the assessment and diagnosis of hyperactivity (Homatidis & Konstantareas, 1981; Ullman, et al., 1981) nor a treatment of choice (Cohen et al., 1981; Dubey, O'Leary, & Kaufman,

1983; Wolraich, 1979), this chapter treats this complaint much like any other presented by parents. It is to be understood that in those cases where there is conclusive evidence of a significant organic factor underlying the problematic behavior, drug therapy may be indicated in conjunction with psychotherapy.

Finally, the treatment described in this chapter is a method that is applicable to inpatient as well as outpatient settings. In situations where parents and children are not living together at the time of treatment, the "family system" may have to be thought of as including people the child is living with presently or other mental health professionals involved with the child and the parents.

HISTORICAL BACKGROUND

One cannot actually speak of treatment of the disturbed parent–child *relationship* prior to the early work in family therapy by pioneers such as Ackerman (1958), Wynne and colleagues (1958), and Bowen (1961). In the early twentieth century the child was treated individually in situations in which his or her behavior disturbed parents. Two choices were available: child guidance clinics and psychoanalysis. The former were an outgrowth of the feminist and mental hygiene movements at the time and offered treatment by a multidisciplinary team: The child was tested by a psychologist and treated by a psychiatrist while a social caseworker saw the parents. The latter was the outgrowth of the work of Sigmund Freud.

The first reported case study of the psychoanalytic treatment of a child was in 1909, the famous case of Little Hans (Freud, 1909), in which Freud supervised the child's father in the treatment of the 5-year-old son's horse phobia. Subsequently Freud's daughter Anna and Melanie Klein developed theoretically divergent schools of psychoanalysis for children (Freud, 1946; Klein, 1955), with Anna Freud's "Vienna School" (which treated only exceptional children) being the first to recognize the importance of work with the family. The theoretic orientation guiding all of the treatment mentioned above was psychodynamic. Symptoms were viewed as the child's inability to cope with unresolved internal conflicts.

By the 1930s, various other types of treatment for children became available, some based on psychodynamic theory such as play therapy (Allen, 1942; Conn, 1939) and release therapy (Levy, 1938), others based on operant conditioning and learning theory, known as behavior therapy (Dollard & Miller, 1950; Eysenck,

1960; Lazarus, 1960; Mowrer, 1950; Wolpe, 1958), as well as group therapy (Slavson, 1952) and others. While the behaviorists were the first to make extensive use of the parents of the child patient in the process of modifying his or her behavior (parent-consultation or parent-training treatment models), it was not until families were begun to be seen from a systemic (Buckley, 1968; von Bertalanffy, 1968) and cybernetic (Bateson, 1971; Maruyama 1968; Wiener, 1954) point of view that one can truly begin to talk about treating the parent–child *relationship*. It was then that the focus for intervention became the interactional patterns between members of the family system, not the individual pathology or faulty learning of the individuals.

Family therapy in the 1980s has assumed a systemic orientation, although many different models have cropped up under that umbrella, such as structural (Minuchin, 1974), systemic (Selvini-Palazzoli et al., 1978), intergenerational (Boszormeny-Nagy & Spark, 1973; Bowen, 1961, 1978), communication-interaction (Luftman & Kirshenbaum, 1974; Satir, 1964; Satir & Baldwin, 1985), strategic (de Shazer, 1982, 1985; Watzlawick et al., 1974; Weakland et al., 1974). In the past decade there has been a movement to develop models that integrate some or all of the developments to date (Feldman, 1985; Kantor & Neal, 1985; Pinsof, 1983). Many family therapists use an eclectic approach and apply different techniques from different models.

It should also be noted that physicians in the field of psychosomatic medicine were among the first to recognize that symptoms are the result of relationships between people. For example, in 1930 the term "parentectomy" was invented by a pediatrician named Peshkin (Harper, 1983) who discovered in his work with asthmatic children that family relations, not allergens, are the bronchospastic factors.

TREATMENT CONSIDERATIONS

Therapists treating disturbed parent–child relationships from a systemic point of view must take into consideration the cognitive, physical, and emotional development of the child as well as the parental characteristics that pertain to their desire and ability to parent. Although the intervention may address the interactional process, that process must be guided by certain societal and developmental norms as well as by the characteristics of those in interaction. In the previous chapter Chilman documents some of the pertinent research in this area, for example, the effect of parents' reactions to their children from birth through adolescence, the effect of children on parents as individuals as well as on their marital relationship, and the effect of the parents' marital status and satisfaction on the children. These studies provide evidence for viewing every case as having idiosyncratic interactional complexity.

A given in any parent–child relationship is the parents' responsibility to promote the healthy development of the child by means of physical and emotional nurturing, guidance, and teaching. Thus, even though the assumptions of systemic treatment models are that behavior is recursive, the solution to the disturbed relationship requires that the parents provide what dependent children need for healthy development and that they feel competent in parenting. This notion then implies that it is the parents who should be viewed as the primary contributors to the solution.

Unfortunately, the simplest, most logical solutions are often not the ones most easily attainable. Therefore, the systemic therapist must assess each system individually and be open to many different ways of constructing solutions with its members to bring about therapeutic results that fit the particular system.

The relationship between parents and their children is the most basic and formative of all human interactions. It strongly affects children's sense of self-worth through adolescence, when it becomes the arena for their struggle for independence. Ideally, parents must gradually relinquish control and permit their children to assume responsibility for their own life decisions. Not only do parents and children rarely agree on when and how this is to occur, but frequently mothers and fathers have differences of opinion about this as well. Ultimately, parents must let go, and young adults must make choices that are best for themselves regardless of what their parents think. But for parents, too, this relationship is vital for self-esteem. They tend to see offspring as extensions of themselves—for better or for worse—and bask in their children's successes and feel guilty about their failures. They are no less ambivalent about their children's gradual and continuous striving for physical and emotional independence than the children are because the success parents want to take credit for also deprives them of the satisfaction of being looked up to and needed.

Thus the therapist must also consider parental behaviors such as permissiveness, authoritarianism, indecisiveness, inconsistency, irritability, and so on when constructing a solution with a particular family, despite the fact that the parents usually initiate treatment and present the complaints from their point of view. The therapist must construct a "frame" of the presented complaint from the verbal and nonverbal information provided during the assessment while simultaneously creating and maintaining a context in which solutions can be found as easily as possible. Because parents decide whether treatment will continue, it is best to use their frame of the complaint in discussing the situation. Creating any defensiveness on their part at the outset of treatment either results in their decision not to return or complicates treatment considerably.

RESEARCH

In their overview of research about the effectiveness of psychotherapy, Lambert, Shapiro, and Bergin (1986) conclude that in general it has a positive effect and is better than no intervention.

The present state of research in the area of child psychotherapy is perhaps best illustrated by the changes Garfield and Bergin made in 1986 in the third edition of their *Handbook of Psychotherapy and Behavior Change*. In the second edition (1978), they included a chapter about "Research on Child Psychotherapy," whereas in the 1986 edition they did not. Instead, they have a chapter on "Child and Adolescent Behavior Therapy." This was foreshadowed by the earlier chapter's report that there is increasingly less material available on child psychotherapy because of the shrinking availability of direct services for children and the strong trend toward behavior and family therapy.

For the past two to three decades behavior treatment of children's "conduct disorders" (as defined at the beginning of this chapter) has dominated the literature. The assumption was that the context of the child's behavior must be modified; therefore, treatment should focus on teaching parents how to handle their child's positive and negative behavior differently. Behavior therapy, with its goal of concrete changes in visible behavior, has also been more amenable to empirical research than psychodynamic models that aim for internal changes in personality structure.

There is an immense amount of literature and research about the methods and efficacy of different types of child behavior therapy, including parent-consultation and parent-training models, which attempt to teach parents to reward, ignore, and communicate differently by various methods such as working with them individually, working with them in groups with other parents, and providing them with parenting manuals. A review of these treatment methods (Atkeson & Forehand, 1978; Dumas, 1984; Forehand et al., 1979; McMahon & Forehand, 1983) indicates that the overall results appear to be positive and that progress has been made.

However, Ollendick (1986, p. 552) concludes that "empirical support for their use is not as strong as it is often surmised . . . since studies are poorly controlled or their external validity is unknown." He goes on to explain that nearly all studies in the area of school phobia, for example, are uncontrolled case reports from which it is next to impossible to determine whether change occurred as a result of treatment. Griest and Wells (1983, p. 49) suggest that the research indicates that we know too little about the "interplay of various family variables." Despite this general criticism, it appears reasonable to consider pursuing the development of approaches that attempt to integrate behavioral and systemic principles such as those initiated by Patterson (1974), Patterson & Fleischman (1979), Patterson et al. (1982), Fleischmann (1981), Alexander & Parsons (1973, 1982), and Barton and colleagues (1985) because they have been shown to have better outcomes than other therapies (i.e., client-centered and dynamic-eclectic) as well as lower recidivism on follow-up studies.

The efficacy of family therapy treatment has been addressed by Gurman and colleagues (1981, 1986). They report that "non-behavioral marriage and family therapy produce beneficial outcomes in about two-thirds of cases, and effects are superior to no treatment" and that "positive results of both nonbehavioral and behavioral marriage and family therapy typically occur in treatment of short duration, that is, 1–20 sessions" (1986, p. 572). The criteria for measuring outcomes in family therapy are subject to great debate. Jacobson (1985) supports the idea that the elimination of the presenting problem is the best measure of successful outcome because that fits the family's goals rather than the therapist's hypotheses. The Brief Family Therapy model described later in this chapter equates successful outcome with the elimination or amelioration of the problem as it is defined by the family.

Furthermore, there is presently much controversy about whether empirical investigation is the most appropriate form of research (Lebow, 1986; Shields, 1986b; Tomm, 1986). The diversity of family therapy treatment models as well as the many internal and external variables of family systems and therapists and their interactions with each other make research design very difficult. So far there have been studies to evaluate interventions (L'Abate et al., 1984; Lea, 1983), outcome (De Witt, 1978; Katz et al., 1975), assessment tools (Forman et al., 1984; Miller et al., 1985), coding systems for measuring the therapeutic interaction (de Shazer et al., 1985; Pinsof, 1980; Shields, 1986a), and models for organizing family issues such as Doherty's Family FIRO Model (Doherty & Colangelo, 1984).

Koss and Butcher (1986) conclude that studies on brief therapy outcomes so far attest to the efficiency of brief methods, but comparative studies of brief and unlimited therapy show no difference in results. Both de Shazer and colleagues (1986) and Weakland and colleagues (1974) have done follow-up studies at their centers on brief therapy and have found a 72% client satisfaction rate with treatment, based on clients' goals.

SOLUTION-FOCUSED TREATMENT

The treatment method described here is Brief Family Therapy (de Shazer, 1982, 1985), a solution-focused model influenced by the work of Gregory Bateson and Milton Erickson. Brief Family Therapy views the complaints that bring clients to therapy as part of the interactions between people rather than as individual pathology. In treatment the client or clients and the therapist (and the team behind the one-way mirror, if there is one) form a therapeutic suprasystem for the duration of treatment for the purpose of constructing a solution to the complaints that prompted the request for treatment. Complaints are seen as troublesome interactional patterns in which the clients are stuck because of the constraints of their perceptions, thoughts, or behaviors. Solutions are seen as either already happening as occasional exceptions to the troublesome interactions or potential exceptions existing in the clients' imagination of which they are not conscious.

Treatment begins with exploring the clients' present view of the situation (frame) to find the already existing alternative perceptions, thoughts, or behaviors on which solutions can be built. If this is not fruitful, then the next step is to investigate the clients' ideas about possible solutions or to help them construct future frames containing solutions that best fit their unique social, cultural, and personal world view.

For example, an 8-year-old boy is brought to treatment by his busy, professional parents for lying and stealing. The mother is home a little more than the father, who travels a lot. As soon as possible the therapist asks for exceptions to the complaint behaviors. The parents cannot think of any. The child offers the information that he does not steal when he is with his grandmother. The parents agree and add that he does not seem to have the need to steal at school, either. He did so only once, when he had a teacher he did not get along with.

The therapist's questioning determines that the difference between situations when the boy steals and lies and when he does not is that he gets attention and affirmation in a positive rather than a negative sense. At home the busy parents focus almost entirely on the complaint behaviors. (This is not pointed out to them, however, because the goal is for them to increase their effective behavior, not to make them aware of mistakes.) The therapist will now try to build on the exceptions mentioned by prescribing a task for the family in which the boy will get more positive attention from his parents.

Brief Family Therapy builds on the strengths of families. The exceptions to the complaints on which solutions are built are the things that are going well. Thus, from the earliest stages of treatment the focus is much less on the details and history of the complaints, so painful for both sides, than it is on the minute details of what is happening when the complaints do not exist.

The format for Brief Family Therapy sessions is that the therapist who conducts the interview takes a break after 30 to 45 minutes to consult with a team (if there is one) or with him- or herself to compose an intervention that will be read to the family. This intervention consists of "compliments," a list of things that members of the family are already doing well (including exceptions to the complaints) as well as a homework task that builds on whatever family members are already thinking or doing that may lead to solution. Sessions are generally spaced 1 week apart until there is a consistent change in patterns for the better; after that, sessions are gradually spaced farther apart until termination.

Almost all parents, no matter how confident and successful they may appear to be, fear that they have failed somehow when they find themselves in the position of having to seek treatment. Similarly, children usually feel guilty whether they show it or not. Therefore, at the beginning of the first session it is very therapeutic to focus on positives—for example, the exceptions to the complaints—rather than on the complaints and to reinforce these positives at the end of the session with compliments (always factually based on material presented by the family in the session) such as (to the parents) "you are a conscientious parent just for being here," or "we can see you care a lot about your child's success in life," and (to the child) "you seem to care a lot about what your parents think about you," or "you have cooperated well here today even though you didn't want to come." This often shifts the family's perceptual frame of the situation radically and contributes to a solution by opening up possibilities for more of the exceptional behaviors to take place as well as for new and different ones to evolve.

COOPERATING

The Brief Family Therapy model is only one of many ways to treat disturbed parent–child relationships. Because limited space does not permit a full description of its solution-focused methods, the focus of this chapter is on the concept of "cooperating."

De Shazer (1982, pp. 9–10) has defined "cooperating" as follows:

> Each family (individual or couple) shows a unique way of attempting to cooperate, and the therapist's job becomes, first, to describe that particular manner to himself that the family shows and, then, to cooperate with the family's way and, thus to promote change.

There are many things that determine how families attempt to cooperate, such as whether they are coming for help for the first time, whether they have had a positive or negative experience in previous therapy, whether they are ready to give up or try just about anything to get help, or whether they have come of their own volition or because someone has ordered it (such as school, court, or a social service agency). Also, some people are open and willing to take direction and follow it, whereas others automatically do the opposite of what is suggested or at least have to modify it in order not to seem too conforming.

The first step the therapist takes to promote a cooperative mode for therapy is to accept the description of the complaint at face value. An example of this follows: Mr. and Mrs. S came to therapy with 3-year-old Brad and their 3½ month-old daughter Peggy. Mr. S, age 32, is a self-employed craftsman who sets his own work schedule and works both at home and away from home. Mrs. S., age 31, studied art and worked in a quilting shop until Brad was born. She and her husband have strong feelings about the desirability of young children having a full-time mother at home as well as a father who can be with them as much as possible. Their presenting complaint was that Brad, who had always been a very bright but demanding child, had become almost impossible to manage lately and was having frequent temper tantrums, saying that he hates them and himself. The referral to our agency had been made by the pediatrician.

During the parents' description of the complaints, Brad whined, kicked the table in the room, and occasionally yelled, "I hate this lady" (referring to the therapist). The parents took turns holding the baby and responding with patience and concern for Brad's feelings. They alternated handing him a toy, holding him on their lap, and politely explaining why he must behave and why they were there. The more patient they were, the more angry he became. Eventually Brad started to poke at the baby to wake her up and to tug at his mother's blouse as though to open it. Mrs. S. explained that since Peggy's birth she has allowed Brad, who had been weaned at 15 months, to nurse again because she did not want him to feel she was favoring Peggy.

The parents also made it quite clear that they had carefully planned for parenthood by reading about child development and various parenting styles and that they have committed themselves to providing a very accepting environment for their children in which free expression is possible. When the therapist asked during one of Brad's temper tantrums whether this was an example of how things are at home and how they handle it, they said it was. They did not believe in corporal punishment, and Brad refused to accept the short time-outs they tried to impose. Until recently they were able to calm him down by talking to him at great length and trying to model loving behavior in response to his anger. Since Peggy's birth they did not have quite as much time and patience for him, which made them feel very guilty.

When asked whether they thought Peggy's birth had anything to do with the deterioration of Brad's behavior, both parents appeared slightly anxious and explained in great detail how they had prepared him for it, how he had even been at the home delivery attended by a midwife, and how he claimed to love the baby dearly. When asked about exceptions, the parents reported that Brad behaved best when he had the undivided attention of one or both of his parents. When the therapist asked about Mr. and Mrs. S's extended family and their thoughts about the complaint, it became evident that both sets of grandparents and siblings had suggested that Brad was spoiled and needed a firmer hand but that Mr. and Mrs. S disagreed with this and, in fact, felt offended by it.

How can a therapist best cooperate with these parents? Clearly they were in therapy hoping that their child-rearing techniques would be affirmed. They were simultaneously acting in a helpless manner and being assertive about how they wanted to raise their children. For the therapist to create a cooperative environment, it was necessary to accept their "frame" and affirm them so that they would not become defensive but in a manner that made them want a solution that was different from the one they were clinging to so desperately.

The therapist took a noncommital stance during the interview. When the parents talked about their extended families' ideas about how to deal with Brad, they occasionally asked the therapist, "What do you think?" The therapist avoided taking sides with responses such as, "Well, you are the parents, and you have the right to decide how to raise your children," or "It is important that you feel comfortable with your decisions."

The therapist read the following message to Mr. and Mrs. S after the consultation break behind the mirror:

> The team and I were very impressed, Mr. and Mrs. S, with the great deal of careful thought and unlimited energy you devote to raising your children. Very few people we see have read as much and thought as much or are as philosophically clear about how they want to raise their children. You both have an extraordinary amount of patience and commitment to parenthood, and we can see you clearly choose to put your children's needs before your own.
>
> We can also see that Brad is a very intelligent, spunky child who has a mind of his own and trusts your love for him enough to express himself freely at all times.
>
> We are not certain how to explain Brad's recent change in behavior. Perhaps it is an adjustment to not being an only child anymore, or perhaps it is just a stage he is going through. He may get over it soon with enough love and patience or it may take time. Each child is different—some shape up and start developing some self-discipline earlier and some later. With Brad it could happen tomorrow, or next month, or in a year or two, or even when he's older like eight or ten . . . [at this point the father gasped and said "Oh, no, we'd go nuts till then," but the mother made no response]. With some children it comes so late that it makes adolescence real hard for parents . . . but parents with enough love and energy can manage. There are things we can suggest to help that process along—to help build that self-disci-

pline sooner, but it may not fit into your philosophy of child rearing, and we really don't think it is right to interfere with people's ideas about how to raise children.

Our suggestion is that you go home and think about all this and continue to do what you feel is best until you see some of the patience and control you are modeling for Brad become part of his behavior. If, however, you decide at any time that you want some help in speeding up this natural process by doing something different, we will be happy to make some suggestions.

The parents appeared both pleased and stunned by the intervention. They said nothing while they bundled up the children to leave and followed the therapist out to the waiting room. She shook their hands and said, "Well, I hope things work out soon for you." Mrs. S, who during the session had appeared to be more defensive about the permissiveness than her husband, said, "You mean you aren't going to give us another appointment?" The therapist answered that she would be happy to see them again anytime they choose to explore some different alternatives for Brad. At this point Mrs. S's cool, controlled demeanor cracked. She looked as though she was going to cry and said, "Please give us another appointment. I'm afraid I'll do someting I regret to Brad if his behavior doesn't change soon. I'm willing to try anything different just to be able to control him." Mr. S looked at his wife, mildly shocked. She noticed and said to him, "Let's try something else. I can't take it anymore." Mr. S's response was, "I've been trying to tell you we're giving in to him too much. I'd like to do things differently."

The couple made another appointment and were told to come without the children. They reported having had a better week with Brad because they had sat down together and talked about some ways of being a little less permissive. During the session the therapist talked with them about setting limits and enforcing them in a firm but loving way and about being consistent. The couple seemed relieved. They cancelled their next appointment because of illness but reported progress. When they came back 3 weeks later they felt that they had complete control over the situation, and their reports of how they handled Brad's demands indicated that, indeed, they no longer had any difficulties in setting limits for him. They reported that he seemed so much happier and calmer since they were firmer.

It may seem logical that people who seek help will want to follow the therapists's suggestion, but this is not an assumption that the therapist should ever make. For many people having to seek help is a sign of weakness or defeat, and a solution to a problem achieved with the help of "an outsider" is less acceptable than the complaint situation. Often improvement through therapy could prove a referring source right, which can be another reason to avoid finding a solution. Therefore, the therapist's acceptance of the family members' view of the complaint gives them the freedom to make their own choices. The resulting feeling of independence builds the necessary confidence to do something different now and perhaps again in the future when another problem arises.

Another aspect of promoting cooperation is assessing the clients' response to the task given at the end of the first session and using this information appropriately. Tasks assigned at the end of the first session depend on whether the family has presented some exceptions or ideas about solutions that can be built on, as described earlier in this chapter. If the task has been carried out as prescribed and there is change for the better, the assumption is that the family will continue to cooperate in this manner, and further tasks can be assigned to build toward a solution.

However, many families "forget" to do the task or modify it to fit their own ideas, which indicates the need for other forms of intervention. In the case of the 8-year-old who was lying and stealing, mentioned above, if his parents had been told, for example, to make a list of all the things they notice about him that they approve of and give him a hug for each one, and the boy was told to notice what he will do in the week to come that makes him feel good about himself, and the parents come back and say that they did not have time to do the task but report some changes for the better, and the boy reports having played a game with his Dad several times this week and having been allowed to help Mom bake some cookies, then this family cooperates by listening to what is said in the session and making use of it in some way but not in the manner they were told to. Therefore, the therapist will cooperate in the future by giving indirect suggestions rather than more explicit tasks.

When the interview produces no exceptions or specific solutions for the future or the complaints are too numerous and vague to provide a focus, an excellent way to create a cooperative climate and to stimulate the family to produce exceptions to their complaints is to give the following task to everyone in the session:

> Until we meet again next week, we want each one of you to notice and report back to us all the things that will happen in the family that you want to continue to have happen.

This task focuses the family away from the complaint on to exceptions, creates an expectation of change with the use of the words "what *will* happen," and provides information about task performance. If the task is performed, then the therapist not only knows that the family will comply directly but exceptions will have been elicited that can be built on in future sessions.

Maintaining the family's cooperation is an ongoing process that must be evaluated session by session. Unfortunately, task compliance is not always a straight road to solutions. For example, let us look at the A Family:

Mr. and Mrs A are 40-year-old parents of 10-year-old Billy and 15-year-old Susan. Both parents work outside the home. Mrs. A works in an office where her hours are somewhat longer and less flexible than Mr. A's, who works in a school system. The family was referred by the school psychologist at Billy's school because he was doing poorly academically and socially despite placement in a special class for difficult children. He was rebellious and uncooperative at home as well. The couple's behavior during the interview indicated that Mrs. A was the more dominant spouse. Susan was described as a model child who requires no disciplining. She seemed disinterested in the session and avoided making any straight replies that would reveal her alliances in the family constellation. Billy tried to hold center stage by being "cute," but he also seemed seriously concerned about his problems, particularly with peers at school.

It was difficult to focus this family on exceptions or ideas about solutions although they admitted Billy was sometimes more manageable on a one-to-one basis than in a group. The complaints were endless. Mrs. A described a long list of attempted solutions, all of which had failed. She implied (and Mr. A agreed) that her husband did not have the patience or commitment to follow through on disciplinary actions she suggested.

How does the therapist cooperate with this family? The parents obviously feel inadequate and defeated. Everyone needs to be affirmed and to experience some hope. The sister's wish to be uninvolved must be acknowledged, as must Billy's wish for improvement. Because there were no concrete exceptions or future ideas offered that could be reinforced and the parents and Billy were focusing on a multitude of negatives, the family was given this intervention message at the end of the session:

> We are very impressed with the concern you have for Billy, Mom and Dad. It is clear you are determined to leave no stone unturned to help

him despite your busy schedules. We were struck with how many different things you have already tried to help him, such as spending more time with him on the weekends, involving him in your hobbies, changing his school, having him evaluated and seen by various therapists, helping him with homework, and talking with his teachers.

Susan, we appreciate your input today. You are obviously very perceptive about your family and what is going on. We appreciate your honesty in saying you try not to pay attention to what happens.

Billy, we are impressed with how well you spoke up and how much you seem to care about not doing well at school. Many children your age would not care about anything except having fun. You also seem to want to have things improve at home for you and your parents.

We would like you all to do something for us for next week so that we can get to know some more about you and how to help you.

To parents: Notice and report back to us what Billy is doing at school and at home that you want him to continue to do.

To Billy: Notice and report back to us what will be happening at school and at home that you want to continue to have happen.

To Susan: You may do either what your parents or Billy do, but you don't have to unless you really want to.

The family returned the week after without Susan who "had to study for some exams." The parents reported that Billy had done well at school 4 out of 5 days and had not had any notes sent home. He had been more cooperative at home and had no temper tantrums. Both mother and father had tried to praise him more and spend more time with him. Billy reported feeling good when he was praised by his parents instead of being yelled at. He had only one fight in school this week and had not upset his teachers as much.

During this session Mr. A's feelings of inadequacy about dealing with Billy became more evident. Mrs. A expressed some concern about this and wished that her husband would take over more with Billy because she was very busy with housework during the evening and on weekends.

Because the family had cooperated with the first session task, the therapist cooperated by responding with another task that built on the positive results of the first one. Two things were important here: (a) for both parents to keep on doing what they had started to do (focusing on what Billy was doing right and rewarding him for it with positive attention) and (b) to respond to Mrs. A's wishes for Mr. A to be more of an equal partner. However, regarding the latter, it was necessary to go slowly (father not to assume too much responsibility too soon), because the cooperative mode of therapy could easily be jeopardized if mother, despite what she said she wanted, felt too

much of a threat to her dominant position in the family and sabo-
taged Dad's efforts. This was the intervention that was read to the
family.:

> To both parents: We are very impressed with your response to Billy
> this week . . . how you praised him on his good days and how you
> experimented with all sorts of other ways of helping him such as
> playing Yatzee with him in the evening. This must be particularly hard
> for you, given the pressures you are both under at work and at home.
>
> To Billy: We are very pleased to hear how well you did at school
> this week—4 days out of 5—and how hard you tried to control
> yourself at home. It is good that you let your Mom and Dad know how
> proud you are about your success. We would like you to keep on
> noticing what you do to make yourself and them feel proud.

Billy was then asked to leave the room, and the rest of the message
was read to the parents alone, in order to protect their image in his
eyes.

> We know you are hard-working people and how much energy it takes
> just keeping the family going on a daily basis. Yet it is clear to us that
> no sacrifice seems too great for you to straighten out this situation
> with Billy.
>
> Now this may sound odd to you, but we have a suggestion that has
> worked with other situations like the one you have with Billy, and we
> are wondering whether you might like to try it out this week. On
> alternate evenings we want you to take turns spending 20 minutes
> alone with Billy just before bedtime. During this time he should set the
> agenda—it can be anything at all as long as it is not destructive. It
> should be a fun time, during which the two of you enjoy each other and
> there is no serious talk about school or any opportunity for his doing
> anything right or wrong. In other words, during this time you just
> listen and accept his ideas, but you do not correct him or judge him.
>
> One more thing: on the days when it is Mom's turn to spend these
> 20 minutes with Billy, Dad, you do someting for her which you think
> she might appreciate, and when its Dad's turn, do something for him
> you think he'd like, Mom.

(The last paragraph of this intervention was intended to alter the
pattern of how the couple reinforce each other.)

When the family returned one week later, the parents asked to be
seen alone first, and Billy was asked to wait outside. Mrs. A looked
terribly angry and upset, and Mr. A looked extremely concerned.

Mrs. A reported that she was at the end of her rope and was going on strike. She was not going to do anything for anyone anymore, and if the family didn't start helping her, she was going to leave home. She was sick and tired of Billy's behavior and Dad's lack of support and of having responsibility for the well-being of the entire family. Mr. A seemed helpless and frightened by the outburst.

A family's response to an intervention can never be predicted with certainty. Although therapists design interventions with specific goals in mind, they must be open and ready to deal with whatever the clients come back with. Sometimes the presenting complaint masks the real reason that brings people to therapy, and signs of improvement in the former gives people the courage to allow what they may perceive as more serious or frightening complaints to surface. Although it would be hazardous to assume that there is a marital problem behind every disturbed parent–child relationship, there are occasions when this may be so.

The therapist in this case considered that possibility and spent the rest of the session exploring the complaints they presented that day. While she allowed ventilation of Mrs. A's anger for a little while to convey understanding, she tried to shift the emphasis to when they got along and functioned *well* together, particularly under stress, in order to find building blocks for a solution. She was also careful to maintain a cooperative mode with what they had originally stated as their reason for coming to therapy, Billy's behavior, lest the couple get too threatened talking about their marriage. For example, she would ask questions like, "What will your husband be doing differently to support you so that you are less frustrated *with Billy?*" rather than phrasing the questions in a manner that implied a marital problem. Billy was never invited into the session that day, and the intervention message to the parents was:

We are very pleased that you are able to talk so openly about your frustrations today. Mrs. A, you obviously are at the end of your rope with Billy and everything else to have to resort to thinking about going on strike or leaving the family, and we can see how very upset you are.

Mr. A, we also recognize your concern for your wife and your feeling of helplessness when you see her so upset, but we also see how anxious you are to be of help. It looks to us like you may need to take over for a while because she really seems in need of a total rest. That is certainly a difficult thing to ask of you because you are a busy man, but we have some ideas how you can organize things around the house so she can recuperate and won't have to go on strike.

Mr. A, we want you and your wife to sit down and decide which basic chores need to be done around the house and which of them Billy and Susan can do and which of them you can do. We also want you to decide what the consequences will be if Billy does not do what he is asked to do. Then you, Mr. A, sit down with the children without your wife and tell them that mother needs a rest and you are in charge from now on. Tell them what you expect them to do and what will happen if they don't do it. You must also make sure they know you mean business about making them pay the consequences for their behaviors.

We want you to continue to spend the 20 minutes a night with Billy by yourself for the time being, without alternating with Mrs. A. We know this will be very difficult for you, but we also can see how anxious you are to be supportive of your wife at this critical time. Give her as much rest as possible. You may consult her at times about decisions you are making when the two of you are alone, but in front of the children you must be in total command.

Mrs. A looked calm and very pleased during this intervention, and Mr. A kept nodding his head in agreement throughout. The therapist accompanied the couple out to the waiting room, told them to come back alone next week, and apologized to Billy for not having had a chance to talk with him today because she had important grown-up business with his parents.

The couple returned a week later smiling. Mr. A had successfully accomplished everything we had suggested, and Mrs. A, who had never before given her husband the opportunity to be in command, felt pleased and impressed. She confessed that "it has been difficult to let Bob speak for me to the kids at first, but I was so tired that it was also sort of a relief. Then I suddenly realized that it really didn't matter if everything doesn't go exactly the way I have it in my mind as long as it gets done."

The confidence Mr. A had gained in being allowed to parent alone with good results increased his assertiveness in a way that continued to earn him respect from his wife and children. In the next two sessions, to which the parents came alone, they disclosed that they were being much more open and direct with each other, which greatly improved their relationship. Mr. A continued to be more assertive and cooperative because he was more confident about what would please his wife. The parents also reported improved behavior on Billy's part at home, that he was doing his homework without any trouble, and that they had less reports from school about disruptive behavior. The case came to a successful termination three sessions later (spaced first 3 and then 4 weeks apart) when the family and therapist felt confident that the changes that had occurred were lasting. Billy was seen separately once at the request of the parents, and the last session included Susan as well.

Finally, how can a therapist cooperate with a family that does not do tasks and refuses to admit to changes for the better even when they are evident?

The P family was referred by the school psychologist at the high school that 16-year-old Joe attends. It was his second year there. Mr. P is a 43-year-old factory worker, and Mrs. P a 37-year-old home-maker who represents a line of jewelry that is sold privately in homes. Mr. and Mrs. P have one younger son, Tim, who is 13. Mrs. P appeared alone with the boys for the first session and said her husband would be late because he wanted to finish watching a television program. The therapist chose to wait to start the session until he appeared, which was about 20 minutes later.

Mrs. P presented the complaint, and Mr. P agreed. Joe had not had any problems until he started high school. He had always achieved acceptable grades with the help of his parents, particularly his mother, who supervised his work carefully and forced him to sit down and do homework every afternoon. He had never been a discipline problem at home or at school. Since the beginning of the freshman year, he had gradually slacked off and was about to fail several courses. As the grades dropped and Joe stopped bringing work home, the parents increased their pressure on him to do well. Mrs. P stepped up her calls to his teachers to see if Joe was lying about his homework, which he was. The more she and her husband scolded and punished, the more he rebelled against all their rules.

There were many rules, some unusually restrictive for a high school student. Mr. P indicated some mild disagreement with his wife about these overly protective rules, which were based on her fears of exposing the boys to wrong values. However, he was in full agreement with his wife about school. Because he only had an eighth-grade education, he felt that his chances in life had been greatly limited. Tim was reported to be a poorer student than Joe but one who tried his best and was not rebellious at this time.

Joe was very cooperative during the session and said that he was upset about failing grades and wanted to do better, but that he just did not want to do the work because it was boring and he could not concentrate on it. He only did well in a drafting course because he liked it a little. As to the home situation, he felt that his parents were much too strict and that they treated him like a little kid.

A vague first session task, that is "notice what will happen in the week to come that you want to continue to have happen," was given to each member of the family at the end of the session because the therapist could not get the parents or the boys to come up with any exceptions or ideas about solutions that they could agree on. The family came back a week later without Tim and reported no improvements, no matter how hard the therapist tried. In fact, they all agreed that things had been worse, particularly because a poor report card was delivered that week.

The split between the father's and mother's ideas about solution became more evident during this session. Mr. P had spontaneously taken Joe off all grounding that week with the hope that more freedom would make him try harder with his school work. Mrs. P, who was angry at not having been consulted, had wanted to increase restrictions. To counteract the husband's decision, she had nagged Joe more, called school more frequently, and monitored his phone conversations even more than usual. All attempts to focus on positives in the past, present, or future were met with more complaints by the parents and Joe. Mrs. P volunteered that they were not bringing Tim anymore for fear these sessions would give him some ideas about misbehaving.

In order to "cooperate," the therapist first had to consider that the task had not been complied with and that the family was refusing to allow a positive focus. His next move was to do something different: not to continue to focus them positively but to join them in their negative frame, but in a manner that would produce some difference. Thus, he began to ask questions like, "Things certainly seem to be going from bad to worse. Do you think they have hit bottom yet?" "What do you imagine things will be like at their worst?" "How much worse do you think they can get?" "What will you do when that happens?"

These negative questions, which must push the family's negative attitude even beyond their own frame, usually lead to the realization on one, or several members' part, that they had better do something different so that things don't actually get as bad as they are imagining. Then, if only one person in the system does something different in response to that, no matter how small a change it may be, it will have a positive effect on the entire system. Usually families respond to having to imagine the worst by giving some example of why things aren't as bad yet or won't become that bad, and this gives the therapist something positive to use for constructing a solution again.

The intervention at the end of this session was:

> We are very concerned about the seriousness of this situation. We can certainly understand how hopeless you both must feel, Mr. and Mrs. P, after all the different things you have tried. We also see that you have high values for yourself and your children and that you will not compromise these at any price. You want your children to profit from what you have learned from life and have things easier than you had.
>
> You both have some clear idea about what is best for Joe, and you are both strong willed enough to stick to what you believe in. That is a good quality, and obviously you have been able to instill that in Joe, because he fights for what he believes in as well. We hope that you'll be able to show him the benefits of learning how to compromise and appreciate other points of view soon, so he can get on with his life.
>
> Joe, we can see how upset you are about the bad report card and how unhappy your parents are with you, but we can also appreciate how anxious you are to be more independent and make your own decisions about how to run your life. Obviously, you are willing to take the consequences for being your own person.
>
> Because you all have pretty strong ideas about what the solutions to this problem are . . . and because things are so bad, we suggest that you don't change anything right now until we can get some more information from you that will help us figure out how we can help. The best we can hope for right now is that things stay the way they are and don't get any worse.

The family returned a week later, still insisting that nothing was better despite the fact that Joe had brought homework home one night and done it and his mother had agreed to permit more freedom in television viewing for the boys. The therapist could not maintain a positive focus and therefore decided to split the family and see the parents and the boy separately. This decision was made primarily because of the developmental needs of a family with an adolescent: for parents to begin to let go and for the young person to take more responsibility for himself or herself. If this same situation arises with a younger child, then the parents are usually seen alone (see the A family above) and the child is only seen if this is necessary for cooperation with the parents.

As soon as Joe had left the room and the parents were alone, they began to fight about their differences in raising him. The therapist asked for exceptions in their parenting when they did *not* differ that, with some persistence on his part, led to some examples that made them realize that both boys behaved best when they, as parents, had first come to some agreement about how to handle a situation.

In his time alone with the therapist, Joe complained bitterly about how unhappy he was at home, at school, and with himself. He felt as if he had no control over any part of his life. He wanted to be a rock musician, and his parents wanted him to go to college; he liked people of all colors and creeds, and his parents wanted to restrict him to seeing friends of his own color and religion; and so on. Again the therapist started to ask about exceptions and helped Joe find some that made him realize that his parents gave him more rope when he conformed to their wishes than when he did not. Naturally, this was not an acceptable solution to him until the therapist asked him, "What do you want for yourself?" Joe answered he wanted more freedom as well as more respect from his parents but that he would not be the kind of person they wanted him to be.

"What's better for you in the long run, having them mad at you all the time or getting more of what you want?" the therapist asked. Joe admitted it would be to his advantage to have them less angry at him but was afraid the price would be too high. The therapist wondered whether there wasn't a price to be paid for anything in life and whether the price had to be all or nothing; whether there weren't some choices about that price, some trade-offs. The rest of the interview changed Joe's perception from the bind, "Either I obey and my parents are happy and I'm miserable/or I don't obey and my parents are miserable and I am still miserable because I feel guilty and they are down on me" to "I have a choice about what I can do to please them so that they can be happier with me and give me more of what makes me happier."

Separate interventions were given at the end of the session. The parents were told that they did not have to follow this suggestion but that it might not be a bad idea if they both met each evening to talk about what Joe had done that day that they both agreed was good. Joe was told that he probably would not want to do what was suggested, but if he felt like it, he might keep track of all the things he chose to do for himself that made him feel good and that also pleased his parents.

These separate interventions were given to reinforce the separate exceptions the parents and the boy produced, which together would lead to a solution for all of them.

The parents and boy were seen separately one more time. In the next session the therapist did not ask them about task performance but only whether anything had been different in the past week. All three reported changes for the better, which were then reinforced at the end of the session. Because agreement about improvement had been achieved, the family was reassembled (including Tim) for three more sessions so that everyone could benefit from as many views as possible about the solution and how it could be maintained.

CONCLUSION

Some aspects of the treatment of the disturbed parent–child relationships with the Brief Family Therapy model have been described here. Although this model considers the uniqueness of every family system and requires the therapist to "cooperate" with the family in various ways to avoid time-consuming defensiveness, the ages of the children and the stages of the family system's development provide some guidelines for appropriate solutions. Regardless of how the therapist envisions a solution to the presented complaints, he or she must construct one with the family that (a) fits their world view and (b) reflects the unalterable fact that parents (or some other responsible adults) must provide the nurturance and guidance children need until they can function on their own.

The essence of this approach is to build on already-existing strengths of families and to help them construct solutions for the future instead of focusing on the history of and the reasons for complaints. The concept of "cooperating" describes how the therapist interacts with the family members during and between sessions in order to help them construct solutions as easily as possible. Unlike models in which therapists try to overcome family members' "resistance" to their ideas of how to achieve the means to a "solution," Brief Family Therapy views therapists as responsible for adapting their interventions to fit the family members' frames. This is not unlike good parenting, which requires parents to adapt their methods to the different needs of each of their children rather than expecting them all to respond similarly. Thus, the therapist models what parents must go through in life in order to achieve more satisfying relationships with their children.

Although research findings indicate a trend toward behavioral and family therapy as the treatments of choice for disturbed parent–child relationships, there are no indications as yet that one treatment model within these orientations is more effective than any other. Brief Family Therapy is only one of many family therapy models in use. It represents yet another way of approaching problems brought to therapy and how to solve them. What recommends it for consideration as a choice in treating families with disturbed parent–child relationships is its positive, solution-focused approach, which helps people replace the despair and insecurity that brought them in for help with hope and confidence from the moment they start treatment.

Of course, this model would require modification for families with severe problems vis-à-vis interaction with defective systems in the environment. These include unemployment, poverty, racism, inadequate housing, poor schools, and the like. These problems may require such strategies as referral to other community services, therapist advocacy efforts, building support groups, and so on. (See, for example, Volume 1 of this series.)

Violence in American Families:

7

HOW MUCH IS THERE AND WHY DOES IT OCCUR?[1]

MURRAY A. STRAUS AND RICHARD J. GELLES

The first half of this chapter examines the extent of violence in American families. It will show that physical assaults occur more frequently in the family than in any other setting or group except the military in time of war and that these are long-standing phenomena. The second half of the chapter is designed to explain the paradox that the family is also the most loving and supportive group by showing that a large part of the explanation for the high rate of violence inheres in the very nature of the family and the society as it is presently constituted.

HISTORICAL AND LEGAL BACKGROUND

Wife Beating

Descriptions of wife beating extend as far back as recorded history, including the Roman Empire, the Middle Ages, and modern times (Davis, 1971). Blackstone's codification of the English common law (1768) asserted that husbands had the right to physically "chastise" an errant wife provided the stick was no bigger than his thumb. As recently as 1867 this rule was upheld by an appellate court in North Carolina.

Despite this, family researchers, therapists, and the public at large almost completely ignored wife beating until the 1970s. The subsequent emergence of research on wife beating by sociologists and criminologists, and the changes in public attitudes and the criminal justice system reflect many factors, including:

1. The general social activism of the late 1960s that sought to aid oppressed groups of all types.
2. The growth in paid employment by married women. This gave more women the economic means to no longer tolerate the abuse that had long been the lot of women.
3. The reemergence of the women's movement. By the mid-1970s the women's movement had made battering a central issue and gave it wide publicity. This sensitized women to the fact that they were being

victimized and provided the ideological justification for leaving a battering relationship.
4. The invention of shelters for battered women. Shelters provided the assistance necessary to make leaving possible and were also ideologically important because they made concrete and visible the existence of a phenomenon that had previously been ignored.
5. The growing public revulsion with violence stemming from the rising homicide and assault rate, violent political and social protest, assassinations and terrorist activity, and the Vietnam War.
6. Disenchantment with the family. The late 1960s and early 1970s were a period of increasingly critical reassessment of the family. This prepared people to perceive a range of negative features of family life, including violence.
7. Changes in theoretical perspectives in sociology, family studies, and criminology. The consensus model of society came under increasing attack by conflict theory models. In the consensus model, society is viewed as a system of relatively harmonious parts that is disrupted from time to time by conflict, and research tends to be focused on what maintains social integration. In the conflict model, society is viewed as a system whose normal state is one of conflict between its parts, and research tends to be focused on the extent and types of conflict, including violence.

Child Abuse

The history of physical abuse of children is also well documented. The historical record demonstrates use of extensive and often lethal forms of violence by parents. Those who have examined the history of child abuse, such as Bakan (1971), Radbill (1974), Newberger and colleagues (1977), and De Mause (1974, 1975), document a history of violence and infanticide dating back to biblical times. The Bible includes the dictum "spare the rod and spoil the child" and chronicles parental violence beginning when Abraham nearly killed his son as a sacrifice. Jesus' birth coincides with Herod's "Slaughter of the Innocents." Infanticide, mutilation, and other forms of violence were legal parental prerogatives from ancient Rome to colonial America. Children were hit with birch rods, switches, and canes. They were whipped, castrated, and destroyed by parents, most often with the consent and mandate of the ruling religious and political forces in the society.

The history of violence toward children in America dates back to the arrival of the Puritans. Laws threatening death to the unruly hung over children's heads, and parents supported their right to whip and punish with Biblical quotations. Religious ideology dictated that all children were born corrupted by original sin and required salvation by their parents. To "beat the devil" out of a child was not just a passing phrase. It was a mandate to provide salvation for their children through physical punishment.

Thus, historically we have a tradition of physical (and emotional) cruelty to children. As a society we have justified this cruelty through religious dogma or by maintaining it is in the child's best interests. This societal mandate and tolerance of physical violence toward children may have been one factor that delayed the identification of child abuse as an important social problem.

When New York charity workers in 1874 tried to get help for the badly abused foster child, Mary Ellen, they found a Society for the Prevention of Cruelty to Animals, but none for children. And so they founded the first chapter of a similar society for children in 1875 (Ross, 1977). Thus, although child abuse was identified as a social problem by concerned church workers, social workers, and private citizens in the nineteenth century, it took almost 100 years after the case of Mary Ellen for violence toward children to be considered a major, national, social problem. It was not until C. Henry Kempe and associates published their classic work on "The Battered Child Syndrome" in the *Journal of the American Medical Association* in 1962 that battering and abuse became a focal point of public attention.

By the end of the 1960s all 50 states had passed laws mandating the reporting of child abuse and neglect and had begun to take steps at least to treat abused children and their families. In 1974 the federal government established the National Center on Child Abuse and Neglect in an attempt to provide a mechanism to increase knowledge about the causes of child abuse and neglect and identify steps that could be taken to prevent and treat abuse.[2]

Current Legal Situation

Despite these important advances, parents have the right to use physical punishment in all but a few countries such as Sweden and other Scandinavian countries. In fact, the new child abuse reporting laws often contain a provision that reaffirms this right.

The legal situation with respect to hitting a spouse is different but not as different as it may seem at first (Lerman, 1981). The common law right of a husband to physically punish his wife has long since ceased to be formally recognized, and wife beating is a crime in every American state because assault and battery are crimes in every state. Beginning in the late 1970s, legislation specifically declaring assault within the family to be a crime was enacted by many states. Despite this and despite the fact that attacks that are serious enough to be termed wife beating are aggravated assaults, police, prosecuting attorneys, judges, and assaulted wives themselves are reluctant to invoke criminal procedures and penalties (Parnas, 1967). Simple assaults such as slaps, pushes, shoves, or throwing objects, which would probably produce legal action if they occurred in a non-domestic setting, are almost never regarded as requiring criminal adjudication when they occur in the home. Thus, the spirit, if not the letter, of the common law lives on.[3]

OFFICIAL STATISTICS OF THE INCIDENCE OF CHILD ABUSE AND SPOUSAL ABUSE

The evidence that the family is as violent as was suggested at the beginning of this chapter comes from a variety of sources. Although there are many discrepancies between the various statistics, none of these discrepancies challenges the supremacy of the family with respect to violence.[4]

Homicide

The most widely available statistics on intrafamily violence consist of data on murders within the family. In the United States about one-quarter of all murders are of other members of the same family (Straus & Gelles, 1986). In other countries, the percentage is much higher. In Canada, for example, 48% of all homicides are within the family, and in Denmark it is 67% (Straus, 1987a). These percentages, however, can be misleading. Canada and Denmark actually have *low* homicide rates. Consequently, the real meaning of the Danish percentage is that when homicide has been almost eliminated in a society, the setting in which it is most likely to remain is within the family.

Child Abuse

Homicide, of course, is the most extreme form of violence. At the other end of the severity continuum is the physical punishment of children. Surveys of parents since the 1920s have shown that almost all parents use physical punishment (Bronfenbrenner, 1958). In between the extremes of physical punishment and homicide, the data become scarce and questionable.

All states now require doctors, teachers, and other human service professionals who know or suspect a case of child abuse to report that case to the child protective services division of the state or local public human services agency. These figures have been collated for the federal government since 1976. In 1976 there were 669,000 reports. By 1984 the figure had grown to 1.7 million—a 258% increase (American Association for Protecting Children, 1986). Of these cases about one-quarter were physical abuse and the remainder were reports of sexual abuse, neglect, or emotional abuse. Although these are the most widely known and used statistics on child abuse, they have a number of limitations. First, they vastly underestimate the actual extent of child abuse because they represent only those cases where the indicators were so obvious that they were noticed and only those cases where the person noticing decided to risk involvement with the legal and welfare bureaucracy. In addition, as noted later in the chapter, the 258% increase does not mean that child abuse itself increased, only that there was a large increase in the *intervention* rate.

Spousal Abuse

Official data are also of limited value for estimating the incidence rate of spousal abuse. The most widely used data on crime in the United States are the "crimes known to the police" given in an annual FBI publication "Crime In The United States." These data do not provide information on wife beating because assaults between spouses are not reported separately from other assaults.

Crime victim surveys such as the National Crime Survey have been tabulated to produce rates of wife beating (Gaquin, 1977). The resulting rates vastly underestimate the incidence of wife beating because the focus of these surveys is on crime and, as noted above, the public tends to consider assaults by a spouse to be a "family problem" rather than a "crime" in the formal sense. Most instances of wife beating are therefore not reported.

THE NATIONAL FAMILY VIOLENCE SURVEYS

The limitations of official data on violence in families outlined above led us to conduct two surveys designed to measure the incidence of child abuse and spousal abuse in nationally representative samples. The 1975 survey describes 2143 families (Straus, Gelles, & Steinmetz, 1980). The 1985 survey, which is the basis for the rates reported in this chapter, describes 6002 families (Straus & Gelles, 1986, 1989). These surveys provide the most complete figures available on incidence rates, although they are almost certainly underestimates (Straus, Gelles, & Steinmetz, 1980).

Method of Measuring The Incidence of Violence

The Conflict Tactics Scales (CTS) (Straus, 1979) were included in both the 1975 and 1985 surveys.[5] The CTS starts by having trained interviewers ask the respondents to think of the times when they had a conflict with their child or spouse or just got angry with them. Respondents are then given a list of tactics that they might have used in these situations of conflict or anger. The tactics ranged from calm discussion to attacks with a knife or a gun. The 1985 version of the CTS (used for this chapter) consisted of 19 tactics, 9 of which refer to acts of violence.[6] The violent acts included in the 1985 version of the CTS are throwing something at the other; pushing, grabbing, or shoving; slapping or spanking; kicking, biting, or hitting with a fist; hitting or trying to hit with something; beating up the other; burning or scalding (for children) or choking (for spouses); threatening with knife or gun; or using a knife or gun. The occurrence of these violent acts was used to compute the following measures of family violence.

Overall Violence

This measure indicates the percent of parents or spouses who said they used *any* of the violent acts included in the CTS during the year covered by the study.

Severe Violence

For purposes of this study, "severe violence" was defined as acts that have a relatively high probability of causing an injury. Thus, kicking is classified as severe violence because kicking a child or a spouse has a much greater potential for producing an injury than does an act of "minor violence" such as spanking or slapping.[7] The acts making up the severe violence index are kicking, biting, punching, hitting with an object, beating up, threatening with a knife or gun, and using a knife or gun (see footnote 4).

Child Abuse

What constitutes "abuse" is, to a considerable extent, a matter of social norms. Spanking or slapping a child or even hitting a child with an object such as stick, hairbrush, or belt, is not "abuse" according to either the legal or informal norms of American society, although it is in Sweden and several other countries (Haeuser, 1985). Our operationalization of child abuse attempts to take such normative factors into consideration. We computed two child abuse rates. Child Abuse–1 is the use by a parent of any of the acts of violence in the severe violence index (see listed above), except that to be consistent with current legal and informal norms hitting or trying to hit with an object such as a stick or belt is *not* included. Child Abuse–2 adds hitting with an object such as a belt or paddle, even though many people do not consider that to be abusive. However, we believe that such acts carry a much greater risk of causing an injury.[8]

Spousal Violence

The problem of terminology and norms is even greater for violence between spouses than for violence by parents. Although spanking or occasionally slapping a child is not usually considered abuse (or even "violence"), our perception is that the same act is often considered to be abusive if done to a spouse. Thus, in the case of violence between spouses, the "overall violence" rate is important.

Wife Beating

Because of the greater average size and strength of men, the acts in the severe violence list are likely to be more damaging when the assailant is the husband. Consequently, to facilitate focusing on the rate of severe violence by husbands, the term "wife beating" is used to refer to that rate.

Incidence of Marital Violence

Couple Rates

The rate of 16.1 in the first row of Table 7.1 indicates that more than one out of six American couples experienced an incident of physical violence during 1985 (or more precisely during the 12-month period preceding the interviews, which were conducted in the summer of 1985). Applying this rate to the approximately 54 million couples in the United States that year results in an estimate of about 8.7 million couples who experienced at least one violent incident during the year.[9]

Most of those violent incidents were relatively minor—pushing,

Table 7.1

Annual Incidence Rates for Family Violence and Estimated Number of Cases Based on These Rates. (Data from the National Family Violence Surveys.)

Type of Intrafamily Violence[1]	Rate per 100 Couples or Children (percent)	Estimated Number Assaulted[2] (millions)
A. Violence Between Husband and Wife		
Any violence during the year (slap, push, etc.)	16.1	8.7
Severe violence (kick, punch, stab, etc.)	6.3	3.4
Any violence by the husband	11.6	6.250
Severe violence by the husband ("wife beating")	3.4	1.800
Any violence by the wife	12.4	6.8
Severe violence by the wife	4.8	2.6
B. Violence by Parents: Child Age 0–17		
Any hitting of child during the year	Near 100% for young child[3]	
Very severe violence (Child Abuse–1)[4]	2.3	1.5
Severe violence (Child Abuse–2)	11.0	6.9
C. Violence by Parents: Child Age 15–17		
Any violence against 15–17 year olds	34.0	3.800
Very severe violence against 15–17 year olds	2.1	.235
Severe violence against 15–17 year olds	7.0	.8
D. Violence by Children Age 3–17 (1975–1976 sample)		
Any violence against a brother or sister	80	50.4
Severe violence against a brother or sister	53	33.3
Any violence against a parent	18	9.7
Severe violence against a parent	9	4.8
E. Violence by Children Age 15–17 (1975–1976 sample)		
Any violence against a brother or sister	64	7.2
Severe violence against a brother or sister	36	4.
Any violence against a parent	10	1.1
Severe violence against a parent	3.5	.4

1. *Part A* rates are based on a nationally representative sample of 6002 currently married or cohabiting couples interviewed in 1985. *Note:* The rates in Part A differ from those in Straus and Gelles (1986) because the rates in that paper are computed in a way that enabled the 1985 rates to be compared with the more restricted sample and more restricted version of the Conflict Tactics Scale used in the 1975 study.

Part B rates are based on the 1985 sample of 3232 households with a child age 17 and under. *Note:* The rates shown in Part B differ from those in Straus and Gelles (1986) for the reasons given in footnote 1.

Parts C and D rates are based on the 1975–1976 study because data on violence by children were not collected in the 1985 survey.

2. The column giving the "Number Assaulted" was computed by multiplying the rates in this table by the 1984 population figures as given in the *1986 Statistical Abstract of the United States*. The population figures (rounded to millions) are 54 million couples and 63 million children age 0–17. The number of children 15–17 was estimated as 11.23 million. This was done by taking .75 of the number age 14–17, as given in *Statistical Abstract* Table 29.

3. The rate for 3-year-old children in the 1975 survey was 97%. See Straus, 1983, Figure 13.4, for age-specific rates from 3 through 17.

4. See "Definition and Measurement" section for an explanation of the difference between Child Abuse–1 and Child Abuse–2.

slapping, shoving, or throwing things. However, the severe violence rate of 6.3 (see second row of Table 7.1) indicates that a substantial number were serious assaults such as kicking, punching, biting, or choking. Thus, the figure in the column headed "Number Assaulted" indicates that of the 8.7 million households where such violence occurred, 3.4 million were instances in which the violence had a relatively high risk of causing injury.

Husband-to-Wife Violence[10]

The middle two rows of Part A of Table 7.1 focus on assaults by husbands. The rate of 11.6 per 100 couples shows that almost one out of eight husbands reportedly carried out one or more violent acts during the year of this study. The most important statistic, however, is in the row for severe violence by the husband. This is the measure we use as the indicator of "wife beating." It shows that more than 3 out of every 100 women were severely assaulted by their partner in 1985. If this rate is correct, it means that about 1.8 million women were beaten by their partner that year. However, along with all the other rates shown in Table 7.1, the wife-beating rate must be regarded as an underestimate. There are a number of reasons for this (see Straus, Gelles, & Steinmetz, 1980, p. 35), including the virtual certainty that not every respondent was completely frank in describing violent incidents. The true rates could be as much as double those shown in Table 7.1.

Wife-to-Husband Violence

The last two rows of Part A show the rates for violence *by* wives. As in the case of the 1975 study, we found that the rates for violence by wives are remarkably similar to the rates for violence by husbands. The fact that women are so violent within the family is in contrast to the extremely low rate of violence by women outside the family but consistent with the results of a number of other studies (Brutz & Ingoldsby, 1984; Gelles, 1974; Giles-Sims, 1983; Lane & Gwartney-Gibbs, 1985; Laner & Thompson, 1982; Makepeace, 1983; Sack, Keller, & Howard, 1982; Scanzoni, 1978; Steinmetz, 1977, 1978b; Szinovacz, 1983). Although the two national surveys and the studies just cited leave little doubt about the high frequency of wife-to-husband violence, the meaning and consequences of that violence are easily misunderstood. For one thing, as pointed out elsewhere (Straus, 1977a; Straus, Gelles & Steinmetz, 1980), the greater average size and strength of men and their greater average tendency toward aggressiveness means that the same act (for example, a punch) is likely to be very different in the amount of pain or injury inflicted (see also Greenblatt, 1983).

Even more important, a great deal of violence by women against their husbands are acts of retaliation or self-defense (Straus, 1980b). One of the most fundamental reasons that a number of women are violent within the family but not outside the family may be that her own home is the place where there is the greatest risk of assault for a typical American woman. This can also be surmised from the statistics on homicide. In 1980 women committed only 9% of the non-spousal murders in the United States but nearly half (43%) of the murders of spouses (Plass, 1986). The main reason is that they are in mortal danger primarily within the family (see Browne, 1987, for examples) as shown by the murder victimization rates computed by Plass (1986). Plass found that women are seldom murder victims outside the family (12% of nonspousal murders) but make up 57% of spousal murder victims (see also Plass & Straus, 1987).

On the other hand, the high rate of assaults by women on their husbands, together with the high rates of violence found in child-to-child, parent-to-child, and child-to-parent relationships (Straus, 1983), suggests wife beating is part of a broader problem of violence in the family and the society. Programs to aid victims and treat aggressors, important as they are, must be supplemented by programs that address the fundamental causes of the overall high level of violence in families and in society generally.

The Meaning and Importance of Violence by Women

The repeated finding that the rate for violence by women in the family or in dating relationships is similar to the rate of violence by their male partners is an important finding about violence in American families. Unless women also forsake violence in their relationships with male partners and children, they cannot expect to be free of assault. Women must insist on nonviolence by their own sex as much as they rightfully insist on it by men. That is beginning to happen. After·years of denial, shelters for battered women are confronting this problem. Almost all shelters now have policies designed to deal with the high rate of child abuse by mothers as well as by fathers, and some are also facing up to the problem of wife-to-husband violence.

The cost of giving publicity to violence by wives is that it is apt to be misused to defend male violence. Our 1975 data, for example, have been used against battered women in court cases and also to minimize the need for shelters for battered women. However, the cost of failing to attend to this problem will ultimately block the goal of being free from violence by men. There may be costs associated with acknowledging the fact of female domestic violence, but the cost of denial and suppression is even greater. Rather than attempting to deny the existence of such violence (see Pleck et al., 1977, for an example and the reply by Steinmetz, 1978a), a more productive solution is to confront the issue and work toward eliminating violence by both men and women. The achievements of the 20-year effort to reduce child abuse and the 10-year effort to reduce wife-beating (see Straus & Gelles, 1986) suggest this may be a realistic goal.

Violence Against Children

Overall Violence Rate

No rates or numbers are shown in the first row of Part B of Table 7.1 because statistics on whether *any* violence is used are almost meaningless unless one takes into account the age of the child. For children age 3 and under the true figure is close to 100%. For example, 97% of the parents of 3-year-olds in the 1975 study reported one or more times during the year when they had hit the child (Straus, 1983, Figure 1). For children age 15 and over, Part C of Table 7.1 shows that the rate is much lower: about one-third of 15- to 17-year-olds were hit by a parent during the year of the study. However, the difference between age groups should not obscure the fact that one-third is still a remarkably high rate, especially considering that the latter group consists of 15 to 17 year olds.

Child Abuse–1 Rate

This measure of child abuse is confined to acts by parents which are almost universally regarded as abusive: kicking, biting, punching, beating up, scalding, and attacking with weapons. The second row of Table 7.1, Part B shows that the reported rate of such indubitably abusive violence was 2.4 per 100 children in 1985. This is almost certainly an underestimate because not all parents were willing to tell us about instances in which they carried out such acts. Nevertheless, if we apply this rate to the 63 million children living in the United States in 1985, the result is an estimate of about 1.5 million seriously assaulted children per year. This is about three-and-one-half times greater than the number of physical abuse cases per year in the official child abuse reports (American Association for Protecting Children, 1986).

Child Abuse–2 Rate

This measure of child abuse (as noted earlier) adds hitting the child with an object such as a stick or belt. Hitting with an object was omitted from the Child Abuse–1 rate because neither legal nor informal norms presume that as "abuse." However, because hitting a child with an object involves a greater risk of injury than does spanking or slapping with the hand, we think the best measure of physical abuse of children is the Child Abuse–2 rate. The third row of Part B shows that in 1985 11 out of every 100 children were reportedly assaulted by a parent in a way that we regard as "abuse." When this rate is applied to the 63 million children living in the United States in 1985, it results in an estimate of 6.9 million abused children per year, which is about 16 times greater than the "official rate" of child abuse.

Abuse of Children Age 15 through 17

Although infants and young children experience the highest rates of child abuse, teenagers are by no means immune. About one out of three parents of a child age 15 through 17 reported having used physical force on the child at least once during 1985—usually one of the acts of "minor violence" such as slapping. However, serious assaults were far from absent. In fact, Part C of Table 7.1 shows that 6 out of every 100 children this age were reportedly victims of a serious assault by one of their parents, including 3.4 per 100 who were victims of very serious assaults.

Violence by Children

Children 3 through 17

The first row of Part D in Table 7.1 reveals that children are the most violent people of all in American families. The rates are extremely high for violence against a sibling—80 out of 100 had hit a brother or sister and more than one-half had engaged in one of the acts in the CTS severe violence list. This came as a surprise, even though it should not have. Had we analyzed the issue theoretically beforehand, it would have been an obvious prediction because of the well-known tendency for children to imitate and exaggerate the behavioral patterns of parents and because there are implicit norms that permit violence between siblings, exemplified by phrases such as "kids will fight."

The rate of violence by children against parents is much lower, as might be expected, because of the strong norms against hitting one's father or mother, but there is still a substantial rate, including 9 per 100 assaults involving one of the acts on the severe violence list.

Children 15 through 17

There is a vast difference between being punched by a 5-year-old and being punched by a 15-year-old—at least with respect to the pain or injury that can result. Consequently, we computed separate rates for violence by 15-to-17-year-olds. The first row in Part E of Table 7.1 shows that even in their late teens, two-thirds of American children reportedly assault a sibling at least once during the course of a year, and in over one-third of these cases the assault involved an act with a relatively high probability of causing injury (kicking, punching, biting, or attacking with a knife or gun).

Finally, the last two rows in Table 7.1 show that teenagers attack their parents about as often as the parents attack each other. The overall violence rate is slightly lower (10 per 100 children this age versus 11.3 per 100 husbands and 12.1 per 100 wives), and the rate of severe violence against a parent (3.5) is midway between the rate of severe husband-to-wife violence (3.2) and severe wife-to-husband violence (4.5).

How Violent Are American Families?

As indicated earlier, the rates and numbers just presented are almost certain to be underestimates. But even taking the statistics at face value, they indicate that violence is a major family problem. However, because many of us are trained to see the loving and supportive side of the family and to discount the "dark side" of the family, these figures are sometimes dismissed. For example, it can be noted that there was violence between the spouses in only 16% of the couples, that is, 84% were *not* violent. Moreover, most of those violent incidents were minor, such as slapping or throwing things.

Suppose, however, that we had studied universities rather than families. It seems unlikely that the findings would be dismissed by saying that "84% of the faculty did not hit a student in 1987 and, in any case, most of those episodes involved slapping the student or faculty member, rather than punching or beating up."

The comparison with an imaginary survey of violence in universities provides an appropriate link to the next section of the chapter because it illustrates one of the fundamental reasons why there is so much violence in the family—the existence of a double standard which tolerates intrafamily violence.

THE CAUSES OF FAMILY VIOLENCE

How can we explain the paradox that women are most likely to be assaulted by husbands or lovers and children by parents? The issue is important both theoretically and practically because information on the causes of child abuse and wife beating influence prevention and treatment. If child abusers or wife beaters are thought to be mentally ill, psychotherapy may be helpful; if husbands hit their wives when angry because they know that the chances of being prosecuted are near zero, criminal penalties may be a deterrent. If parents hit their children because they are at their wits end and do not know what else to do, then strategies such as teaching parenting skills and providing other assistance to beleaguered families are appropriate. Consequently, the following section outlines some of the key causal factors. (See Gelles & Straus, 1979, and Straus and Hotaling, 1980, for additional causal factors).

High Level of Family Conflict

One of the most fundamental factors accounting for the frequency of violence in families is that the family is a group with a high level of both conflict and commitment. Part of the reason for the frequency of conflict within the family is that unlike colleagues in a work setting, the family is concerned with more than such limited aspects of a person as work skills. The family cares about "the whole person," that is, about every aspect of a person's life. Thus, there are more things over which conflict can occur. Moreover, when conflict does occur, the deep commitment makes emotionally tinged arguments common. A disagreement over preferred types of music might occur with work colleagues, but it is unlikely to have the same emotional intensity as when parents favor Bach and children favor rock. The likelihood of marital conflicts is further multiplied because the partners are men and women, thus introducing differences due to the different orientations and interests of the two sexes. The family, in short, is the prime locus of the "generation gap" and the "battle of the sexes."

Although the family by its very nature tends to be high in conflict,

conflict is also high in academic departments and congressional committees, yet physical violence is practically nonexistent in such settings. Clearly, other factors must be taken into account to explain why violence is so much more frequently used to deal with conflicts in the family rather than in other groups.

Cultural Norms

One of the most important differences between the family and other groups that helps explain the much higher rate of violence in families is the fact that there are cultural norms that permit or require violence. These norms are difficult to perceive because norms that prescribe love and gentleness within the family dominate perceptions of family relations. Consequently, it is difficult to see that there are also contradictory norms legitimizing the use of violence (as defined in footnote 3) between family members. These rules are sometimes explicit or even mandatory, including, for example, the right and obligation of parents to use an appropriate level of physical force to train, protect, and control a child. As previously indicated, almost all parents use physical punishment at some time—for example, 97% of the parents of 3-year-old children (Straus, 1983). Moreover, most parents feel obligated to do so if the child persistently misbehaves, which is in marked contrast to other institutions of society. Even prison authorities are no longer permitted to use corporal punishment.

In husband–wife relations similar norms are present and powerful, but they are largely implicit and taken for granted and therefore largely unrecognized. Just as parenthood gives the right to hit, the marriage license is also a hitting license. As with other licenses, there are rules governing its use. For example, the spouse must be engaged in some serious wrong as perceived by the assailant and "won't listen to reason." Many of the men and women interviewed by Gelles (1974) expressed this with such phrases as "I asked for it," or "She needed to be brought to her senses."

The idea of the marriage license as a "hitting license" does not reside only in the folk culture. Despite important recent statutory reforms, it remains embedded in the actual operation of the legal system. Many police officers believe that husbands do have the right to hit their wives provided the injury does not require medical treatment. In at least one city this was called the "stitch rule" (Field & Field, 1973). If a wife wants to press charges, until recently she was discouraged at every step in the judicial process. Police officers refuse to make arrests, prosecuting attorneys do not bring the case to court, and judges dismiss cases or suspend sentences in the small fraction of cases that do reach the court (Field & Field, 1973). Under pressure from the women's movement, this is changing, but slowly. The 1985 survey revealed that only a very small percentage of men think that a legal sanction would occur if they assaulted their wife (Carmody & Williams, 1987). And they are correct. This same survey found that of the more than 600 instances of assaults by husbands, the police were involved in only 6.7%, and an arrest was made in only five cases. Thus, the chances of legal sanction if a man assaults his wife is less than 1 in 100 (Kaufman Kantor & Straus, 1987). The probability is even lower in cases of assaults by a woman on her husband.[11]

Family Socialization in Violence

In a certain sense it begs the question to attribute the high rate of violence in the family to norms that tolerate, permit, or require such violence. If norms permitting violence exist for the family, why are there different norms for stores, churches, or university departments? There are a number of reasons, but one of the most fundamental is that the family is the setting that most persons first experience physical violence and the setting that establishes the emotional context, meaning, and uses of violence. Learning about violence begins with physical punishment, which as noted above is experienced by over 97% of American children. Physical punishment aims to teach that certain types of behavior are not condoned, but it also provides several unintentional lessons.

The first of these additional lessons is the association of love with violence. Studies in England (Newson & Newson, 1963) and the United States (Straus, 1983) show that physical punishment typically begins in infancy with parental slaps to correct and teach. Parents are the first and usually the only ones to hit an infant. For most children this continues throughout childhood. Children therefore learn that those who love them the most are also those who hit. Second, because physical punishment is used to train the child in morally correct behavior or to teach about danger to be avoided, it establishes the moral rightness of hitting other family members. The third lesson stems from the fact that parents often refrain from hitting until the anger or frustration reaches a certain point. The child therefore learns that anger and frustration justify the use of physical force. These indirect lessons become a fundamental part of the child's personality and are later generalized to other social relationships, especially to such intimate relationships as those of husband and wife and of parent and child. This is confirmed by the finding that the more physical punishment experienced as a child, the higher the rate of hitting a spouse (Straus, 1983; Straus, Gelles, & Steinmetz, 1980). Many children do not even need to generalize the pattern of violent behavior to other family relationships because they can directly observe role models of physical violence between husbands and wives. At the societal level the near-universality of physical punishment and the millions of children who observe violence between their parents lays the groundwork for the cultural norms discussed next.

Gender Inequality

Male dominance in the family and in society generally is an important cause of family violence and is also important for explaining why beaten wives so often stay with the assaulting husband.

The empirical evidence is clear: Male-dominant marriages have the highest rate of wife beating (Straus, 1973; Straus, Gelles, & Steinmetz, 1980; Straus & Hotaling, 1980), and societies in which male-dominant marriages prevail have higher rates of marital violence than more egalitarian societies (Straus, 1977b) because force is ultimately necessary to back up the right to have the final say (Goode, 1974).

Gender inequality continues to be a factor accounting for wife beating in the United States because, despite the trend toward a more egalitarian family, many husbands still claim the right to be regarded as the head of the family and to have the final say. This fact is obscured by egalitarian rhetoric. Nevertheless, countless legal and administrative rulings and procedures and innumerable taken-for-granted customs assume that the husband is the head of the family. Husbands also continue to dominate because society favors men over women: Salaries of women employed full time are about one-third lower than are salaries paid to men, and money is a source of power. Male dominance is also supported by the prevailing practice of men marrying women who are younger, shorter, and less educated. Because superior age, physical size, and education are a basis for exercising power, the average marriage begins with an advantage to men. If the initial advantage changes or is challenged, many men are willing to use their greater size and strength to maintain the privilege of having the final say (LaRossa, 1980).

Gender inequality also helps explain why beaten wives remain in abusive marriages. As recently as the 1980 United States census about one-half of all married women with children had no earned income of their own. The other half earned only about one-half of the male wage. When marriages end, children stay with the mother in over 90% of the cases. Women have the main financial responsibility in such cases because child support payments are typically inadequate and typically ignored after a year or two. No-fault divorce has worked to the economic disadvantage of women (Weitzman, 1986). Many women stay in violent marriages largely because the alternative is bringing up their children in poverty.

Other Factors

Many other factors contribute to the high rate of intrafamily violence in the United States, even though they do not explain why the family is, on the average, more violent than other groups. Within the space of this chapter, it is only possible to briefly identify three of these factors.

Stress

Stress and frustration are frequently cited as causes of violence, and the empirical evidence shows a correlation between stress and all types of violence, including child abuse and wife beating. For example, data from the 1975 National Family Violence survey show that the greater the number of stressful events experienced by a family, the higher the rate of marital violence and child abuse (Straus, 1980a; & Kaufman Kantor, Straus 1987). In addition to specific stressful events that impinge on families, there are chronic stresses such as poverty that are also strongly associated with child abuse and spouse abuse.

Alcohol

Almost all studies that have investigated this issue find a strong association (Coleman & Strauss, 1983; Kaufman Kantor & Straus, 1987). However, even though heavy drinkers have two to three times the violence rate of abstainers, most heavy drinkers do *not* engage in spousal abuse or child abuse (Kaufman Kantor & Straus, 1987).

Societal Violence

There is considerable evidence that the higher the level of non-family violence in a society, the higher the rate of child abuse and spousal abuse (Straus, 1977b). Ironically, this carryover of violent behavior from one sphere of life to another seems to occur when the societal violence is "legitimate violence" rather than criminal violence. Thus, Archer and Garter (1984) and Huggins and Straus (1980) both find that war produces an increase in interpersonal violence. Straus (1985) constructed an index to measure state-to-state differences in the extent to which violence was used for socially legitimate purposes such as corporal punishment in the schools or expenditure per capita on the National Guard. The higher the score of a state on the legitimate violence index, the higher the rate of *criminal* violence such as homicide (Baron & Straus, 1988) or rape (Baron, Straus, & Jaffee, 1988).

SUMMARY AND CONCLUSIONS

Although previous analyses comparing the 1975 and 1985 National Family Violence Surveys (Gelles & Straus, 1987, Straus & Gelles, 1986) suggest that there has been a substantial reduction in the rates of child abuse and wife beating, it is obvious from the rates reported in this chapter that American society still has a long way to go before a typical citizen is as safe in his or her own home as on the streets or in a workplace.

The Causes of Family Violence

No single factor such as male dominance or growing up in a violent family has been shown to account for more than a small percentage of the incidence of child abuse or spousal abuse. However, a study of the potential effect of 25 such "risk factors" (Straus, Gelles, & Steinmetz, 1980) indicated that in families where only one or two of the factors existed there were no incidents of wife beating during the year studied. On the other hand, wife beating occurred in 70% of the families with 12 or more of the factors. Similar results were found for child abuse. Thus, the key to unraveling the paradox of wife beating appears to lie in understanding the interplay of the numerous causal factors.

The Future

During the period since 1965 the age-old phenomena of child abuse and wife beating underwent an evolution from "private troubles" to "social problems" and, in the case of wife beating, to a statutory crime. Every state in the United States now employs large numbers of child protective service workers, and there are national and local voluntary groups devoted to prevention and treatment of child abuse. There are more than 750 shelters for battered women, whereas none existed in 1973, and a growing number of counseling programs for batterers and family dispute mediation programs. Criminal prosecution of violent husbands, although still rare, is increasing.

Each of the steps just listed is essential to reduce the level of child abuse and wife beating and to protect victims. However, the root causes of child abuse and spousal abuse lie in the very nature of the family and of other aspects of society. Consequently, social services for abused children, shelters, counseling, and prosecution are unlikely to have a major or lasting effect unless they are part of a larger process of changing certain basic characteristics of the family and the society. These characteristics include the incidence of violence outside the family (ranging from corporal punishment in schools to executions and bombing countries we accuse of engaging in "state terrorism"), social norms tolerating violence between spouses (providing the violence is not serious enough to produce an injury), the use of physical punishment in child rearing, poverty and unemployment, racism, and gender inequality within the family and in society at large.

NOTES

1. The data for this study are from the National Family Violence Resurvey, funded by National Institutes of Mental Health, Grants RO1MH40027 and T32MH15161. This research is part of the Family Violence Research Program of the Family Research Laboratory, University of New Hampshire. A program description and list of publications can be obtained by writing to the Family Research Laboratory, University of New Hampshire, Durham, NH 03824. The Family Violence Research Program also has been supported by the National Institutes of Justice, the Centers For Disease Control, the National Center on Child Abuse and Neglect, the National Science Foundation, the Conrad Hilton Foundation, the Eden Hall Foundation, and the University of New Hampshire. It is a pleasure to acknowledge the support of these organizations.

2. See Nelson (1984), Parton (1985), and Pfohl (1977) for analyses of the reasons why the long-standing problem of child abuse emerged as a social problem during the 1960s and 1970s.

3. The reasons for this are complex and would take far more space than is possible within this chapter. See Straus (1976) for an analysis of the role of gender inequality and Straus and Lincoln (1985) for an analysis of the general question of the

consequences—positive and negative—of invoking the criminal justice system to deal with illegal acts, including theft and assault, that occur within the family.

4. The focus of this chapter is not on all the "abuse" or "violence" that can go on within the family but on *physical violence* as one type of abuse. Moreover, as will be seen later, even restricting the focus to physical violence leaves important issues unresolved. For children, where is the line between "physical abuse" and "physical punishment"? In view of these issues, it is essential for readers to know that the definition of violence used for purposes of this chapter is: *An act carried out with the intention, or perceived intention, of causing physical pain or injury to another person.*

This brief definition, although essential, does not provide an adequate conceptual framework for understanding violence. A more adequate discussion is presented elsewhere (Gelles & Straus, 1979), including an explication of this definition and an analysis of alternative definitions. As pointed out in that article, the fact of a physical assault having taken place is not sufficient for understanding violence. Several other dimensions also must be considered. However, it is also important that each of these other dimensions be measured separately so that their causes and consequences and joint effects can be investigated. Among the other dimensions are the seriousness of the assault (which can range from a slap to stabbing and shooting), whether a physical injury was produced (which can range from none to death), the motivation (which might range from concern for a person's safety, as when a child is spanked for going into the street to hostility so intense that the death of the person is desired), and whether the act of violence is normatively legitimate (as in the case of slapping a child) or illegitimate (as in the case of slapping a spouse) and which set of norms is applicable (legal, ethnic or class norms, couple norms, and so on).

5. The CTS has been used and refined in numerous studies of family violence (e.g., Allen & Straus, 1980; Cate et al., 1982; Giles-Sims, 1983; Henton et al., 1983; Hornung et al., 1981; Jorgensen, 1977; Steinmetz, 1977; Straus, 1973). Three different studies have established that the CTS measures three factorially separate variables (Jorgensen, 1977; Schumm et al., 1982; Straus, 1979): reasoning, verbal aggression, and violence of physical aggression. The reliability and validity of the CTS have been assessed in several studies over the 15-year period of their development. See Straus (1979) for evidence of internal consistency, reliability, concurrent validity, and construct validity. Other investigators have confirmed some of these findings. See, for example, Jouriles and O'Leary (1985), Jorgensen (1977) and Schumm et al. (1982).

6. The 1985 rates reported in this chapter are higher than those found in the paper comparing violence rates in 1985 with those found in the 1975 survey (Straus & Gelles, 1986) because the need for comparability meant that the analysis could not use the 1985 additions to the CTS list of violent acts (described earlier) and also could not use the 1985 additions to the sample (children under 3, single parents, and information about marriages that had recently been terminated).

7. It should be recognized that in most instances the outcome from being kicked, although painful, does *not* result in an injury. However, absence of injury does not remove it from the category of an abusive act. Our distinction between minor and severe violence parallels the legal distinction between a "simple assault" and an "aggravated assault." An aggravated assault is an attack that is likely to cause grave bodily harm, such as an attack with a knife or gun, irrespective of whether the person attacked was actually injured.

8. From a scientific perspective, it would be preferable to avoid the term "abuse" because of the definitional problems just mentioned and because it is as much a

political and administrative term as a scientific term. Despite this, we use "abuse" for two reasons. First, it is less awkward than "very severe violence index." Second, it is such a widely used term that avoiding it creates communication difficulties.

9. These statistics and the analysis that follows are not confined to women who are legally married to their male partners. Unmarried cohabiting women and women who are divorced or separated are at least as likely to be victims of assault by their partner or former partner as are married women (Gaquin, 1978; Stets & Straus, 1988; Yllo & Straus, 1981). Such assaults tend to be ignored by the public and the criminal justice system in essentially the same way as assaults on married women.

10. For convenience and economy of wording, terms such as "marital" and "spouse" and "wife" and "husband" are used to refer to couples, irrespective of whether they are a married or a nonmarried, cohabiting couple. For an analysis of differences and similarities between married and cohabiting couples in the 1975–76 study, see Yllo (1978) and Yllo and Straus (1981).

11. Although it is essential to recognize the criminal nature of spousal abuse and child abuse, it is also essential to recognize the limits and possible negative effects of criminal sanctions, especially imprisonment. The dilemmas posed by use of criminal sanctions are illustrated by the refusal of parents to participate in criminal actions in cases of sexual abuse when the offender is another of their children. These and other dilemmas associated with invoking the criminal justice system in cases of intrafamily crime are discussed in Straus and Lincoln (1985).

Strategic Rapid Intervention in Wife Beating

8

J. SCOTT FRASER

A woman, after having been beaten by her husband, comes to a therapist who compassionately tells her that she does not deserve this abuse and strongly urges her to leave him. The woman returns to her husband but not to the therapist. A battered woman repeatedly withholds information and denies the extent of the abuse during ongoing couples therapy. The couple discontinues treatment, and the battering recurs. Another woman stops therapy after months of exploring her family history to uncover the reasons why she accepts abuse. The battering continues. A battering husband goes to a therapist after his wife has left him. His wife returns, and neither husband nor wife is seen by the therapist again. A battered woman drops legal charges and returns again to her husband from a shelter despite the shelter workers' frustration and concern. The woman is killed.

These are only a few of the common scenarios encountered by therapists and advocates attempting to intervene in wife battering. The all-too-frequent occurrence of wife abuse in our society is not only tragic and dangerous, it is a compelling problem and a frustrating one for those of us attempting to help. On one hand, the violent results of the abuse are appalling and create outrage in those of us encountering the participants. On the other hand, the social, economic, and family interactional patterns involved are often so insidious and endemic as to defy our best direct attempts to stop them.

The focus of this chapter is on the treatment of wife abuse by their male partners; it recognizes but does not attempt to discuss the reverse but much less common problem: husband abuse by wives. Most of the reviewed and recent societal and professional response to wife abuse is little more than 12 years old. Starting with the work of Erin Pizzey at Chiswick House (one of the first battered women's shelters in London, England) and her influential book, *Scream Quietly or the Neighbors Will Hear* (1974), a number of other influential works followed. These works include Steinmetz and Straus'

AUTHOR'S NOTE: I gratefully acknowledge the help, support, and perspective of my wife, Beth Morrow Fraser, in writing this chapter.

Violence in the Family (1974), Dell Martin's *Battered Wives* (1976), Lenore Walker's *The Battered Woman* (1979), Dobash and Dobash's *Violence Against Wives: A Case Against Patriarchy* (1979), and Straus, Gelles, and Steinmetz' book, *Behind Closed Doors: Violence in the American Family,* 1980), to name a few. These works, along with others that have followed, and accompanied by the nation-wide battered women's shelter movement, have helped to raise the visibility of wife battering as an intolerable problem and have in-creased our knowledge of its nature and the characteristics of its participants. This movement also has begun to provide viable alter-natives for women who wish to protect themselves or to leave their partners. Although the front-line therapist or advocate has consider-able knowledge available about the problem, there are still relatively few theoretically sound and socially or clinically practical tools to help initiate change. Often the clinician's or advocate's best efforts at intervention in multiple levels of social, legal, or family systems seem to fail and, at times, may even exacerbate violence. Such attempts frequently create alienation of the clients from helpers and burnout and disillusionment in clinicians and advocates.

This chapter addresses some of these problems. The position taken here does not claim to be a solution for all ills in the area of family violence intervention. It will, however, present a point of view regarding the process of early intervention in wife battering. The strategic rapid intervention discussed is not only based on a systemic perspective common to a significant portion of the wife battering literature (Gelles & Straus, 1979; Giles-Sims, 1983; Straus, 1973; among others) but also goes beyond many of the more static descrip-tions, using much of what we know about battering system patterns. Essentially, the approach attempts to use what is usually a set of pathogenic processes and turn them to positive ends.

THE STRATEGIC PERSPECTIVE

The strategic perspective discussed here is most accurately de-scribed as a process/constructive view (Fraser, 1984a). It is based on the work of the Brief Therapy Center of the Mental Research Insti-tute (MRI) in Palo Alto, California (Fisch, Weakland, & Segal, 1982; Watzlawick, Weakland, & Fisch, 1974). Although the work of Haley and his colleagues (Haley, 1973b, 1976, 1980) is also referred to as strategic, their work has been judged to have a set of distinctly different assumptions and goals (Fraser, 1986b) and should be distinguished from the MRI–based approach discussed here.

This strategic view describes couples and families as ever-changing, fluid, open systems of interaction. System interactions are initiated from small changes or variations that may occur either accidentally or due to some life-cycle change. The system members then interact around this variation in attempts to either assimilate it into ongoing family patterns or to accommodate those patterns to the change. This process generally produces some elaboration or evolution of the system, either minor or major, gradual or rapid. The system members' patterned transactions, or *process,* as well as their individual and shared ideas, or *constructs,* are what interact to both guide and be shaped by this general process. These processes and constructs derive from both cultural and historical norms and traditions as well as from the unique history of patterned interactions of each separate couple or family. Interaction cycles may be either gradual or rapid, and longer-standing patterns are made up of short, repetitive cycles. Whereas patterns judged to be positive are termed virtuous cycles, patterns judged to be negative are termed vicious cycles.

According to this view problems are seen as vicious cycles of often well-meaning attempts to adjust to a variation or perceived difficulty. The major problem is that variations on the same solution pattern are often attempted over and over again. This occurs despite the fact that the very solution attempt itself may be making the problem worse instead of better. It is often necessary for one or another party not only to stop the solution pattern but also to actually reverse it. From the strategic view if the process of a relationship system can be understood and accepted, then dissonance is more likely to be introduced, and the system process turned beneficently toward more positive ends.

STRATEGIC RAPID INTERVENTION

Strategic rapid intervention takes the above ideas and employs them at system crisis points (Fraser, 1986a). The goal is to introduce small but significant change in the given system, thus increasing the chance of interrupting a vicious cycle and initiating a virtuous one. System crisis points are chosen for intervention because these are usually the times of greatest system pattern agitation and offer the greatest openness for the relationships to accept new options.

Because detail on the therapy session model, phases, and process of strategic rapid intervention have been presented elsewhere (Fraser, 1986a), only a brief overview is covered here. Generally, phases of an interview session move in an overlapping way from joining to information gathering, to consensus on the problem as defined, to a brief break, to a problem-solving phase and concluding with a summary of the session, the problem defined, and the plan. The therapist focuses on questions such as: What is the problem as defined similarly or differently by all involved parties? What have they done about it, and how has this worked? What do they usually do about problems like this? What have others told them to do? What are the clients' characteristic language, ideas, and motives? What are the clients' positions on the prospect of change and in relationship to the therapist as a helper? What are their most modest goals in solving the problem? How do these mesh with the therapist's goals, given a knowledge of the common processes of this problem in our culture and the unique patterns of this particular couple, family, or larger system?

Therapists must be careful not to duplicate currently malevolent system patterns but instead use the general problem cycle to introduce dissonance and shift the process toward a positive end.

STRATEGIC INTERVENTION IN BATTERING

In strategic rapid intervention, the major thrust is to identify, adopt, and use inherent system forces and channel them toward new and more desired ends. In this process, insidious cycles and patterns that have historically led to greater closure and increased potential for violence are directed instead toward increased openness and safety.

The primary goals of strategic rapid intervention are to decrease isolation, equalize power differentials, disqualify violence as an accepted option, increase the woman's perception of self-respect and control, and increase the man's acceptance of responsibility for his actions while offering new options. To these ends it is important for the intervenor to be aware of both the common patterns that generally contribute to increasing closure and violence as well as the unique positions, ideas, and patterns of each relationship encountered.

Battering as a Critical Event

Most intervenors, whether therapists or advocates, first will encounter a battering relationship shortly after an incidence of violence. A therapist also may be confronted unexpectedly with spousal violence in a couple currently in therapy. Such surprises usually occur because the therapist has either not attended to existing patterns that may have predicted this or has so consistently seen the couple together that their common process of colluded secrecy, intimidation, and protection have disguised the situation.

Nevertheless, whenever such a violent incident does present itself, direct action is called for. A crisis such as this is a classic dangerous opportunity for the system members as well as for the therapist. For the woman, the danger of the incident lies in the possibility of a beating. Its opportunity lies in the limited time during which the couple has increased motivation to end the fear and pain of violence and find new options. For the man, the danger lies in an increased loss of control and the potential loss of his partner. Its opportunity lies in limiting the increasingly ineffective use of violence and opening new, safer, and more effective interactions. For the therapist, the danger lies in the responsibility to ensure the current and future safety of the victim while not alienating the couple from help. Its opportunity lies in the increased yet time-limited ability to access a dangerous, semiclosed system and help move it toward more openness and safety.

Assessment

As a semiclosed system, a battering relationship by its very nature tends to limit output or information *to* the outside and prevent input or intervention *from* the outside. This is especially evident when both parties are seen together. Denying, minimizing, or excusing the violence as attributable to some historical or external reason are common when couples are seen together. Disclosure of the violent patterns in couples therapy may, in fact, be ill-advised given the documented history of such disclosures precipitating new violence following the session (Bograd, 1984; Coleman, K. H., 1980). Although this runs counter to traditional, system-based couple therapy that encourages that couples be seen together, it is consonant with a strategic approach that not only allows but also encourages that system members be seen separately as needed (Fisch et al., 1982). Such separation can allow more open disclosure while providing the intervenor the opportunity to attend to the unique values, motives, language, and position of each party. In a tightly closed system, such brief separation may cause considerable anxiety in both parties over the increased possibility of disclosure and separation yet may serve well as a small initial step toward reopening the system. Therefore, if both parties are available at initial contact, it is strongly recommended that they be seen separately.

The Woman

When initially encountering the woman, it is most important to learn first her reasons for contacting a therapist. If the contact is by phone, it is important to learn if the man is present and/or if a violent incident is currently in progress. If an incident is in progress, it is best to learn where she is and if there are children involved, to get police or others to the site, and to get her and any children to a safe place. If the man is present, the woman may not be able to speak freely, and the therapist may need to ask questions that are easily answered by "yes" or "no." If the contact is in person, it should be determined if a battering has recently occurred. If so, safety needs are again paramount. The woman may be reluctant to disclose this information, and, if so, should be told to take her time in discussing it. Pressure may only cause her to withdraw further. She must be sure that the therapist understands the sensitive nature and potential danger of such disclosure.

In the meantime, any evident injuries should be noted and inquiries made as to whether they have been attended to medically. It is not uncommon for women not to seek outside medical help out of fear of discovery, shame, or embarrassment for themselves or their partner. If unattended injuries are present, their treatment should become one of the therapist's current major goals. If possible, the woman should be accompanied by a supportive person during any medical treatment, and clear documentation of injuries should be encouraged in the event of future legal actions.

Another pertinent initial question if battering has been recent is whether the man is with the woman or knows of her current location. If the battering phase is still in progress and if the man is either closely adjacent or knows of her location and her attempt to seek help, both she and the intervenor may still be in imminent danger. Precautions should then be taken to have security personnel available, maintain safe separation of the couple, eliminate weapons, and provide for safe exit. Women have been seriously injured or killed in the process of leaving or seeking help, and those intervening with them can be in similar jeopardy. In these instances, it is most critical that the intervenor have information and access to community resources such as safe and confidential shelter for the woman (whether organized or informal) and knowledge of and access to the law enforcement and legal systems for sanctions and protection.

Once again, however, it is most important to attend to what the woman is *asking for,* whether or not she is involved in an acute battering instance or some other phase. She may, indeed, be asking for help with her physical injuries, safety, and escape. In this event direct aid, with only some minor cautions added, may be appropriate and effective. On the other hand, even when in acute danger, she may in fact be asking for help for her partner, help in maintaining a low profile, help in keeping her relationship together, or a number of other things. If these requests are not attended to and respected, no matter how illogical they may seem to the intervenor, the woman may be unlikely to align with the intervenor and follow through with directives. A woman concerned for the welfare of her partner, for example, is more likely to get medical attention for her injuries for his sake than for hers. Accepting the woman's motives and building on them to move toward positive goals is a key point here.

Even if a woman is directly requesting escape and safety, it is important for the intervenor to remember the realistic dangers involved in the move and the potent economic and social factors mitigating against it as well as the compelling forces of such a semiclosed relationship system to draw her back. Without discouraging the woman from leaving, it is important to prepare her for such forces by mentioning them as strong reasons why she may find herself not leaving or returning soon. If she is then pulled back, she is less likely to feel guilt or shame and will be more likely to continue with or recontact the intervenor.

Questions should be asked about the duration, frequency, and intensity of the violent pattern. Is this the first incident, or has it recurred many times? How frequently has it occurred? Is it becoming more frequent or severe? Is property being damaged? Has the violence progressed to pushing, slapping, fists, or weapons? Are children involved? If alcohol or drugs are a problem, by whom are they used, and are they seen as a cause or excuse? Each of these questions must be pursued gently, with a sensitivity to the woman's possible embarrassment, vulnerability, self-protectiveness, and need to defend her most important relationships.

Pagelow (1984) has suggested that one of the most critical points in the evolution of a battering relationship is how the woman responds following the first incident of physical violence. If she makes it clear in multiple and forceful ways that she will tolerate no further instances of violence, calls in outside authority, or leaves, future incidents and escalations of violence are much less likely to occur. When first meeting a woman following an initial violent incident, then, it is important to assess how she perceives the incident, how she sees her role in it, what she has said and done with her partner, and what others have said to her, if anything. If she has expressed intolerance, not accepted blame, and not excused her partner for one reason or another and if others have supported her in this, the intervenor must strongly reinforce her position while commenting on the dangers of an escalating cycle.

If, on the other hand, she has seen this as an isolated incident, accepted blame, excused her partner, and feels that it will never happen again and if others have either not been informed or have questioned her on what she did to provoke her mate, she is at greater risk for future violence. The intervenor's position is more delicate as well, in that the woman's assumptions need altering, yet this must be done without encouraging defensiveness and alienation. The woman can be told that no one deserves to be hit, but whether she, her partner, or her social network will believe or act on this is an open question.

Pagelow (1981) learned that most women found the first instance of violence to be completely unexpected, and the majority had assumed it would never happen again. This is strongly reinforced by the classic honeymoon or loving respite phase that typically follows the acute battering (Walker, 1979). Such common responses as the batterer's remorse, apologies, outpourings of kindness and favors, and promises that it will not recur tend, very reasonably, to decrease the woman's anger and recriminations. In the beginning, she is likely to see this as hopeful—that this is the real man she married, that maybe she was at fault, and that, after all, he was drunk, upset with work, or angry with the kids, and so on. Later on these respites may become the only instances of intimacy or relative safety in the relationship. No matter how long the battering has gone on, the loving respite phase tends to pull the woman back in, reinforces the violence, and further closes the system. This is a powerful and difficult force to turn toward a more positive end.

Whether this is the first or the fortieth incident of violence, it will be useful for the woman to recount the most recent incident in as much detail as possible. This can be helpful for the woman by not only allowing her to share the incident with a supportive other, but it also can serve to maintain or heighten the stark reality of the battering and the extent of its danger. For the intervenor, such a detailed description may provide vivid information about both the generic and unique patterns of the relationship as well as the phases of its cycle.

The woman's resources (economic, intellectual, and social) must be assessed to determine the extent of her personal power, control, and potential independence in relationship to her partner. The stronger these resources are, the better the potential is for rebalancing and opening the system. Particular deficits should be noted so that improving on them can become potential goals. Equally important is the extent and nature of the woman's social network. It is especially important to find out who is in this network, if anyone, and what she has shared with them. It is helpful to know how they have responded to her and what she thinks of their position. No matter what their position is, if the woman has not accepted it or reacted against it, it is unwise for the therapist to take a similar stance, no matter how much sense it makes. If others have told her to leave, she may have become more isolated from them through her feeling that they don't understand her reasons for staying and through their frustration over her continuing to stay. In this case no matter how compelling the reasons, if the intervenor urges her to leave, this very stance may reinforce the cycle of isolation, alienate the client, and drive her further into the closing relationship.

Instead an acceptance of the reasons, both emotional and practical, that the woman is choosing to continue the relationship is much more likely to cement an empathetic therapeutic alliance. In such an alliance, the woman is more likely to freely evaluate these factors and open her options rather than defending them and thus closing off her choices. In relating to a battered woman, a prime goal is to *align with* and *empower* the woman. Although it is very tempting to try to convince her that her position may be wrong or to take charge of her decisions, such behavior may actually both alienate the woman and further deprive her of what power she currently has.

The woman should be offered as many choices as possible, and her decisions should be respected. Only in this way can she be empowered, and the therapist maintains the ability to alter future interactions. If the woman feels that her decisions are accepted, she

is much more likely to listen to and accept the further interventions
of the therapist. Whether she chooses to leave or stay in the relationship, she is much more likely to collaborate with the intervenor
on how, when, with what reasons and cautions, and with what new
options or skills she is pursuing her current course. The therapist's
method and purpose must be aligned with and utilize current patterns in order to employ their power to introduce dissonance and
new direction into the system. This becomes more evident as the use
of the cycle phases are discussed later.

The Man

As with the woman, when assessing the man it is important to
attend to what he is asking for and the phase of the battering cycle he
is in. Additional factors unique to him include the extent to which he
accepts responsibility for his behavior and to which he abuses alcohol or drugs, accepts or feels entitled to the use of violence to
achieve his ends, and justifies his behavior by adopting a variety of
excuses.

In most instances, a male in a battering relationship contacts a
therapist because he feels in jeopardy of losing the woman. Thus,
therapy is often viewed as a lever to regain control. It is also possible
that some men contact a therapist early in a cycle's evolution because they feel repulsed and alarmed by a seemingly alien and
impulsive violent interchange. In such instances, control of the violence is sought in order to maintain or regain the relationship rather
than to regain control of the relationship despite the violence. In
either case, remorse following a battering incident is likely.

One way of distinguishing the classic "repentance" of a loving
respite phase from remorse over the violence itself is to attend to
what the man is asking for. For the intervenor to assume that the
man's goal is to eliminate violence may be a grave error. On the
contrary, most men may be reluctantly willing to control their violence in order to regain the relationship. The therapist is better off
assuming this position until proven wrong rather than vice versa. In
fact, many men seek help in validating their position that their wife is
at fault or has a problem that must be fixed. As with the woman, a
gentle acceptance of what the man is requesting goes further in
establishing a working relationship than does preconceived assumptions, rejection, or correction.

If the man is encountered during the violent phase of the cycle,
until proven otherwise, he should be considered dangerous to the

woman and others aiding her. If there are mandatory arrest laws in the community, this is the time when police should be called in. If the community requires that a complaint be filed against the man, the woman and/or the intervenor, if the intervenor was a witness, would be strongly advised to do so. Although the potential for violence is briefly escalated during arrest and although the process of court hearings and the possible consequences of dropping charges once filed may be burdensome for the woman, the potential for future deterrence of violence through such arrests appears to be well worth the risk (Sherman & Berk, 1984). Such action may not only increase safety but also helps to introduce the kind of immediate social sanctions that are characteristically absent from the semiclosed system characteristic of wife abuse.

The man, similar to the woman, may be secretive about the nature of the relationship and downplay the role or the extent of the violence. Whether attributed to embarrassment, shame, or indifference, this is common to this kind of semiclosed system. During the loving respite phase, however, when a therapist is most likely to encounter the man, he is considerably more likely to disclose about the relationship and to admit his part in the violence. Later on during the tension-building phase such relative candor may sharply decrease or be markedly absent. Again, as with the woman, it is important to take advantage of any initial accessibility to find out as much as possible about the patterns of the relationship and the phase and extent of the cycle. The most recent battering incident should be reviewed in as much detail as possible from the man's perspective, and the extent of concordance with the woman's description should be noted. This not only makes it harder for the man to deny the violence but also gives some indication of the degree of openness and agreement within the couple. Close attention should be paid to the language used and to the implied causes of the violent incident as described by the man. This language and these premises may be used later by the therapist to build toward new actions.

The extent to which the man accepts and assumes the traditional male role for himself and the traditional female role for the woman should also be noted. Where he places himself and his partner on such implicit dimensions as dominance/submission, and control/freedom, along with his assumptions on how labor should be divided or decisions made, is important, among other things, to understanding and aligning with his position to shape it toward new ends. The extent to which these roles and values reflect his own family of origin and/or the couple's current subcultural context are also important to attend to. The more similar these roles and assumptions are to these historical and current contexts, the more difficult they are to directly refute or redirect. For battering men some common histories are an authoritarian family structure; paternal violence toward the mother; a hierarchical, authoritarian job in business, the military, or the police; or participation in a machismo-based street or ethnic sub-culture.

These factors also relate to the man's position on whether he feels justified in the use of violence in controlling others and to whether he sees it as useful. Of course, situational correlates such as the woman not obeying, not performing up to expectations, or attending too much to others outside the relationship may also be offered as just reasons for strong correction. The more the man perceives the violence as justified and useful, the less likely he is to be open to direct challenge or alteration. In fact, such direct challenge most often feeds right into his position of escalating counterargument and results in the rejection of outside intervention.

The final factors to be attended are the extent to which the man adopts a number of excuses to explain or justify the violence. One of these is alluded to above is the implicit traditional role of the man as king of his own castle, decision maker, corrector, and guardian. This excuse assumes his ultimate right, or mandate, to power and control. Other excuses, however, may be used to excuse the violence. One of the most prevalent is that of drug or alcohol use. As noted earlier, although correlated with battering, substance abuse has *not* been determined to cause battering (Gelles, 1974; Pagelow, 1984). Never-theless, both men and women in battering relationships generally relate to it as a cause or excuse. The general stance of, "I had too much to drink and didn't know what I was doing" or similar positions must be negated. If substance abuse is present, another subgoal is its treatment or at least its negation as a cause or excuse. Other excuses are those that imply medical problems, job problems, or other stresses. These, as with substance abuse, are areas that must be respected and attended to as realistic contributors to the pattern of violence. At the same time, the less an excuse can be used as a justification for violence, the more responsibility the man has for new choices.

A final note on excuses: The man may very well be entering therapy in order to be labeled a "help seeker" or "one who is sick" and thus out of control. This may not necessarily mean that he wants to change anything. Instead, he may be attempting to use the help-seeking status to convince the woman not to leave or to return. Or, the sick status may become a new reason to justify, excuse, or otherwise not own responsibility for the violence. These reasons are insidious, but if noted and accepted by the intervenor, they also may be taken toward positive ends.

Other than the above information, the nature and extent of the man's social network must be determined. Has he shared his situation with anyone? If so, what has he shared, with whom has he shared it, and what have their responses been? Generally, he does not reveal much, and what might have been shared may have been skewed to downplay the violence and/or support the reasons for it. Others may have broadly overlooked or supported his reasons for or use of violence, or they may have rejected and chastised him for it. It is most important to determine his position in relation to these others' responses. If he feels supported by others in his use of violence, does not see it as alien or problematic, and has rejected any others' suggestions that it is so, then the intervenor is well advised not to directly challenge it initially unless there is a strong guarantee of immediate and powerful social sanction such as arrest and incarceration.

If the goal of the intervenor is to alter or reshape the couple's interaction from within rather than to serve as a representative of strong social sanctions from without, then direct confrontation only undercuts this goal by producing immediate alienation. The therapist may be more able to disqualify the violence not by sanctioning it but at least by not challenging it initially. As the intervention proceeds, the violence may then be disqualified gradually as too dangerous an option for the man or the woman, not as useful as other options, or running counter to other goals or values of the man.

This is a sensitive issue. Although it is tempting for the intervenor to revile the violence, this stance may not only reduce the intervenor's options to eliminate it but also may in some instances escalate its potential and further close the system to future help.

A final point on assessing the man relates both to aligning with his general goals and to danger. Any intervenor must realize that there is a potential in any battering relationship for danger to the life of the man, the woman, or both. If the system has become tightly closed, and the man loses hope of achieving his goals, his self-respect or the respect of others, or his partner, suicide and/or homicide may occur. This is especially possible if a tight cycle of jealousy and dependence

has developed. For this reason, among others, it is generally important to accept and align, at whatever level possible, with the man's
broad goals and to collaborate on new ways of achieving them. Such
a position, as with the woman, empowers the man in new ways while
avoiding the despondence of perceiving that all paths to achieving his
goals have been cut off or lost.

Intervention

In the strategic model of rapid intervention, assessment and intervention go hand in hand. In the interview process, information
gathering and initial steps toward intervention are woven together
gently from the very start (Fraser, 1986a). Nevertheless, as the
interview moves from joining, through information gathering, to con-
sensual problem formulation, there is an increasing movement toward more explicit interventions. Such interventions are usually
solidified during a brief break in the session and delivered during the
problem-solving phase (Fraser, 1986a). In a semiclosed, battering
relationship the goals are to decrease violence, isolation, and closure
while balancing power differentials. In the strategic rapid intervention model, the global means to these ends are to gain access to the
system by aligning with its process and to introduce dissonance and
new direction through utilizing the force of the system's patterns
toward new ends. In this process, there are a number of useful
therapeutic stances. Several of these positions are reviewed next,
followed by a few representative case examples.

Going Slowly

Most change is anxiety-provoking, if only because it represents
movement from the familiar and predictable to the new and unpre-
dictable. No matter how painful current situations may appear, this
draw toward the predictable and the reluctance to embrace the
unknown is always present to some degree. The advantage of a crisis
state is that it does tip the balance toward considering new options.
However, if people are pushed too quickly toward change, sooner or
later they will begin to feel reluctant and dig in their heels. "Going
slowly" is often a welcomed and empathetic stance on the part of the
intervenor.

Predicting, Ascribing, and Prescribing

*When in doubt, always discuss the possibility that the battering-
cycle phases may occur.* If the man and woman are not aware of such
a cycle, it is helpful for them to learn of it. Then if it occurs in their

relationship, it is harder for either partner to overlook it. If the cycle does not occur, so much the better. Once a pattern is seen, it becomes difficult for participants to react within it as they had before. This information introduces important dissonance and thus possible choice.

Predict the probability of future escalation. In most cases such cycles escalate toward increased violence, injury, and/or death. It is helpful for the participants to review the progression of their own conflicts as expressed in shouting, damaging objects, pushing, slapping, hitting with fists, kicking, or using weapons. A comparison of this movement to the common progression may help each partner realize future dangers and increase the probability that future escalations are labeled as evidence of an insidious cycle. If offered in a concerned yet supportive way and if more severe violence does indeed occur, such predictions are likely to increase the credibility of the therapist in future contacts. Such discussions also allow for a review of current alternatives to violence.

Predict the possibility of a return to old patterns. This stance is not unrealistic, considering the predictability of old patterns and the unpredictability of new patterns. It also allows return to the therapist without shame if there has been backsliding. Furthermore, once aware of the possibility of such backsliding, the clients may become more armed against it and may be strengthened in their determination to follow through with their changes. If there is a return to old patterns, it is much easier to discuss the reasons with the therapist, consider if this path is the best, and discuss new options. The clients win either way.

Ascribe new, malevolent motives to old patterns. A general goal here is to impugn current actions or patterns so that they are more difficult to perform and still have the former value. For example, when a woman is determined to return to the man, the therapist can get her to agree that she will not just return but also will test whether the battering cycle will actually recur. If it does, the therapist can discuss alternatives for deescalation and safety. This alteration of motives may also alter interaction. A woman's apologies may be recast as placations. Making continual adjustments and taking on added responsibilities may be recast as taking responsibility away from the man. The man's rage may be recast for him as the ultimate loss of control or as conceding control to the other. Innumerable variations on these themes are possible. A major tack is to help alter an undesirable pattern by aligning it with a motive or outcome that is undesired by the client.

Ascribe old, beneficent motives or outcomes to new actions or patterns. If the goal is to introduce and increase the probability of new actions, then old, destructive patterns not only must be impugned but also new, constructive options must be offered a positive "halo." If the man's motive is to correct his wife, then he may be encouraged not to correct her so as to allow her to learn by her "mistakes." If the husband has been jealous, it might be suggested that the only way he will know if she is choosing him freely is to offer her more freedom. Or, the continual checking on his wife's activities might be cast as playing right into the hands of anyone who would like to see his wife driven from him. The woman may offer her husband the option of learning new responsibilities by doing less for him. The woman who is in the constantly self-sacrificial position of doing for her husband or children might be encouraged to branch out and do more for herself. This can be done by describing her as an "empty pitcher" who must sacrifice by giving more to herself so as to be able to give more to others. Or, a "tough love" approach may be encouraged. The woman can be shown how to protect the man or her children from future escalations and help them learn new limits by enduring the pain of letting him be arrested. Such reframing is a delicate process that must be adapted to the particular concepts, values, and motives of the people involved.

When old patterns appear highly likely or inevitable to recur, prescribe them with slight variations and for new reasons. Violence should *not* be prescribed. In fact, it should be ruled out for both partners as dangerous, along with a full range of other reasons why violence runs counter to the couple's individual and/or joint goals. In so doing, a range of new options should be built in for both partners. However, it should be remembered that when old patterns, which were formerly done spontaneously, are then prescribed to be done deliberately, it is either be more difficult for them to be performed or their performance will now be perceived as more awkward or unnatural. This has been referred to as the so-called be spontaneous paradox (Watzlawick et al., 1974). If, in addition, new and slightly different variations and motives are included, then the potential for further pattern alterations is increased more. If the old pattern is attempted but cannot be performed, then the former process has been interrupted. If it is performed with difficulty and slight alterations, the pattern has been altered. Such small shifts may then be amplified.

For example, the wife, determined to return home, can be told that she may "have to do so" in order to be sure that a battering cycle is actually occurring. She can be encouraged to keep mental or written notes on each interaction with her partner or try new alternatives to test whether they will be allowed or restrained. These actions, if performed, have the potential to interrupt the normal process. Or, during the classic tension-building phase, when both partners commonly "walk on eggshells" in an attempt to avoid conflict, they may be encouraged to enact minor, deliberate disagreements to "let off steam" or to "learn more about their styles of conflict resolution."

Using Positions and Cycle Phases

Determine and use the clients' position on change. As stated above, most clients are ambivalent about change, even when it holds positive prospects. Typically, clients request the elimination of discomfort while all else remains the same. Beyond this, however, some participants in battering relationships may be particularly reluctant to change. Although there are numerous practical and ideological reasons for this, attempting to directly convince someone to change who does not want to may be folly.

A more productive approach is to determine what elements in their relationship the man and woman want to retain, regain, or amplify. Then new actions are encouraged in service of these goals while current patterns are implicated in undercutting these goals. This position is one that uses the concepts of first- and second-order change (Watzlawick et al., 1974). For example, the man who is struggling to control his partner may be encouraged to try a number of new behaviors (which may previously have looked like giving up or giving in) in order to truly regain control at a higher level.

Determine and use the clients' position on the therapist's authority. Members of a semiclosed system are likely to be suspicious and guarded, and they often actively reject outside intrusion, especially by perceived authority. It is important for intervenors to remember this, along with the fact that no matter how the therapist feels about his or her own role, clients are likely not only to see the therapist as a change agent but also as an authority figure. To the extent possible, then, the intervenor should actively disengage from an authority position with the clients. This may be achieved by variations of a "one down" and aligned stance.

First, aligning with each system member's plight, values, and motives can help him or her feel that the therapist may be an advocate and not an adversary. Second, this position can be amplified by attributing the majority of control and sanctioning power to external agents such as the police, courts, and social agents other than the therapist. The intervenor's position can then be defined as a compassionate advocate for the man and woman with each other as well as between themselves and external authority. This is an enviable position for the intervenor, who can empathize with each partner while presenting the possible undesired consequences of a given course of action.

For example, the therapist can say to the man: "I can sure understand your frustration with this situation, yet I'd hate to see you fly off the handle with Mary and then have the court down your throat again. I'll support you all I can in this, but if you miss more work by being in jail, they may fire you. So, as hard as these new options are, they may be worthwhile to keep everyone off your back."

A similar stance with the woman might be: "Lord knows, you don't need anyone else meddling in your family! That's why I'd hate to see this violence get any worse. I know that you don't want to see the kids involved, and you don't need to give the Children's Services people any excuse to take them away. So, as hard as they are, that's why I think it's worthwhile to take these new steps."

Another variation on this theme involves using clients' reactivity to external authority to help them move forcefully into new behaviors or to reinforce them once new behaviors are adopted. An example is: "Although I don't believe this, I think that the judge sees you as one more bad dude to put away, and he's waiting to see you pop Mary again to confirm his predictions. That's why I'd like to see you prove him wrong by taking these new positions."

Determine and use each person's position in relation to his or her partner and their children. Once each partner's motives in regard to other family members are identified, these motives can be used by the therapist as the driving force for new, more constructive actions. This is important, because apparently beneficent motives such as the wish to help or protect may be currently fueling unproductive or dangerous patterns. Conversely, what may appear to the therapist as currently malevolent motives such as revenge, jealousy, or control may be enlisted to motivate new and more desirable patterns. An example of this is when a woman is encouraged to have her partner removed from the home to protect the children or to help him understand that he has overstepped his limits. With a man, encouraging his partner to do something outside the home may serve as a test of her loyalty, an avoidance of alienation, an opportunity to avoid her subtle control, or a lesson in how to do things right in the real world.

Use the acute battering phase to enter the system and introduce safety, new information, and sanctions against violence. Although the acute battering phase represents the point of greatest danger for the participants, it also offers rare opportunities with these often unapproachable systems. First is the chance to introduce some safety in the form of having the woman and any children move to neighbors, relatives, or available shelter. This option is rarely considered by most women at other times. Not only does this aid the woman and children by increasing safety at an acutely dangerous point, but it also moves her physically out of the closed relationship while introducing new information regarding the relationship to significant others. The opportunity for new information and resources to be introduced to the woman is also increased, although whether she is able to use them constructively depends on the situation and the woman.

Second, this crisis offers a rare opportunity to introduce social or legal sanctions against the man's violence, including family or social network disapproval, sanctions from the workplace, and immediate arrest or incarceration. Such sanctions are rarely available in the semiclosed, battering relationship, and, as noted earlier, they have been found particularly effective in reducing future battering as long as the sanctions are clear, strong, immediate, and consistent (Sherman & Berk, 1984). Finally, the opportunity to introduce new information and options to either or both of the parties involved from the intervenor is increased. Nevertheless, the points made in earlier sections above on assessing and entering a battering relationship must be remembered. Recall, for instance, that too forceful an entry by an intervenor with too much new information is likely to be perceived as threatening and can cause a premature reclosure of the system.

Use the loving respite phase to initiate new options and patterns. The police, emergency shelter, and medical personnel are most likely to encounter the battering participants at the acute phase, but therapists most commonly see them first during the loving respite phase. Even though this is the most common phase in which therapeutic help is sought, it is possibly the most insidious in its potential for further closing and tightening the relationship spiral. The apologies, promises, attempts at protection, veiled shame, denial, and implied threats of this phase tend to seduce both parties into assuming that things will be all right now without any major alterations in their basic patterns.

In this phase, a man who feels that he may lose his partner without some show of good faith may enter therapy to gain the status of a "help seeker." He may also show his goodwill by showing concern for his partner's well-being and at least some distress over his actions. The opportunity of this phase presents itself during only a limited time and must be taken advantage of quickly. Some people have described this phase as a chance to play a "con game" with a "con artist." Possibly a better way of viewing the situation is that if a man has been used to manipulating information, power, and control to get his way, he is likely to do that now. Furthermore, if it has worked and he has, until recently, had most of the power in the relationship, he is unlikely to give up this pattern unless he experiences less threat of loss from new, better options. Intervenors often are seen as a threat to be neutralized, and the help-seeker status is one to be added to others that have excused violent behavior such as "sick," "drunk," "stoned," "angry," "overstressed," and others. A major tack here is for the therapist to accept the man's willingness to be seen as a helper and a help seeker and thus use this motivation to introduce new action and information.

For example, a woman who has never sought medical attention for her current or past injuries might be induced to get such attention if the intervenor has her partner talk her into it as a show of his concern. At this point in order to maintain safety, increase candor and information flow, begin the process of individuation, and enhance therapist control and maneuverability, partners are most often seen separately. Conjoint meetings are best used infrequently early on and mainly for a specific, prearranged purpose. This may also be a time for the man to further extend his goodwill by allowing his wife some minor outside contact or by allowing her to participate in a group.

When working with men or with couples, a clear no-violence contract that spells out the conditions of future interaction and the consequences of future violence is most helpful. The man is most likely to engage in such a contract at either the point when his wife is in a shelter, when he has been arrested or is under court order, or during the early loving respite phase. Such contracts make clear the intolerance of violence and its future consequences, but they are actually only as good as they are enforceable through some external authority. A vague, unenforceable, or easily negated contract loses its impact and thus should be avoided.

Another goal of this phase is to neutralize any of the multiple rationalizations that the man or woman have used in the past to excuse the violence or make it look somehow involuntary or out of the man's control. These may include claims of physical or emotional ills or the influence of alcohol or other substances. These may be ruled out or neutralized by having the man submit to medical or substance-abuse screening while he is still attempting to convince his partner that he is earnest about seeking help. She may also be educated separately about the patterns of alcohol or other substance abuse and informed that they do not necessarily cause violence. If the man submits to such screening and treatment, his options for using the problems as an excuse for violence are thus narrowed or ruled out. If he refuses such treatment, he then makes clearer his stand that he is not in fact as willing to change as he might have originally seemed to his partner.

As with other excuses, such as anger or rage, the general approach is to gently demonstrate that the man does have levels of control and does make choices. The overall process with a man who is attempting to "cool out" or neutralize the therapist is to draw him into the position wherein he must either collaborate with treatment, which neutralizes his ability not to be responsible for his actions, or reject the treatment and thus make his refusal to change more obvious.

Finally, the loving respite phase is an ideal time to engage either or both parties in either batterers' or battered women's groups. The goals for these systems are to decrease social isolation; increase social networks, inputs, resources, and sanctions; and offer new information and options. The most important factor in achieving and maintaining such engagement lies in each party's belief that the group may help achieve his or her own goals, whatever they may be.

Use the tension-building phase to prescribe new ways of disagreeing. One of the classic characteristics of the tension-building phase is initial attempts of one or both parties to maintain calm and safety by avoiding disagreement. This is followed by growing tension and minor irritation, followed by eventual blow-ups, usually over seemingly minor or even illusory issues. A major objective in this phase is to undercut this early "walking-on-eggshells" phenomenon by prescribing a series of structured, minor spats. This is generally done when there is treatment access to both parties and when there can be considerable control, practice, and prediction of interactions. Within such a format, each party is helped to review the usual process of their quarrels, the range of options available to them in a disagreement, and a range of new alternatives to practice such as calling time out, leaving the scene, and so on.

The goals of such prescriptions are several. First is to undercut the pervasive fear and avoidance of disagreement, increase comfort with assertion, and recast quarrels as learning experiences. The second is to make it clear that each party has a range of choices in any interaction. The third is to help introduce dissonance into the couple's pattern of disagreements. One way is through practicing new skills of engagement and disengagement. The other is more subtle. The mere fact that they are choosing to disagree implies their volitional control, thus counteracting prior beliefs that one or both parties are out of control in a disagreement or that disagreements occur spontaneously. Furthermore, deliberately attempting to fight makes the action awkward and artificial, and there may be times when the couple just can't pick a fight even if they try. This can be a refreshing relief to partners who have been afraid that they would blow up at the drop of a hat.

There is a range of options in employing these prescriptions. An initial prescription, or one employed when there is access to the woman only, is for each party to wait for the next minor disagreement and take careful mental or actual notes of all aspects of the interaction to learn from it. The more detailed these notes are the better, including the topic, setting, what occurred before and after, how they felt at each stage, and what they did and said as well as how their partner interacted with them. If complied with, this exercise breaks up the usual spontaneity of the interaction that may result in a lessening of its intensity to say nothing of what may be actually learned by the observations.

Another variation is for each party to be given the task of engaging the other in a disagreement. Each is to try to guess when the other is trying to pick a fight and to observe what can get the other one going. Finally, neither party is to tell the other when he or she is picking a fight until the next session when the exercise is discussed. This exercise emphasizes each member's part in initiating and collaborating with a quarrel. It further operates by undercutting the spontaneity of their quarrels and disqualifying their points of disagreement by leaving in question whether they are made in seriousness or for the purpose of the exercise. Other variations can include practicing time outs or leaving the scene. Each exercise should be combined with a clear contract prohibiting violence, including options and consequences if it does arise. Often in-session practice and role play precedes these exercises, including the creative variation of role playing "dirty fighting" so that each party can identify, label, and agree on what they won't do.

It cannot be emphasized enough here that the above interventions should not be considered as merely telling battering couples to fight. Such directives for couples to practice disagreeing are designed to interdict a particular phase of the cycle and are responsibly predicated on enforceable nonviolence contracts and tightly predictable and practiced control of the interaction. This is not a cavalier approach to mere symptom prescription. Such prescriptions are implemented only after it is assured that there are multiple new options for both stopping and leaving the interactions. It should also be remembered that without such allowances for minor disagreements during the tension-building phase, further violent escalations are highly probable. Thus, such directives not only help decrease the probability of future violence, but if a more intense disagreement does arise, it is more likely to be controlled and have greater options for deescalation and safety.

If the couple remains together or in contact, any course of treatment or intervention that lasts more than a week or two after initial contact is conducted during the tension-building phase. Thus, there is an inherent force toward the couple avoiding any disagreements, a downplaying of the seriousness of the cycle and their need to change, an increasing probability of more tension, and an eventual violent recurrence as treatment goes on. The probability of one or both parties dropping out of treatment increases as time goes on, which underscores the need to take quick advantage of early-phase processes and opportunities. Further, if the tension-building phase can be undercut by contradictory actions to actively yet safely practice altered disagreements, then there is some promise that the battering cycle may alter. If it does not alter and if the intervenor has postured him or herself in a supportive and accepting position, then either party, but especially the woman, may choose to reengage with the intervenor to either further alter or end the battering relationship.

The major goals of the strategic rapid intervention model are to introduce small yet significant system changes through using existing system constructs and patterns. Initial deviations may then amplify in a positive cycle through the strength of system interactions. It is a flexible metamodel that can easily incorporate and enhance other current intervention alternatives as well as support the need for political or social intervention to alter cultural biases. By understanding and using current patterns, intervenors can learn to break vicious cycles through the use of the cycle's own force. In this way, they can advocate without having their attempts contradict their goals.

OTHER APPROACHES AND RESEARCH

The focus on battering relationships and the development of intervention modes for dealing with them are both relatively recent, and there is relatively little process or outcome research on intervention effectiveness, including the one described above. This section gives an overview of the current range of alternate intervention modes. These modes include shelters, women's groups, assertiveness training, batterer groups, self-help groups, and arrest options.

The growth and spread of battered women shelters is about 10 years old (Pagelow, 1984). Such shelters may be free-standing, housed in local YWCAs or other agencies, or consist of a series of safe houses. Frequently, the facilities house both women and children, and individual and group counseling is generally available along with support groups, some opportunities for employment, and legal advocacy resources. Such shelters may also house battered-women hotlines and affiliate with batterer's groups. The exact location of the shelters, however, is often kept a secret, and strict security measures are implemented. Shelters exist to offer women a safe option at times of high danger and provide resources to often resourceless women, along with information on the nature of battering. There is often a broad but explicit emphasis on leaving the relationship. These shelters will continue to serve an unmet need, yet questions frequently arise as to how effective they are in either stopping the battering or ending the relationships. A common phenomenon is the revolving door through which a significant group of women seem to pass in and out of the shelter.

Snyder and Fruchtman (1981) conducted a multivariate cluster analysis of the social histories of a sample of 119 women admitted to a shelter. They then developed a typology of five different relationship patterns, which they used to discriminate among the women and differentiate the utility of treatment options. They suggest, among other things, that couple counseling focusing on identifying cues leading to angry exchanges might be most useful for that set of women who have stable marital relationships with infrequent battering and who return to their partners from the shelter with a 90% rate. In contrast, they suggest that the remaining groups may require interventions aimed at more independent living, including vocational, educational, and legal counseling. They note, however, that given that 43% of these women return to their partners at least temporarily, outlining other community resources and options in the event of further violence is in line for all of these women.

Several small-sample studies suggest a number of other variables that predict whether women will return to their partner or leave after being in a shelter. Butchorn (1985) focused on the nature of women's support networks and their decision to stay or leave. In analyzing the support networks of 29 women who came to a suburban shelter, she found that 86% of the networks were encouraging the woman to leave the batterer. Of those who left, 95% of their networks had encouraged leaving. Of those who returned, 70% had networks that encouraged leaving. Those who left had experienced daily battering for which they held their partner responsible. They felt responsible for leaving rather than trying to find solutions, and they received network feedback that they were capable in their roles and would receive network support if they left the batterer. Those who returned to their partners had experienced battering once a week for which they felt the need to find a solution. They did not hold the batterer responsible and received network feedback that they were not competent in their roles and would receive little network help if they left the batterer.

Hilbert and Hilbert (1984), in analyzing data on 35 battered women's shelter residents, found that the age of the victim; severity, frequency, and length of the battering relationship; victim income; and length of shelter stay predicted outcome with 80% accuracy. The older the woman, the more frequent the abuse, the greater the presence of the woman's own income, and the longer the shelter stay, the more likely it was that the woman would not return to her partner.

In support of some of the above results, Aguirre (1985) in a large-scale study concluded that the wives' economic dependence on their husbands almost always ensured that they would return. She conducted a sophisticated variant of statistical regression analysis on the results of 1024 shelter residents' survey responses from shelters across Texas. Not only did she find that economic dependence or independence was the highest and sole predictor of staying or leaving but also that the more shelter resources used by the woman during the stay, the more probable it would be for her not to return to her mate.

Women's groups or victim's groups are often conducted in shelters but are also held elsewhere. These groups provide information and perspective on the battering cycle; disseminate information on economic, social, legal, and employment resources; offer support for the women and normalization of their emotions; and provide models of alternative patterns through other group members. There are few standard formats for these groups, and they have thus been poorly researched. One recent resource for structuring such groups is the text *Talking It Out: A Guide to Groups for Abused Women* by Nicarthy, Merriam, and Coffman (1984).

An ancillary and often conjoint mode of intervention is the assertiveness group for women. In this type of group, there are more standard psychoeducational formats. They consist of distinguishing assertiveness from aggression and include considerable role playing and homework assignments (Ball & Wyman, 1978; Martin, 1976). The goal is to provide new skills along with practice in their implementation, with the expectation that it is the woman's right to assert her own wishes in her relationships. Increasing confidence in handling situations in an assertive way outside the relationship may increase self-esteem and may aid a woman in feeling less intimidated, more in control of her situation and less afraid of leaving an intolerable situation (Jansen & Myers-Abell, 1980).

A series of studies by O'Leary and his colleagues (O'Leary & Curley, 1986; O'Leary et al., 1985; Rosenbaum & O'Leary, 1981) offer some cautions on the use of assertiveness training with battered women. These researchers have concluded that wives' lack of assertion is often quite functional given a history of battering. Their data analysis of the battering histories of 51 abused wives indicated that wives' assertion and disagreement was the single most highly correlated factor with abuse. They recommend that where the probability of abuse is great, assertiveness training without the involvement of the husband and the control of the therapist may be unadvisable. It is thus best applied to general situations and issues outside the marital unit until the assertion/aggression distinction is well learned. Even then, women should be informed of the potential risks so that they can make informed choices.

Turning to intervention modes for men who batter, Gondolf (1985) has set out a typology of men's services that classifies them into mental health programs, shelter adjunct programs, and self-help programs. Mental health programs focus on impulse control and stress reduction through individual, couple, and group counseling. Stress management, anger control, and conflict resolution techniques are often combined with substance abuse treatment and individual counseling. One innovation is court-ordered counseling programs, yet the drawbacks lie in male resistance to therapy and its social stigma plus the tendency of some counseling programs to overlook cultural tolerance of violence and sexism that might support male violence and control.

Shelter adjunct programs focus on group counseling for males by intervenors with expertise in domestic-violence patterns. They coordinate services and interventions for men and women with the frequent use of explicit, complementary contracts. An innovation in such programs is community-based intervention systems that help educate police and courts as well as men who batter in ways to control and decrease violence toward women. Some drawbacks to joint programs, however, are men's frequent resentment of shelter staff and the possible jeopardy of women's safety and privacy.

Self-help organizations stress peer counseling formats that are free from social service stigma; these programs emphasize antisexist education and peer pressure for self-control and self-respect. Innovations in this mode lie in the organization of men for social action, yet these groups have been criticized for their potential for encouraging male separatism and potentially subtle support for sexist attitudes, along with their possible inability to assess more extreme problem patterns and intervene in them.

Some programatic examples are those of Sonkin and Durphy (1982) and Neidig and Friedman (1984). Sonkin and Durphy focus on men alone in their handbook that offers useful exercises and homework, which can be used alone, in a group format, or as an adjunct to counseling. The information is presented clearly and allows for guidance and practice, yet it presumes considerable motivation on the part of the man, which is unusual in the absence of external sanctions. Gondolf (1985) also outlines an approach with similar elements.

The Neidig and Friedman (1984) program is a couple-oriented group approach, which was developed out of work with the Marines. They also present a clear text that details a curriculum including both class exercises, handouts, and homework assignments in a cognitive and behavioral mode. This is an excellently conceived and described program, yet the authors themselves point out several limitations. These are that the program works best when there is some external sanction or pressure on the man from the court or the workplace and when the man sees the violence as uncomfortable or alien rather than useful and his right.

In another approach that appears to work with couples, Deschner (1984) has designed and studied an anger control group approach. This includes educating the couples in the assessment and identification of anger cues along with providing alternatives and the prominent use of time-out procedures. A study with a small, nonrandom sample showed favorable, short-term outcomes with this method.

Several programs similar to these in various parts of the country are currently collecting data on their effectiveness; however, this work is not yet complete. Along these lines another useful resource is the handbook for Batterers Anonymous (Goffman, 1984), which outlines the structure and process of running self-help counseling groups for men who batter women along with providing resources for participants. There is no current research on Batterers Anonymous groups, yet their popularity is spreading.

The final intervention mode is one at the sociocultural level, one that is a natural extension of the work pointing out the great power and resource differentials between men and women in most cultures and particularly in battering relationships (Bowker, 1983; Dobash & Dobash, 1979; Martin, 1976; Straus, Gelles, & Steinmetz, 1980; Walker, 1979). It is also a logical and practical extension of the shelter movement and has grown out of similar social action, particularly in the Minneapolis/St. Paul area. This intervention mode is mandatory arrest and incarceration for batterers. Traditionally, there has been a tacit approval of male violence in our culture, particularly with couples whose privacy is reluctantly invaded. The logic behind this intervention is that immediate, automatic, and negative sanctions for violence against women is particularly critical within semi-closed, battering relationships. Mandatory sanctions are recommended not only to introduce prohibitions, increase safety, and rebalance power but also to take the burden of pressing charges and initiating prosecution off the shoulders of women who are already likely to feel both threatened and powerless. Such interventions achieve, in part, the overall goals of decreasing both a power differential and isolation, mentioned earlier in the chapter. Much of the family systems therapy approach has been recently criticized for overlooking these prominent power differences by assuming equal influence of all system members (Bograd, 1984; McIntyre, 1984).

Strong research support for the mandatory arrest approach has been provided by Sherman and Berk (1984) and Berk and Newton (1985). In the Minneapolis Spouse Abuse Experiment, Sherman and Berk did a large scale study in which the police randomly applied one of three treatments to a sample of 315 incidents of wife battery. They either arrested the offender, ordered the offender from the premises for 8 hours, or offered "advice," which in some cases could include informal mediation. In examining follow-up data from police reports and from victim interviews, it was concluded that arrest was by far the greatest deterrent to incidents of future violence. In their follow-up study, Berk and Newton (1985) replicated these findings and reaffirmed, with some additional refinements, the deterrent effect of mandatory arrest on future violence. Sociocultural system level interventions such as mandatory arrest, along with the development of shelter and advocacy programs, thus appear to be potentially effective modes of intervention in the battering cycle. They, along with the modes discussed earlier, deserve further support, application, and study.

9
Understanding the Families of Children in Foster and Residential Care

JAMES K. WHITTAKER AND ANTHONY N. MALUCCIO

Having a child placed out of the home in foster or residential care may take on very different meanings for the biological family, the substitute caregiver, the child, and the larger community depending on the reasons for and the circumstances surrounding the placement. Consider, for example, the differences between the following placements:

A developmentally disabled adolescent receives regular periods of respite care in a community-based group home

A behavior-disordered school-aged child from a low-income, single-parent family is placed in therapeutic foster family care, among other things, to reduce the risk of abuse and neglect

In the former instance, "placement" is likely to be viewed positively by parents, caregivers, the larger community and, perhaps, the child as a temporary support to a family experiencing life stress. In the latter case, placement is all too often seen as a substitute for a family that has failed. In both situations biological families, substitute caregivers, and the child need to work out issues of loyalty, division of labor (and affection), and communication. For professionals working with families in or at risk of out-of-home placement, a knowledge of the characteristics of families whose children are candidates for foster and residential placement as well as knowledge of the characteristics of the placement settings are requisites for effective helping.

This brief introductory chapter explores some of what is known about children and families entering various kinds of out-of-home placement. Chapter 10 explores some of the practice approaches for engaging these families as partners in the helping process.

THE DEMOGRAPHICS AND POLICY CONTEXT FOR SUBSTITUTE CARE OF CHILDREN

A central demographic factor underlying present policy for all out-of-home services for children and youth is that in the aggregate such children represent less than 1% of the nation's 0- to 17-year olds

(Select Committee on Children, Youth, and Families, 1983). This fact may explain in part why group care and foster care have not ranked higher on the national policy agenda.[1] The overwhelming majority of American children reside with one or both biological parents or in adoptive homes, as shown in the Table 9.1 from the report of the Select Committee. As of 1982, 14 million young people—or 22% of all children under 18—were living in a single-parent family with either their mother or father. Some 23 million young people—or 37% of all U.S. children under 18—were living in something other than a family where both biological parents were present.

The relative lack of visibility of foster care—unlike concern for the developmentally disabled (approximately 10% of the population)—may be either the cause or consequence of the situation described by Steiner (1981, p. 144):

> Foster care has been no First Lady's "principal interest," nor has a secretary of HEW taken it on as a personal crusade. Consequently, it did not receive the high-level attention in the late 1970s that was briefly accorded mental health policy and the dangers of cigarette smoking. Because foster care neither makes a substantial difference in the federal budget nor involves millions of people, it does not automatically command attention. Scandal does provide occasional visibility, but it is scandal usually limited to childrearing practices in a particular setting rather than intolerable scandal entailing fraud in benefit claims or other continuing misuse of public money.

Whether foster care will become a "First Lady's interest" remains to be seen. Yet it is all the more amazing, given the small percentage of children in care, that foster care reform did surface on the national political agenda, culminating in the passage of PL 96–272, the Adoption Assistance and Child Welfare Act of 1980.[2] The intent of this act is to provide permanent homes for children cast "adrift" in the foster care system with no clear plans for permanent placement either through return to biological parents or placement for adoption. For those families at risk of disruption, the act mandates that "reasonable efforts" to prevent placement be carried out and requires a judicial review before such placement is made. Various other provisions have to do with conducting an inventory of all children in the foster care system and providing special subsidies for adoption of "special-needs" children. The means for achieving these objectives include development of statewide information systems, case review procedures, judicial review of placements, preventive family-

Table 9.1
Family Environment

Residence	Children (millions)	Percent
Both biological parents	39.3	63%
Mother only	12.5	20
Father only	1.2	2
One biological parent and one stepparent	6.2	10
Grandparents or other relatives	1.6	2
Foster parents, other nonrelatives, or in institutions	0.4	1
Total	62.4	100%

Note: Calculated from unpublished data from the March 1982 *Current Population Survey Data,* U.S. Bureau of the Census. Proportions adopted and living with remarried parents estimated from the 1976 and 1981 National Surveys of Children, and from Paul Glick "Children of Divorced Parents in Demographic Perspective," *Journal of Social Issues,* 35, 170–182, 1979. (Report of Select Committee, 1983:8.)

oriented services, and development of statewide plans for child welfare services. In general, staged implementation of various reform components is required for continuance of federal funding to the states for foster care payments, although the present administration has given the states considerably more latitude in determining compliance than was the case with the original regulations from the Department of Health and Human Services.

The concept of "permanency planning," so central to the aforementioned child welfare legislation, is defined by Gambrill and Stein (1985, p. 38) as follows:

Permanency planning refers to activities undertaken to insure continuity of care for children. If children cannot remain in the care of their families of origin, the goal of permanency planning is to place them in a living arrangement that has the greatest likelihood of providing continuity over time, with preference to relationships that are legally binding. Alternatives for permanency planning in order of preference are (a) maintaining the child in his or her own home, (b) restoring children who are in out-of-home care to their biological families, (c) termination of parental rights and adoption, (d) court appointment of a legal guardian, or (e) planned long-term foster care. As Pike, Downs, Emlen, Downs, and Case (1977) have said, permanency planning refers to an *intention* recognizing that this outcome cannot be guaranteed. . . . Permanency planning supports the value that our society places on family life and the best interests of the child, which we assume are best served within a family unit.

This definition extends the focus of permanency planning efforts (a) to children already in the substitute care system who need either to be reunited with their biological parents or freed for adoption or other long-term guardianship arrangements and (b) to those children and families at risk of disruption who, through intensive, in-home preventive services, can avoid the placement of their children. Although permanency planning has now achieved a permanency of its own in the landscape of child welfare, it has by no means lost its capacity to generate spirited debate as to intent, procedures, and desirable outcomes. For at its core, permanency planning is, as Wiltse (1981, p. 13) says, a question of "subtle" rights and values:

> When we speak of every child's right to permanency and continuity of care . . . we are endeavoring to express a very subtle kind of right and one not easily reduced to statutory expression or articulated in an agency manual. It is more a concept of what every child needs to grow and develop as a human being.

The problems in operationalizing and defining these "subtle rights" continue to occupy some of the leading investigators and scholars in social work, law, psychiatry, and child development (Goldstein, Freud, & Solnit, 1979; Stevenson & Siegel, 1984; Wald et al., 1980; Zigler, Kagan, & Klugman, 1983). While it is still too early to assess the overall impact of PL 96–272, the U.S. Children's Bureau recently estimated that both the total number of children in foster care and the mean length of stay have declined markedly since the Shyne and Schroeder (1978) national estimate study (U.S. Children's Bureau, 1983). What is not entirely clear is the condition of those children who were reunified with biological families or referred for adoption. A recent review by Barth and Berry (in press) suggests that children who were reunified or who did not enter placement fared less well on a number of indicators than those who were placed. Additional follow-up studies are needed.

Other findings of interest that we have gleaned from several studies subsequent to the passage of the legislation are as follows:

1. There are approximately equal numbers of males and females in foster care.

2. The percentage of the foster care population that is minority appears to be 40% to 45%.
3. About 70% of children in substitute care reside in foster family homes.
4. Return to parents and relatives is the placement goal for 40% of the children in substitute care, while 49% actually do return home.
5. Three-fourths of the children who entered foster care did so because of family-related reasons, and over three-fourths of these were for abuse and/or neglect (U.S. Children's Bureau, 1983).

These findings suggest several things. First, the "case" for placement of any sort in the future will be more difficult to make and will rest on the presumption that reasonable efforts have been made to keep the child and family together. Second, out-of-home placement will increasingly be time limited and used primarily as a therapeutic tool to help rehabilitate the family rather than as an attempt to rescue the child. Finally, the overwhelming majority of children in care for reasons of abuse and neglect and the available evidence on treatment outcomes suggest that a strictly child-focused strategy devoid of an aggressive and comprehensive family intervention component will not succeed in reintegrating children and families.

In the area of residential services, a relatively recent census of children and youth in group care revealed several findings pertinent to the topic of family involvement. This survey, for the year 1981, updates an earlier survey conducted by Pappenfort in 1965 (Pappenfort et al., 1973; Pappenfort et al., 1983). The survey included residential facilities in virtually all streams of care—mental health, juvenile corrections, and child welfare, for example—and identified the following trends:

1. While the number of residential group-care facilities has increased markedly since 1966, there has been a decline in the total number of children and youth in group care.
2. The rate of growth in numbers of facilities has been concentrated in the category of juvenile facilities for children and youth considered delinquent or status offenders and in mental health facilities.
3. Facilities in all categories have declined in size over the past 16 years. In 1966 less than 50% of the facilities surveyed had fewer than 26 children and youth in residence. The majority of all facilities surveyed in 1982 were of that size or smaller.
4. Among the facilities surveyed in 1982, the number of children were almost evenly divided among public and private facilities. Slightly more than one-third of all children were in juvenile justice facilities, one-fourth were in mental health facilities, and about one-fifth were in

child welfare facilities. The remainder of children were in short-term care facilities.

In all there appeared to be something on the order of 125,323 children in group care in 3914 facilities in 1981, down from 155,905 in 2138 facilities in 1965. The drop in placement figures reflects both a decline in actual children in care and a decline in the rate of group-care placement—from 19.9 per 10,000 youth in 1965 to 17.3 for 10,000 in 1981 (Pappenfort et al., 1983).

Permanency planning and deinstitutionalization have made occasional changes in the placement destinations of children and youth. In certain streams of care, nongovernmental services play a major role. For example, 92% of children and youth in group-care services for the emotionally disturbed received that care in nongovernmental voluntary and for-profit agencies. Proprietary care is apparently on the rise and presently serves 4.5% of all children in group care and 8.5% of all children in nongovernmental group care (Pappenfort et al., 1983). Some analysts are concerned with what appears to be a shift of youngsters (e.g., as a result of the removal of status offenders from the juvenile justice system) from more traditional service systems to private drug rehabilitation and psychiatric residential settings, which are often for-profit (Schwartz et al., 1983). Similarly, several investigative accounts in recent years have documented abuses in voluntary placements in religiously oriented group-care services that often avoid not simply public funding but also public licensing (Taylor, 1981; Wooden, 1976). These latter two categories of group care— private, psychiatric placements often funded directly by third-party payments and private, voluntary placements in religious institutions that avoid both public funding and licensing—constitute what some have called the "hidden sector" of group care.

CHARACTERISTICS OF CHILDREN AND FAMILIES IN RESIDENTIAL PLACEMENT

Studies of the characteristics of children placed in residential care provide rich details of the composition of families with children in placement. A recent 2-year analysis of the characteristics of 10,000 children placed in residential care in California between 1982 and 1984 revealed that 52% of all children in the sample came from homes with single-parent families (Fitzharris, 1985). Twenty-five percent lived with families in which both biological parents lived together or in which a biological parent resided with a stepparent. The most frequent condition that led to placement was an inability to control the child in the home. This condition accounted for 65% of all placement factors classified as "deficiencies in parenting" (Fitzharris, 1985).

Children are beset by a number of problems at the time placement decisions and referrals are finalized. In the California sample Fitzharris (1985) found that 83% of all children in out-of-home care had multiple problems at the time placement was made. These included specific acts committed by the child and physical or psychological problems present prior to placement. The data revealed that the children in care were mostly disturbed children who were unable to function in the biological family without outside assistance or support (Fitzharris, 1985).

Parents also experience a variety of problems prior to placement. Studies report that a large percentage of children referred to treatment programs come from families marked by poverty, poor education, single parents, and residence in high-crime neighborhoods (Shaw & McKay, 1969). Working with families experiencing multiple problems poses special challenges to treatment personnel. Wahler and his associates (1979), among others, suggest that families living in conditions such as poverty and chronic unemployment tend to become trapped and socially isolated. These investigations suggest that social isolation has a negative impact on a family's ability to respond to treatment efforts. Because entrapped families lack natural helping networks and appropriate sources of support in the community, their participation in specific treatment programs may only be superficial and provide no tangible results (Dumas & Wahler, 1983; Hawkins & Fraser, 1983).

These findings suggest that singular service strategies that target multiple-problem families may not be adequate to overcome the effects of environmental variables present in the family's daily life. Single interventions such as parent training may not be sufficient to meet the needs of families with children in placement who are experiencing overwhelming life circumstances or who lack basic family management skills (Doherty, 1975). Community-oriented services that seek to identify, create, and maintain support networks of children and families may be one effective method of supplementing specific interventions directed at improving parents' skills and level of functioning (Whittaker & Maluccio, 1986). Strategies that strive to increase parental self-esteem while teaching needed parenting skills may also be an effective way to involve families of children in care who are experiencing multiple problems (Webster-Stratton, 1985).

Some studies of children and families in substitute care indicate that parents frequently experience depression and feelings of guilt and failure when a child is removed from the home (Jenkins & Norman, 1975). The bond uniting parents and child does not dissolve while a child is in placement. If we ignore the contributions that family members can make to a child's treatment process, this may intensify feelings of self-doubt, depression, and guilt for both children and parents.

In the area of outcome research, recent reviews of the effectiveness of residential services for children and youth reveal few positive long-term results (Durkin & Durkin, 1975; Whittaker & Pecora, 1984). Although some programs have proven to be effective in altering the behavior patterns of youth during treatment, such changes have seldom been maintained following treatment (Allerhand et al., 1966; Jones et al., 1981; Taylor & Alpert, 1973). Troubled children often return to their former behaviors upon discharge, failing to generalize behavioral changes accomplished during treatment to situations in their daily lives in the community.

These findings have important implications for program development in children's residential care. Increasingly, treatment efforts have begun to focus on environmental or ecological factors that appear to make an important impact on the child's successful long-term adjustment (Lewis, 1982; Whittaker & Maluccio, in press). Such factors include the availability of support from family and peer networks and the presence of supportive environments in school and the community at the time of discharge as well as concrete assistance with housing, employment, and related family problems (Jenson et al., 1986).

Direct parental involvement and family support in the treatment process for children and youth removed from their homes are among the strongest predictors of a child's ability to successfully adapt to the community following placement (Doherty, 1975; Fanshel, 1975; Rowe et al., 1984; Taylor & Alpert, 1973). Residential agencies must develop closer links to families and other sectors of the community. The increased involvement of families in treatment processes and the development of social support networks for children in the community may enable young people who improve during residential placement to generalize gains made during treatment to their natural environments (Whittaker, 1986; Whittaker & Garbarino, 1983). In the area of foster family care, the research of Fanshel (1975) and Fanshel and Shinn (1978) suggests that involvement of the biological parents in the placement process, as measured by frequency of parental visitation, is the best predictor of the child's eventual return to the family of origin.

Barriers to Parental Involvement

If continued family interaction is so important to a child's success during and after treatment, why have residential and foster placement facilities failed to develop effective methods of working with parents? Whittaker (1979, 1981) identifies a number of factors that might explain the limited involvement of parents in children's out-of-home care. These include (a) lack of financial resources to provide family services to parents of children in care; (b) the location of residential treatment facilities in rural or isolated areas; (3) sociocultural differences between treatment personnel or foster parents and biological parents; (d) limited roles for involvement offered to parents; (e) parental guilt for the inappropriate behavior exhibited by their child; (f) parental fear of continued failure to change their child's behavior; and (g) multiple family problems such as inadequate finances, family disorganization, legal difficulties, and the sheer difficulties involved in parenting a difficult-to-manage child.

A variety of practice methods are required to overcome the complex problems and barriers that inhibit parental involvement in children's out-of-home care. The increase of parental involvement requires agencies to examine their existing policies of care and treatment that limit family participation in all phases of children's out-of-home placement. If lasting behavioral change is desired, it is not sufficient to treat children in isolated, residential facilities and then have them return to environments that earlier supported their problem behaviors (Hawkins, 1985). Many parents can provide important assistance prior, during, and after placement that can help children generalize behavioral change accomplished during treatment to situations in their everyday life. Maluccio and Sinanoglu (1981) and Jenson and Whittaker (1987) offer a variety of practical approaches for engaging biological families in the process of placement. Chapter 10 examines many of these strategies in detail.

EMERGING TRENDS AND ISSUES IN WORK WITH FAMILIES OF CHILDREN IN OUT-OF-HOME PLACEMENT

If the findings from the previously cited California study of children and families are more generally applicable, considerable attention must be paid to the development of service strategies designed to reach single-parent and blended families (Fitzharris, 1985). Single-parent families and divorced/remarried families constituted 52% and 18% of the study sample of families who are candidates for residential care. Only 17% of children came into placement from families where two biological parents were present in the home.

As noted, the most frequently cited problem by parents presenting a child for residential care in the California study was an inability to control the child (Fitzharris, 1985). Intuitively, this suggests the need to teach parenting skills, with the objective of improving child-management skills. The overrepresentation of single parents in this study plus the numerous problems of most of the families, however, suggests caution about overreliance on providing parenting-skills training without also augmenting and enhancing social supports. Dumas and Wahler (1983) found such a single strategy insufficient to meet the needs of socially isolated, low-income mothers who experienced difficulty managing their child's behavior. Program developers would do well to think about packages of intervention that combine social support facilitation and parenting-skills training for such families (Whittaker, Schinke, & Gilchrist, 1986). These should not be viewed as substitutes for the basics of adequate income supports, health care, nutrition programs, and the like.

As the outcome research so clearly indicates, "success" in residential care, however defined, is largely a function of the supports available in the posttreatment community environment and has much less to do with either the presenting problem or the type of treatment offered. Consequently, what has come to be known as the "ecological perspective" has profound implications for family work in children's residential services (Whittaker, 1979). It encourages us to view the residential environment as the complex interplay of many different elements both within and outside of the formal service context. Notable here are the quality of the linkages between the residential program and the family, the neighborhood, the peer group, the world of work, and other present and future sources of influence over behavior in the community environment.

The "Massachusetts experiment" in deinstitutionalization high-lighted the importance of these community linkages as they interact with the formal service program (Coates et al., 1978). One potential implication of this trend for service personnel is that they will be spending less time in direct treatment of children and more time working with and through the environment, particularly in creating and/or maintaining social support networks and comprehensive sets of services as needed by each family (Whittaker, 1979; Whittaker & Garbarino, 1983). Specifically, this means factoring the environment and the family more prominently into the service equation, whether that service occurs in a residential treatment center or the child's own home. For example, it will accomplish the following:

> Teach children *and* families practical skills to effectively cope with their proximate and distal environments through life-skills training.
>
> Enhance naturally occurring support networks where they exist and help create them where they do not. The carefully conducted research of Wahler and others cautions against overreliance on interpersonal-skills training as the sole form of intervention (Dumas & Wahler, 1983; Whittaker, 1986).
>
> Operate on the premise that "environmental helping" is not synonymous with "aftercare": It begins prior to placement, continues during place-ment, and lasts as long after placement as it is needed (Jenson & Whittaker, 1986).

The emerging practice innovations that involve parents in their child's out-of-home placement program are encouraging. Efficient delivery of these interventions should bring about more effective programs and positive results for troubled children and families. Questions to be considered include:

1. What organizational and structural changes are necessary to imple-ment interventions for children and parents in the context of residen-tial treatment?
2. What are the appropriate staff positions and professional roles associ-ated with the provision of services to parents of children in treatment? What role might case managers and case-management systems per-form in coordinating the efforts of treatment centers, parents, and community resources? What roles can informal helpers play?
3. Where should treatment facilities place resources for parents and children? Should funding efforts be focused on improving treatment

services during placement? Should greater funds be allocated for the provision of posttreatment and after-care services?

Evaluations that address the effectiveness of existing family intervention services could provide agencies and policy makers with information about the costs and benefits of providing structured parental involvement in out-of-home settings. Unanswered questions include:

1. Which components of parental involvement, for example, parent support groups, educational groups, and family therapy, are most effective for various types of troubled children and different family constellations?
2. What are the corresponding costs of these components?
3. What are the most important variables in a parent's involvement in treatment services for children? How do these variables affect specific treatment outcomes? How important is frequency of contact? Does duration of involvement in treatment services have an impact on specified child-behavior outcomes?
4. Do current interventions directed at parents of children in treatment accurately identify and measure appropriate indicators of behavior change?

Finally, on a political level much work must be done in organizing the parents of children and youth in care as well as the children themselves. The Who Cares? movement in Britain, a gathering of children and youth in all forms of substitute care (Page & Clarke, 1977) as well as recent innovations in South Carolina and Victoria, British Columbia, offer useful prototypes for how to proceed. In certain streams of care, for example, the parents of children with developmental disabilities are well-organized and become an effective force for the improvement of service provision.

In sum, work with families of children in foster and residential care presents a powerful challenge to professionals. On the positive side, parents are, perhaps, our greatest untapped resource in working on issues related to out-of-home placement. Chapter 10 identifies some promising strategies for building family involvement.

NOTES

1. For additional analysis of why foster care reform has lagged behind other initiatives, see Steiner (1981).

2. Only the briefest overview of this legislation—its antecedents and consequences—are offered here. For further detail, see the comprehensive reviews of issues leading up to the reform provided by Maluccio (1977) and McGowan and Meezan (1983). See also Allen, Golubuck, and Olson (1983); and Maluccio, Fein, and Olmstead (1986).

10

Helping the Biological Families of Children in Out-of-Home Placement

ANTHONY N. MALUCCIO AND JAMES K. WHITTAKER

When children and youth must live away from their homes—in foster families, group homes, or residential care programs—practitioners working with them are called on to help with a number of emergent issues. These include helping children and parents cope with the impact of loss and separation; maintaining the child's sense of belonging, continuity, and family identity; facilitating the child's adaptation in a new family system and environment; promoting the child's growth and development; providing rehabilitative services to the parents; and, above all, responding to the child's need for permanency planning, that is, the need to grow up with a family offering "continuity of relationships with nurturing parents or caretakers and the opportunity to establish lifetime relationships" (Maluccio, Fein, & Olmstead, 1986, p. 5).

This chapter addresses primarily the last issue in the belief that practitioners working with youngsters living away from home should be guided by the following overriding goal: helping the children and their families to reestablish their homes or, if necessary, implementing alternate permanent plans, such as placement with relatives, adoption, or permanent foster family care. The chapter delineates selected programs, methods, and principles useful to professional staff, foster parents, child care workers, and others as they seek to accomplish the goal of a permanent home for children in their care. The focus is on working with biological families, following the ecologically oriented, family-centered approach to child welfare introduced in the preceding chapter.[1]

ECOLOGICALLY ORIENTED, FAMILY-CENTERED CHILD WELFARE PRACTICE

The ecologically oriented, family-centered approach embodies a number of themes that should be highlighted because they provide the theoretical and philosophical rationale for the practice principles, programs, and methods to be considered in this chapter. These themes include:

1. The concept of the family as the central unit of service or focus of attention, whenever possible and as much as possible. Human beings can best be understood and helped within their significant environment, and the family is the most intimate environment of all. It is here that children chiefly develop and form their identities and many of their competencies. The family has the potential for providing resources throughout the life cycle, especially as its members are sustained and supported by various services (Hartman & Laird, 1983).

2. The view of family members as engaged in ongoing, dynamic transactions with each other and with their environment and in a continuous process of growth and adaptation.

3. The conception of families as "open systems" who are spontaneously active and essentially motivated to achieve competence in their coping with life demands and environmental challenges.

4. A shift away from emphasis on "treating" clients toward teaching or helping them develop coping and mastery skills.

5. The premise that varied environmental opportunities and social supports are necessary to sustain and promote each person's efforts to grow, achieve self-fulfillment, and contribute to others.

6. The conviction that appropriate supports should be matched to the person's changing qualities and needs in order to maximize the development of his or her competence, identity, autonomy, and self-fulfillment.

7. The philosophy of permanency planning, particularly the belief that every child is entitled to live in a family—preferably his or her own biological family—in order to have the maximum opportunity for growth and development. Permanency planning is "the process of taking prompt, decisive action to maintain children in their own homes or place them permanently with other families" (Maluccio, Fein, & Olmstead, 1986, p. 4). In each case there should be careful assessment and extensive effort to maintain children with their own families or to make other permanent plans when it has been demonstrated that the parents cannot care for the child.

WORKING WITH BIOLOGICAL FAMILIES

Practitioners in foster family or group-care settings are presented with various challenges and opportunities to work with biological parents and families as an integral feature of treatment. As discussed in this chapter, by exploiting these opportunities and maximizing family participation, we can help members to mobilize their resources and become partners in permanency planning for their children.

Biological Family as the Focus of Attention

To begin with, as various projects have demonstrated, the family's own environment can be employed as the arena in which practitioners intervene to help strengthen overall family functioning and communication, including parenting skills and parent–child relationships (Bryce & Lloyd, 1981; Horejsi et al., 1981; Kaplan, 1986; Kinney et al., 1977; Maluccio & Sinanoglu, 1981; Maybanks & Bryce, 1979; Sinanoglu & Maluccio, 1981; and Stein et al., 1978). Although there has not been rigorous evaluation of these projects, the indication is that many parents (as well as other centrally involved child-caring kin such as grandparents) can be rehabilitated and helped to plan responsibly for their children through provision of comprehensive help involving both counseling and support services, emphasis on skill training, and systematic case management based on principles of decision making, goal setting, and contracting.

The term "parents" is emphasized throughout this paper because they are the persons most usually involved in caring for their children. However, it should be recognized that other kin such as grandparents and stepparents are often centrally involved in this function. Practitioners need to be aware of both variations in family cultural norms and in family forms.

Even in situations in which children cannot be returned home, family members can participate in the planning process in a way that reflects their caring, helps maintain their dignity, and frees the child to move into another family (Jackson & Dunne, 1981). A common denominator in these programs is that parents and other child-caring kin are regarded as human beings with feelings and needs of their own rather than being approached primarily in relation to what they offer or mean to the child. The agency accepts its responsibility to these family members in their own right.

In particular, the growth of the family therapy movement (e.g., Minuchin & Fishman, 1981) has led to the application of various family treatment approaches as alternatives to placement of children out of their homes or as methods of speeding up the reunification of placed children with their families. For example, some agencies employ intensive family therapy with multiproblem families that have children at risk of placement in substitute care (e.g., Kinney et al., 1977). These programs stress the importance of viewing the family from an ecological perspective: Assessment and intervention focus on the family's transaction with its kinship system over the generations; boundary definitions; communication patterns; internal dynamics; and interactions with schools, community institutions, and other social and economic networks. Intervention strategies are directed not only toward engaging the family in treatment but also toward changing the social and economic systems that influence it (e.g., Tomlinson & Peters, 1981).

Through these and other approaches, practitioners can create many opportunities for involving parents (and other closely involved family members) in the helping process, thereby helping both them and their children. In addition, there is the challenge of preserving family ties as much as possible. The natural bonds between children living away from home and their family members continue to be prominent for these members as well as for the children long after they are physically separated, reflecting the significance of the biological family in human connectedness and identity (Jenkins, 1981; Laird, 1979). Practitioners should therefore regard the goal of preserving family ties as a major imperative of services to children in out-of-home care and their families.

Parent Visitation

A key means of accomplishing the preservation of family ties is for family members to visit children living away from home. Research has demonstrated the importance of these visits as the best single predictor of the outcome of placement and, therefore, as the "key to discharge" (Fanshel, 1975). In their longitudinal study of foster care in New York City, Fanshel and Shinn (1978, p. 96) found that children who were visited frequently by family members during the first year of placement "were almost twice as likely to be discharged eventually as those not visited at all or only minimally."

As noted by Aldgate (1980), family contact can have various beneficial results such as assuring the child that he or she has not been rejected; helping the child understand why he or she cannot live at home; preventing the child's idealization of home and family; and helping the family members maintain their relationships with their children. These results are not obtained automatically; they require the extensive involvement of practitioners with parents and other involved kin through such means as aggressively reaching out to them, facilitating visiting arrangements, highlighting visiting as a central component of the service agreement, preparing child and family for the visit, monitoring the visits, and discussing their impact with family members and children. In addition, other writers have called special attention to a neglected dimension: the significance of sibling relationships and the importance of maintaining sibling ties while children are in placement (Ward, 1984).

Restructuring the Family's Environment

Along with regarding the family as the unit of service, a major function of professionals is to help families restructure their environment and modify or enrich it so that it is more suited to their needs and qualities and more conducive to their positive functioning. Indeed, in response to the multiple needs of biological families in basic life areas, many agencies stress the provision of intensive services and environmental supports to the child's family before placement, during placement, and in the after-care period. These comprehensive programs seek to avoid placement or reduce its duration and reunite children with their own families by strengthening the coping and adaptive capacities of parents and other kin by providing them with concrete services as well as counseling.

Some exemplary programs are described in Jones, Neuman, and Shyne, 1976; Kaplan, 1986; Kinney and colleagues, 1977; Sherman, Neuman, and Shyne, 1973; and Weissman, 1978. A major feature of these programs is collaboration among various community resources. Especially noteworthy is the approach of the Lower East Side Family Union in New York City to avert or limit foster care; this is a difficult task that involves careful coordination and monitoring of services provided to at-risk families by a variety of agencies (Weissman, 1978). Such an approach takes into account the complex personal and environmental factors that affect family functioning and structure. There is also sensitivity to the needs, qualities, and values of minority group families and children who are overrepresented in foster care (Mech, 1983; Olsen, 1982).

Restructuring the environment in specific case situations can be accomplished in different ways, as discussed by various authors (Brown et al., 1982; Maluccio, 1981a; Whittaker & Garbarino, 1983). Often, it is realistically difficult for individual practitioners or agencies to achieve major changes in the family's environment. Yet in many cases much can be accomplished by helping families identify actual or potential resources in their social networks such as neighbors, friends, members of the kinship system, or other informal helpers. For instance, the extended family may provide resources to help a parent care for a child so as to avert placement in an unfamiliar institution or foster home, reduce the duration of placement, or help the child maintain his or her family identity while living away from home.

In other cases, restructuring the environment may mean involving family members, usually parents, in a self-help group or introducing a new person such as a homemaker or parent aide. Self-help groups especially can be valuable with family members from varied socio-economic and ethnic backgrounds (Whittaker & Garbarino, 1983). For example, Leon and colleagues (1984) describe a self-help group for Hispanic mothers who appeared to benefit in a number of ways: building personal relationships and mutual support systems with others sharing similar concerns and interests; feeling free to relate their problems and express their anxieties as parents; strengthening their self-esteem and increasing their self-confidence in parenting; and learning how to negotiate the various service delivery systems.

Various studies also suggest the value of complementing professional help with the services of paraprofessionals such as home-makers and older persons who model effective parental behavior and coping skills (Davies & Bland, 1978; Miller, K. et al., 1984). These aides can help meet the basic needs of families, enrich the family's environment, and prevent placement or replacement. They provide parents and others with better opportunities to learn skills, fulfill needs, and develop competence. The introduction of a new, supportive person such as a grandparent figure or homemaker aide can help meet the needs of parents themselves and enhance their capacity to give to their children.

The strategies for helping biological families considered thus far in this section relate primarily to rehabilitative work. In addition, agencies and workers might well become involved in advocacy and social action to help resolve the systemic or societal problems that lead to out-of-home care in the first place. There is ample evidence of a high correlation between entry into foster care and social problems such as poverty and racism. Research has demonstrated that almost all children in foster care come from families with insufficient income, limited social supports, and multiple needs in such areas a health and mental health, education, housing, employment, and family relationships (Fanshel & Shinn, 1978; Fein et al., 1983; Shyne & Schroeder, 1978). Moreover, as noted in Chapter 9, these problems have been increasing in recent years as a result of reductions in public assistance and related federal and state programs.

For these reasons the importance of providing preventive and supportive services to families cannot be overemphasized, especially to vulnerable families with children at risk of out-of-home placement. This has been explicitly recognized by PL 96–272, The Adoption Assistance and Child Welfare Act of 1980, which requires public agencies to provide a range of preventive and supportive services as outlined in Chapter 9. In this regard it should be stressed that an essential function of practitioners is to advocate for individual families to help them obtain needed assistance.

Parents as Resources

The ecological orientation further encourages practitioners to regard parents and other involved kin as resources on their own behalf, as partners in the helping process rather than simply as carriers of pathology. As we shift from a pathological view of families to a competence orientation, we are better able to identify strengths in them and involve them in growth-producing activities (Maluccio, 1981b). As they are given adequate opportunities and supports, parents and other family members can mobilize their own potentialities and nurture adaptive strivings.

As demonstrated by the frequent success of self-help groups such as Parents Anonymous in helping families that experience child abuse or neglect, family members should be recognized as having strengths through which they can often help each other. Practitioners should aim toward empowering clients to accomplish their purposes and meet their needs through individual and collective efforts, as Solomon (1976) has argued in her book on empowerment in black communities. For parents of children in foster care, working together to obtain needed resources for a better life for themselves and their children can be a good way to counteract feelings of powerlessness and promote competence and self-esteem. For example, some agencies have helped biological parents form self-help groups or parent organizations. Participation in such activities can lead to new and more effective helping roles for families as they go through the experience of advocating on their own behalf and influencing changes in the service delivery system (Carbino, 1981).

Encouraging parents and other kin to become involved in parent-training programs is another way to help them to develop and use their potentialities. Biological families of children in foster family care or group home care frequently need help in the area of parenting; they need to learn or relearn skills to enhance their child-caring capabilities.

Opportunities for parenting training may be offered directly by the agency or treatment center or through community resources such as schools, family service agencies, child welfare agencies, and self-help organizations. Although the effectiveness of training programs is yet to be established empirically, practitioners report that many biological parents and other kin can make use of these resources, especially in conjunction with counseling services or other treatment programs (Abidin, 1980; Turner, C., 1980). Further experimentation with parent-training programs specifically geared to the needs and qualities of families of children in foster care would be useful.

As with any professional intervention, it is important to assess with the families what is needed. For instance, do they recognize any needs around their parenting? What are the areas in which they need to build or improve skills in child care? What satisfactions or dissatisfactions do they find in their own lives, apart from being parents? What about their relationships with spouse, friends, relatives, and other significant persons? What is their competence in areas such as interactional skills, behavior management, and cognitive development?

Participation in parent-training programs geared to the needs and qualities of parents and other kin might serve to increase their sense of satisfaction, enhance their competence, and lead to more constructive involvement with the children in their families.

After-Care Services

Practitioners also must help biological families once a child leaves out-of-home care to be reunited with his or her family (Fein et al., 1983). After-care services have long been neglected in child welfare practice, even though various studies have shown that continued professional and community supports are necessary to maintain the gains made by children and families during placement (Taylor & Alpert, 1973).

As found in an investigation of the outcome of permanency planning, many biological families need basic services in the after-care period, services such as housing, employment, financial assistance, recreation, and counseling (Fein et al., 1983). A prominent role for practitioners, therefore, is to link families and children with needed community agencies and resources and to monitor the provision of services once the child returns to the family. In short, as noted in

Chapter 9, after-care services constitute a vital link in the continuum of child, youth, and family services.

Contraindications

In certain situations continuing family involvement may well be inappropriate or even damaging to the child. It appears that many families can be either sufficiently rehabilitated to be able to maintain, sustain, or resume care of their children or can be helped to accept their inability to do so and participate in making an alternate permanent plan. But there are also families who are so severely disturbed or disorganized that they are not able to respond or cannot be helped toward rehabilitation.

In these cases practitioners are compelled to ask: How can we manage to help the family overcome its difficulties within a time scale that does not damage the child? How far do we go in trying to help these families? When is it time to give up? When should we move decisively to make another plan for the child?

As discussed elsewhere (Maluccio, Fein, & Olmstead, 1986), there are certain factors that workers should consider in resolving these questions, although precise prescriptions are not available:

1. Age of child. In general, the younger the child, the more quickly a decision about a permanent plan must be made in order to facilitate the child's bonding with parental figures.
2. Time. A family's potential for rehabilitation "over time" is not enough. There must be an ability to rehabilitate within a "reasonable length of time" as determined on the basis of careful assessment of the child's developmental level, sense of time, and needs.
3. Previous efforts at rehabilitation. Where comprehensive and quality services have previously been provided for a sustained period with no indication of progress, the value of additional efforts can be questioned.
4. Chronicity of problems. When history reflects no time of stability for a family and dysfunction has been a "way of life," there is less optimism about the potential for positive change. This is especially so when there is an established pattern of child abuse or neglect or extensive history of incapacitating drug addiction.
5. Familial investment. When families, especially parents, are unwilling to participate in rehabilitative efforts despite energetic, repeated, varied, and creative attempts to enlist their participation, an extended length of time is inappropriate.

ROLES OF FOSTER PARENTS AND CHILD CARE STAFF

Thus far we have focused on the roles of practitioners such as social workers in working with the biological families of children living away from home. (Unfortunately, the important roles of other professionals such as teachers, physicians, psychologists, and nurses are beyond the scope of this chapter.) Their roles are complemented by the contributions of foster parents, group home parents, and child care workers. In some ways the roles of these persons are even more significant than those of social workers and other child welfare staff because they live with the children and deal with them on a day-to-day basis in relation to crucial life events.

In addition to direct work with children in their care, foster parents, group home parents, and child care workers also play—or could play—a prominent role with biological families, especially by providing supports to parents of children in their care. Playing such roles more widely and effectively, of course, is not simple and requires changes in the field of child welfare, particularly greater professionalization of foster parenting and child care work. This includes improved salaries and working conditions and other rewards for foster parents and child care workers, respect for their important contributions, and acceptance of their position as integral members of the service team.

The movement toward the professionalization of foster parents and child care staff has begun, albeit at a slow pace, and child welfare agencies and child care centers are considering or implementing significant changes. For instance, Watson (1982) proposes a new model of foster family care in which the foster family is regarded as a temporary *extension* of the biological family rather than its *substitute,* as has been true traditionally. The foster family, in other words, should become an integral part of the overall treatment program and help promote the adaptive functioning of the biological families. Following such a perspective, foster parents can become allies of biological parents and other child-caring kin and can be more actively involved in the treatment plan on behalf of each family as long as their roles are clarified and they are provided with adequate supports and rewards. They can be involved as resources for biological families through such means as role modeling or serving as family aides (Davies & Bland, 1978; Ryan, McFadden, & Warren, 1981). They can be trained to work cooperatively with biological parents and other kin, as considered in a manual by Lee and Park (1980).

Similar changes are occurring in the area of residential child care, with various centers moving toward transforming group care into a family-supportive system. It is increasingly recognized that residential treatment programs can contribute to the welfare of children and youth living away from home or at risk of out-of-home placement through such strategies as (a) intensive work with families and children who have been placed to facilitate reunification with biological families; (b) provision of respite care, day treatment services, and the like to prevent out-of-home placement; (c) evaluation of children to determine the most appropriate permanent plan (Weitzel, 1984); (d) preparation of children for adoption (Powers & Powell, 1983; Weitzel, 1980); and (e) recruitment and orientation of adoptive parents and provision of postadoption supportive services (Weitzel, 1984).

Whittaker (1979, 1981), Carlo (1985), Finkelstein (1981), and others have written about new directions in group child care. For example, they have described programs designed to change the residential treatment center into an effective resource or support system for parents and other relatives. In these programs the staff recognizes the family's own needs as well as importance of family to the child and mobilizes agency and community resources on behalf of parents and the family as a whole. As noted by LeCroy (1984, p. 90), "perhaps the most significant recent change in residential treatment services is an increased commitment toward parent involvement," and, it could be added, the involvement of other child-caring family members. Group child care centers and other foster care agencies are increasingly engaging parents and other involved kin in the therapeutic process as well as the child care program in general, through such approaches as including them in staff meetings and particularly in case conferences affecting their children; enabling them to participate in the ongoing care of their children, such as by participating in school conferences; involving them as consultants in training programs; and employing them as child care aides. (Blumenthal & Weinberg, 1984; Bryce & Lloyd, 1981; LeCroy, 1984; Maluccio & Sinanoglu, 1981).

In sum, foster parents and child care staff can help the biological families of children in their care directly in a variety of ways: (a) supporting biological families in their efforts to cope with life stresses, reestablish themselves, and resume care of their children; (b) reaffirming the importance of permanence and sharing the belief that children must know where they will grow up; (c) maintaining the involvement of biological families by consulting them about decisions affecting their children; and (d) modeling parenting skills for biological families through such means as discussing and demonstrating discipline techniques; role playing communication between parents and children; eliciting ideas from the families about better ways of interacting with their children; and modeling the ability to enjoy the child, "relaxing with the child, finding the child in one's self, playing with the child" (Maluccio, Fein, & Olmstead, 1986, p. 178).

As already suggested, having child care staff and foster parents involved in these activities directly with biological families requires a redefinition of their roles as full-fledged members of the service team. In addition, there is a need to redefine the relationships between biological parents and kin and foster parents or child care staff. In contrast to the traditional pattern of keeping them apart or in competition with each other, biological parents, foster parents, and child care workers should be helped to regard themselves as partners in a shared undertaking, with common goals and mutually supportive and complementary roles.

PROMOTING THE COMPETENCE OF FOSTER PARENTS AND CHILD CARE STAFF

Working with children and parents can be demanding and draining, particularly for foster parents and child care staff. It is beyond the scope of this chapter to consider the impact of out-of-home placement on foster families and child care workers or ways of helping them carry out their challenging roles. These issues are examined elsewhere (see, for example, Ainsworth & Fulcher, 1981; Carbino, 1980; Carlo, 1985; Eastman, 1985; Kruger, 1983; and Maluccio, Fein, & Olmstead, 1986). However, it should be stressed that if foster parents and child care workers are to play a stronger role with biological families we need to do much more to support and enhance their competence. Although it is clear that child care workers and foster parents play *the* most important helping role in the lives of children and youth placed in child care, they continue to be in some ways an oppressed group, with low pay, low prestige, and excessive demands on their energies, with consequently high rates of burnout and turnover.

Our typical response to these issues is to provide training programs. Training can be helpful, but it is only a partial answer because it does not address the systemic causes of the difficulties involved. To address these causes, we must provide a more rewarding, supportive, and enriching environment for child care workers and foster parents, especially as we ask them to deal with a more and more demanding group of children and families and as we place higher expectations on them. In our efforts to create such an environment, it may be useful to apply some of the basic principles of the permanency-planning philosophy to child care workers and foster parents themselves. And so we might ask ourselves some questions:

1. What are we doing to contribute to the stability, continuity, and sense of belonging among child care staff and foster parents?
2. How can we prevent burnout, a rapidly increasing phenomenon among child and youth care staff?
3. How does the work environment promote the personal and professional growth of child care workers and foster parents? What is the quality of the staff development program? Is there a career ladder? How adequate are the salaries paid to these workers? What provisions are made for vacations?
4. How are child care workers and foster parents involved in policy formulation, program development, and administration? Is there a collaborative, democratic model in which they are regarded as active and respected participants?
5. What are the administrative and supervisory practices in regard to providing psychological support to staff members and foster parents in order to encourage and recognize each person's efforts and achievements?
6. What kinds of services and treatment approaches tend to be most effective with which kinds of families over a long period of time?

NOTE

1. Working with families of children in out-of-home placement also requires understanding and knowledge in additional areas that are beyond the scope of this chapter, including guides for child and family assessment, criteria for decision making regarding the issue of placement, dynamics of the placement process, and impact of placement on children and families. (For discussion of these topics, see Janchill, 1981; Maluccio, Fein, & Olmstead, 1986; and Stein & Rzepnicki, 1983.)

11

Public Policies and Families

CATHERINE S. CHILMAN

This chapter briefly discusses some of the salient aspects of public policies and families. It is a prelude to the next chapter that addresses legislation and policies concerning troubled family relationships and is very like one with a similar title in other volumes in this series.

DEFINITIONS OF FAMILY WELL-BEING

It can be argued that the chief goal of public policies concerning families is the promotion of family well-being. There are many conflicting definitions of this term, a term that often includes the words "strong families." To traditionalists, strong families are apt to mean patriarchal ones in which members marry as young adults "until death do us part," have a number of children, refrain from the use of artificial contraceptives and abortion, and follow traditional sex roles with husbands as the only (and adequate) wage earners and wives as full-time homemakers and mothers. Such families are often conceptualized as "stable and strong." They present a united front to the outside world, regardless of the divisions and conflicts that may occur within them.

A more modernist view is that strong families are ones that function in such a way as to promote the physical, social, psychological, and economic well-being of each person, both as members of the family and as autonomous individuals. This well-being is viewed in process terms, that is, each family member, young *and* old, is capable (in fact, needful) of growth and development throughout the life span. The processes of this kind of family system support individual growth through respect for the autonomy of each family member and through the nurturance of each member as an integral part of a caring, interdependent, intimate family group. Following such a definition, family stability is not necessarily seen as desirable if stability means that marriages should be permanent regardless of their quality and parenthood should be perpetually selfless regardless of the problems that offspring may present in their adult years as well as their younger ones (Terkelson, 1980).

PUBLIC POLICY PROCESSES

As in the case of "family well-being," the term "policy" has numerous definitions and interpretations. A full discussion of this topic alone could fill many volumes. For the present purposes, however, the term means public (i.e., government) policy and is conceptualized as a series of processes. Moreover, the primary emphasis is on *federal* public policies as constituting the most general approach. Public policy by itself might be thought of as a guiding principle of government, such as "every child in the United States shall receive a high quality of education," a familiar and enticing principle! However, the principle does not move beyond the enticement (and probably vote-getting) stage unless it is developed into legislative proposals, which then must be passed by Congress and signed by the President.

The outcome of these processes is affected by highly political forces. Typically, numerous lobbying groups as well as individual citizens become involved. Action by Congress and the President is strongly influenced by these groups and individuals, most especially by strong, well-financed national lobbies.

The process is far from finished, however, even if legislation is approved and signed. Appropriations that provide *adequate funding* must be made by Congress, and this funding is strongly influenced by the nature of political support for and opposition to the legislation. Then, too, relevant federal departments must be provided with administrative personnel, processes that are also affected by political considerations. Following these steps, administrative guidelines must be developed.

The legislation then moves for its further financing and implementation to state levels. In turn, state governments must develop programs that are to be carried out by local units of government. These units, then, need to further develop and administer programs so that they actually reach the individuals and families for whom the legislation was intended. The degree to which this legislation is funded and implemented at state and local levels also depends on political considerations within the various units of government and, ultimately, on the views that individual local staff members may have about the matter. Even more ultimately, the ways in which these programs are used or not used by individuals and families is strongly affected by *their* particular attitudes, values, and behaviors in relation to the services offered. (Consider government-supported family-planning programs, for instance.)

Furthermore, if it happens that some person or persons question the constitutionality of the law and this challenge reaches the Supreme Court who, in turn, finds the legislation in violation of the Constitution, the entire process will be moved back to square one. In short, there is a long series of processes that must occur for a policy to have real effect: a study in the many trials and triumphs of a democracy in a federal (national–state–local) system![1]

Although ideally public policy development and implementation is a rational process based on the best scientific knowledge, rational process is only one piece of the much larger policy puzzle. For instance, findings from scientific research are often brought into the policy process to provide a patina of rational respectability to a piece of legislation that more fundamentally has pragmatic political purposes.

The complex, lengthy, political processes described above may well be discouraging to those who wish to affect public policies. To be effective, it is often useful for individuals to select a few policy issues that seem to them to be crucial, to affiliate with groups (often representative of one or more of the human services professions) who share their concerns, and to keep informed and politically active with that group or groups and follow the legislation through its many processes: congressional and presidential legislative actions, budget appropriations, development of administrative guidelines, state and local implementation, and court challenges. It also helps to know one's elected local, state, and federal representatives and to join and contribute to the political party of choice as well as campaign organizations for candidates supporting desired public policies.

In general, it is unproductive to complain, as many do, that public policies are "just a mess of politics." Within the American system of government, "politics" is a process of democracy in action. As discussed above, the many processes involved are heavily affected by pressures from politically active individuals and groups. Thus, the way for human service professionals to affect policies is to become politically active themselves, especially through knowledgeable, well-organized groups. To simply criticize and stay outside of the process is to pass the power to others who *are* actively involved and often involved with pushing agendas that are not in the best interests of families in trouble, especially poor and minority families who have relatively little power themselves.

A major point to the policy chapters in this series is to provide both a knowledge background and stimulus to readers to involve themselves, to one extent or another, in political activities to affect public policies that play such a large part in the lives of troubled families. An ecological approach to services for families clearly implies that concerned human service professionals should involve themselves, to one degree or another, in policy- and planning-oriented political activities as well as in the provision of direct services, the major focus of most practitioners serving families today (1987).[2]

FAMILY-RELATED POLICIES

This leads to another definition: family policies or family-related policies. Again, policies referred to here are public, that is, government policies. Again, the term "family policy" has numerous meanings and involves numerous controversies. As of the mid-1980s the term was attracting increased attention, sparking heated debates covering the entire political spectrum from the extreme conservative political right to the extreme liberal left. Virtually everybody appeared to be "pro-family" and in favor of supports for family well-being, including supports for their economic and occupational well-being. But as we have seen, definitions of family and family well-being have many interpretations. To some the term "public family policy" may mean that certain kinds of families and family-related behaviors, as determined by government action, should be promoted and other kinds officially opposed.

On the other hand, many others hold that "family public policies" should be defined as including all government policies and programs that have an impact on families; they also tend to believe that government should not impose a particular standard of family roles and functions on its citizens. The concept that family policies consist of all policies affecting families has lead in a number of directions, including that of family-impact analysis, a term that became popular during the Carter–Mondale administration of the late 1970s (Zimmerman, 1982).

Family-impact analysis takes a rational planning approach to family policy. It seeks to gather large bodies of data concerning numerous public programs that affect families and to assess their effects through complex statistical analyses of relevant data. Impact is measured by demonstrated or probable effects on birth, marriage, divorce, separation, illegitimacy, employment, and income. These statistics are primarily provided by the U.S. Bureau of the Census, the National Center of Vital Statistics, and the U.S. Department of Labor. Moreover, numerous studies of various aspects of family well-being and of program effectiveness of family life, broadly defined, have been carried out by numerous government agencies and universities as well as by human service public and private organizations. Findings from these investigations are also used to supplement the above data. Many of these studies are also discussed in the relevant chapters of this series.

Senator Patrick Moynihan, who has had a long-time interest in family policy, writes that in essence family policy focuses on the outcomes of other policies. He sees family welfare as being the business of numerous social and economic programs at national, state, and local levels and holds that their impact on families can be assessed, at least in part, by analyses of family data, as discussed above (Moynihan, 1986).

Kamerman and Kahn (1978), who have conducted extensive surveys of family policies and programs in this and other countries, define family policies in ways that are close to Moynihan's conceptions. They hold that family policy consists of activities funded and sponsored by government that affect families directly or indirectly, intentionally or unintentionally, whether or not these policies have specific family objectives. They write that family policy is both a perspective and a set of activities. As an activity it includes such family-specific programs as family-planning services, food stamps, income maintenance, foster care, adoption, homemaker services, day care, child development programs, family counseling and therapy, and employment services.

All of the above views include, or can include, the concept of family-impact analysis. This analysis has considerable merit primarily because it recognizes the huge network of government programs that impinge on families. This analysis also calls for the application of survey data as well as many kinds of research, both basic and applied, to the formation and analysis of public family-related programs and policies. However, family-impact analysis by itself cannot be expected to change public policy. Those who apply its methods will have major problems if they fail to recognize and deal with the many political processes that are also necessary to actualize policies as shown above.

Also, family-impact analysis is deficient if it merely takes the passive approach of simply analyzing what effects government programs and policies will have or are having on families. An active approach is also needed in which the needs of families are the primary consideration and planning activities are then directed to formulating what programs and policies, both existing and not yet existing, are needed.

Another and far more conservative view of family policy was presented by President Reagan's Working Group on the Family in 1986 (Washington Cofo Memo, 1986). Their report called for less government infringement on the rights and responsibilities of families. State-funded day care, income assistance through public family allowances for children, school feeding programs, and national health care systems were all seen as socialistic evils that undermine American families and the larger society. The report called for local, volunteer assistance to families in lieu of federal/state government programs. On the other hand, government should take an active stand to affect cultural patterns perceived by the working group as being hostile to families; these patterns included drug use, pornography, and "bigoted" stands against religions.

The report also saw economic expansion as essentially a profamily program. Such expansion could be brought about, the group stated, through such measures as low taxes, control of inflation, and the end of "social spending schemes." The report further stated that old principles that prevent erosion of family rights and responsibilities through court actions, dominance by public education, and control by social programs must be reaffirmed. Senator Moynihan called this report not so much an analysis of public policies and families as a "conservative tantrum." Indeed, it seemed to reflect some of the main aspects of the extreme conservative position. Furthermore, the report illustrates the principle that *all* aspects of the functioning of society can be viewed as relevant to family policies. It also shows that the field of family policy is highly sensitive and readily politicized.

Family issues deeply engage the heart as well as the mind. They touch upon the most intimate, significant aspects of our lives, the central identity each of us derives through our total development from infancy onward. Family issues include our most private and personal attachments, values, and beliefs. For many, probably the majority of Americans, family issues are closely intertwined with religious ones. And a basic principle of the American credo is a separation of church and state. Probably all religions see the guidance and succor of families as being central to their function and sharply different from those of government.

Furthermore, individual and hence family freedom from government interference is also basic to the American tradition. Millions of immigrants from the early 1600s to the present have come to this country in search of this freedom. Thus, the very words "family policy" can serve as a red flag to many of our citizens of all political persuasions.

Schorr (1986) writes that it is preferable to plan for wide-range public policies and programs that families need rather than advocating for family policies per se because the former term is less sensitive and controversial than the latter. Moreover, many such programs can be offered as services that may be chosen or not, depending on the values and beliefs of individual families and their members, thus safeguarding principles of freedom.

FAMILIES VERSUS SOCIETAL RESPONSIBILITY

The concept of "family responsibility" is another controversial and complicated one that usually arises in debates about families and policies. It lies at the heart of many issues. Although our traditional cultural patterns hold that it is desirable for families to be self-reliant and self-supporting, responsible toward each of their members, and independent of any public aid, virtually *no* family in today's highly urbanized, technological society is totally independent of the services provided by large networks of external systems, both private and governmental. Government-aided and/or regulated systems within the country that are crucial to the well-being of virtually all families include transportation in its many aspects, water supplies, waste disposal, fire and police protection, dependable money supplies and insured savings bank deposits, public education systems, public health services, social security provisions, the court systems, and so on. And international programs aimed at implementation of foreign policy and national defense as well as improved international trade, theoretically at least, provide important assistance for every individual and family in the country.

Although many of these forms of assistance are more or less taken for granted, sharp arguments quickly arise over such issues as special income, health, employment, housing, child care, and education assistance targeted to the poor and near poor. Such programs are highly visible, are incorrectly seen as inordinately expensive, and are often viewed as replacing family responsibilities—with many of these responsibilities fundamentally being the traditional functions of women, including child care; nursing care of the ill and disabled; and stretching the food, housing, and clothing dollar through home production. Some traditionalists claim that keeping these kinds of responsibilities within the family actually enhances the well-being of families. However, if we return to our earlier definition of family well-being, we can see that this well-being is eroded, rather than supported, if the basic survival and developmental needs of families and all their members, including wives and mothers, are not met. An overload of economic adversities or severe illnesses or handicaps may make it impossible for some families to handle problems such as these without the supplementary assistance of public programs. Although conservatives often argue that private voluntary efforts should provide the assistance needed, our society has become too urbanized, costly, and complex for these activities by themselves to make much of a dent on the host of problems that many families encounter today. These voluntary efforts can be helpful as a supplement to, but not a substitute for, necessary family assistance programs.

As shown in the foregoing chapters, families in our complex, technologically advanced society have only limited control over their own physical health and over mobilizing the frequently costly resources for treatment of the physical illnesses and disabilities that may afflict family members.

A careful analysis of the points listed above can lead to the recognition that many of the relationship problems faced by families today are not solely a result of irresponsible actions on their part; rather, to a large extent they are a result of a combination of factors external to families. These include the many employment, community, financial, and depersonalizing stresses of modern society. Thus, a number of public policies and programs are needed to promote and support the positive relationships in families and their members, as is discussed in more detail in Chapter 12.

NOTES

1. Other legal challenges regarding legislation and its administration may be raised through the courts at various local, state, and regional levels, but a discussion of details concerning this, and other, issues affecting public policies transcends the space constraints of this chapter.

2. Although the foregoing paragraphs may seem like a high school lesson in civics, it is my experience that the majority of citizens including graduate students, many academicians, and human service professionals fail to understand a number of the

principles sketched here. These principles grow out of my experience and study as a university professor, as a former staff member of the (then) U.S. Department of Health, Education and Welfare during the 1960s, and as a former staff member of various state governments and private social agencies.

It was my common government experience during the 1960s that both academicians and human service professionals outside the federal government sought to impress me with their views of what policies and programs were needed because they assumed I was an "influential policy-maker." In actuality, the executive branch of government (i.e., the President, his Cabinet, and the staff of the various federal departments) cannot create public domestic policies (with "domestic" referring to policies _internal_ to this country) without supportive legislation and appropriations as provided by congressional action. Also, any staff actions must be within guidelines provided by the relevant legislation. Furthermore, federal staff members need to be sensitive to the reactions of citizens, as groups and as individuals, at local levels because these citizens may protest to their Congresspeople if they object to any part of federal programs and the way they are administered.

Thus, it seems to me that the term "federal domestic policy makers" tends to be a fallacy if it refers to federal staff personnel, because their options are limited by many factors. In fact, given the constraints, it is something of a miracle that federal "bureaucrats" can act at all. Similar comments apply to local and state governments, but our focus here is on the federal government.

Family Law Policies and Programs: 12

TOO LITTLE, TOO LATE?

MARGARET J. NICHOLS

This chapter uses the author's family law knowledge and experience to discuss common legal issues affecting families who come into contact with various courts. United States courts have affirmed repeatedly that the family is our most fundamental social institution. "It is through the family that we inculcate and pass down many of our most cherished values, moral and cultural" (*Moore v. City of Cleveland*, 1977). Legal definitions of "the family" affect how courts respond to cases involving spousal relations, child–parent–state relations, reproductive freedoms, sexual preference, differing lifestyles, and family dissolutions. But are courts any better than other social institutions at defining their vision of the family?

On a strictly technical level, courts define family as a group of two or more individuals related by blood, marriage, or adoption. In reality, individual judges bring fairly traditional personal backgrounds to family matters. For many, families are comprised of husband and wife and children in which the males are wage earners and the females are homemakers. Yet judges often deal with nontraditional families, as traditional families constituted only 31% of families with children (and 16% of all families) in 1983 (Kamerman, 1987). Even progressive judges may find it hard to give up deeply ingrained views, inadvertently allowing cultural values to slip in as standards against which the presenting family is judged.

Like the rest of society, the courts continue to strive to reflect the best thinking in society as they cope with its problems. Unfortunately, they do so at the most ineffectual level—after the family has come to the attention of government authorities. Courts should be used as resources of last resort for families who cannot otherwise resolve a problem. Yet sometimes it takes court action before social resources of any consequence are made available to a struggling family. Effective family policy would surely address the needs of troubled families earlier.

LEGAL PRINCIPLES AFFECTING VIOLENT FAMILIES

Spouse Assault

Although available data are somewhat contradictory, it is difficult to address spouse assault in a sex-neutral way: "With the exception of homicide in which males and females are almost equally victimized by their spouses, women tend to suffer the most serious injuries in cases of spouse abuse" (Star, 1987). From a Texas study one may conclude that no fewer than 15% of abused spouses are males (Stachura & Teske, 1979). For purposes of this brief essay, discussion is couched in the somewhat simplistic terms of male batterers and female victims. The point is that family violence has become an issue for the courts and that some legal techniques seem to help stop the cycle of violence.

Women today may be no better protected than they were when the Constitution did not include them as citizens. Protections that police and the criminal justice system provide for strangers involved in a bar brawl are often not afforded to women beaten at home by their mates. James Bannon, the Executive Deputy Chief of Police in Detroit, has reported that police officers avoid domestic violence situations both because they do not know how to cope with them and because they share the cultural view that these are individual problems, not public issues. No one, he observed, is more thoroughly socialized in masculine roles than police officers. For many police officers, women still are considered property. Believing this, there is some paradox in sending police officers to intervene in family violence (Bannon, 1975).

Suits Against the Criminal Justice System

Women's groups in the late 1970s and 1980s sought their own solutions. One was to sue municipalities, police departments, and prosecutors on behalf of the victims of violent family attacks. Victims alleged that the criminal justice system had failed to handle their family violence cases appropriately. Usually such cases are characterized by lengthy histories of calling for police assistance in which no arrest or removal of the assaultive spouse occurs. Women frequently are discouraged from completing a criminal complaint, either directly or indirectly, by cumbersome procedures. In some instances the woman is advised to seek safety outside of her home. While practically speaking this may be good advice, it serves to embolden the batterer by showing that he can get away with abusiveness. In these ways, the crime is trivialized, and the victim receives no real protection or justice.

Several lawsuits brought by women against municipalities and the police resulted in large damage awards. Findings of negligent performance of mandatory duties have had far-flung effects on police procedures and training and other aspects of the criminal justice system. States and local police departments are passing laws or implementing new policies permitting arrests without a warrant if there is reasonable cause to believe that an assault has occurred. Some mandate arrest where there is evidence of injury or that a weapon was used in the assault. Arraigning magistrates (judges or their assistants who decide whether there is enough evidence to hold a trial) are being encouraged to require that the alleged assailant have no contact with the survivor as a condition of release pending trial.

Policies for prosecutors (state or district attorneys) in Wayne County, Michigan (including Detroit), have been changed to require prosecutors to defend a decision not to prosecute. Perhaps more significantly, they must consider issuing more than misdemeanor warrants if there are injuries or if a weapon was used. Some courts and prosecutors are using specially trained court personnel to assist victims in understanding the court process and knowing when and where to appear and what to expect. The goal is to increase convictions, because of all studied intervention techniques, arrest and prosecution are the most likely to stop the cycle of violence. Studies show that only after such a firm response does the system have any chance of effecting improvement in the behavior of many batterers through counseling or other interventions (Berk & Newton, 1985).

It is important to be familiar with police, prosecutorial, and judicial policies concerning domestic violence, as they represent the most universally available protections for victims of family violence. It is useful to learn the conditions that may be imposed on accused and convicted assailants. Probation and personal recognizance orders, which place conditions on release from custody, are better victim protection than anything available through civil injunctive processes, which are usually inaccessible or too costly for many victims anyway. A civil injunction requires the victim to hire an attorney and initiate the judicial process, while probation and personal recognizance orders place restraints on the behavior of persons convicted or accused of a crime at the initiative of the courts. Knowing the limits within which the criminal justice system must work and putting it on notice that it may be held accountable under those policies for failure to perform can ensure that improved policies are more than just paper policies and may point out inadequacies of unrevised manuals.

Individual Suits for Protective Orders

Civil injunctions are a way to intervene in the cycle of spousal violence. They involve prohibitions, initiated by victims and imposed by courts outside the criminal law, and prohibit defendants from having contact with victims. All states allow for injunctive relief upon a showing in a civil case that the person seeking protection has been beaten or threatened in such a way that a reasonable person would be afraid. In the event the abuser violates the injunction, the victim must seek enforcement through the issuing court. Some states have enacted special protective order provisions, which provide the police with primary enforcement power.

Although injunctions are mere pieces of paper, the sense of many practitioners is that they work when the victim can afford to use them. In many instances physical violence ceases when the assailant is put on notice that the courts will impose sanctions if violence recurs. There are dangerous individuals, however, for whom these orders may act as "red flags" or as no deterrent. Predicting who will respond this way is mostly a matter of carefully interviewing one's client and perhaps a sixth sense born of experience. For these clients only secure shelter can protect them, particularly in the period immediately following a victim's flight.

The facility for obtaining civil injunctive orders or of enforcing them depends not only on the laws of a state but also on availability of knowledgeable attorneys and favorable attitudes among judges. Attracting legal help depends in part on the promise that crisis counselors and social workers will be available to support the non-legal needs of the client.

Survival issues, such as those discussed below, will affect the success of any court intervention, civil or criminal. Victims require considerable assistance to be able to appreciate their worth, their right to be free from abuse, and their ability to remain safe. Economic issues will seem overwhelming unless resources within public agencies are developed to facilitate getting food and shelter allowances quickly. Finding housing, particularly for poor women with children, is often difficult. Employment or job training and child care for working mothers are key needs. It is important to know the eligibility criteria for local agencies and federal relief programs. With therapeutic and logistical support, more attorneys will be willing to provide needed legal services. Helping victims of domestic violence requires nothing less than adequate resources and effective social and legal agency cooperation. However, studies are generally lacking as to the effectiveness of many of these services.

Working Toward Changes Within the System

Lobbying on behalf of the abused, particularly at the state and local levels, has produced some results. National legislation, which created the Office of Domestic Violence in the late 1970s, was abandoned by the Reagan administration, leaving states to handle the problem. Forty-three states and the District of Columbia have legislation allowing for civil protection, as described above. Several states permit warrantless arrests on the basis of reasonable suspicion. Now in most states a police officer must witness an assault before making an arrest. Some states, however, have changed their statutes to allow for arrest if the officer has reasonable cause to believe an assault has occurred. Even when desirable policies are in place, those administering them must be trained to make the best use of them (Star, 1987).

Those without training specific to the cycle of family violence cannot effectively assist members of such families. What happens to people locked into a cycle of codependent violence is incomprehensible to most people, even to many otherwise trained in behavioral dynamics. Because many intervenors such as the police, prosecutors, attorneys, and social workers have no personal perspective from which to understand why a woman remains in or returns to a violent relationship, they consciously or unconsciously blame her for the violence. This reinforces her already low self-esteem and makes even more unlikely her ability to stop the violence.

Criminal justice system personnel seem to be particularly hard on victims and difficult to train to understand family violence and act appropriately. Yet the response of the police, prosecutors, and judges is so vitally important that it cannot be ignored. Court and police personnel appear to learn best from their peers. Therefore, training efforts probably should come from respected members of their own agencies in conjunction with training by competent assault crisis counselors. When properly approached, the training academies and seminars for new police, prosecutors, and judges may add family violence education to their curricula. Effective use can be made of such studies as the U.S. Attorney General's Task Force on Family Violence (1984). After hearing testimony from victims, police, prosecutors, and shelter workers, task force members recommended that federal and state authorities implement changes such as obtaining convictions to make clear that offenders' behavior is cruel and intolerable, issuing protective orders and stern personal recognizance terms to protect victims, and using a wide range of alternatives in sentencing to break the cycle of violence.

Another approach to changing entrenched views of police and court personnel is through involving prosecutors, chief judges, chiefs of police, shelter workers, and others in task forces that examine family violence in their communities and how community systems respond. Dialogue among participants will help to engender an appreciation of the common frustrations and limited effectiveness of the present system of justice and heighten awareness of the resources available to better approach the problems.

The results of advances in urban environments often do not extend beyond county lines. Rural communities, with fewer resources and advocates, are slower to change. Still, there are encouraging studies and reports from areas where police and court procedures have improved. Reports that show beneficial results from changes in policies and procedures should be widely disseminated in journals that rural police, prosecutors, and attorneys are likely to read and respect. Local results may vary, but there is some reason to believe that police chiefs and judges, when properly educated, can assert that beating another person is a crime and that it makes no difference that the criminal is a friend or a member of the family.

Human service professionals, including lawyers, social workers, and others, can do and have done a number of other things to approach the problem, including establishing hotlines where victims can call for advice and comfort and shelters to provide safe living quarters. By 1985 there were 700 shelters in the United States that, in addition to safe, temporary housing, often provide economic and legal assistance as well as help in locating permanent living arrangements. Some also offer support groups for victims. Other programs include groups for batterers to help them control assaultive behavior and victim assistance programs that help victims through court appearances and other contacts with the criminal justice system (Star, 1987).

ABUSE AND NEGLECT OF CHILDREN

As of 1984 there were about 275,000 children living in foster care (Rosen, Fanchel, & Lutz, 1987). United States courts handle over 200,000 cases each year in which the abuse or neglect of children is alleged (American Bar Association, 1981). For some judges these cases are a small part of those appearing in their courts. In other courts, commonly called juvenile courts, such cases are everyday events. Wherever heard, these cases are treated differently than other matters. Courts with jurisdiction over children as victims or as alleged delinquents have been and continue to be the most controversial of all courts dealing with families. Juvenile courts are criticized on the one hand for permitting too many children to be victimized and castigated and on the other for interfering in families that do not feel they need to be "fixed."

Child protection statutes attempt to ensure that child-rearing goals are met by legally requiring caregivers to meet certain minimum requirements for the education, health, and safety of children. These statutes also prescribe how those duties are to be enforced. Given the increasing isolation of families and the poverty in which many families live, raising children has become increasingly difficult to do well. Yet even impoverished parents have legal duties that they are not free to abandon as long as their children are in their care. The difficulty in defining grounds for intervention in families is to avoid being so broad that the statute is too vague to be properly implemented or so reduced in scope that it permits numerous mistreated children to be excluded from court jurisdiction. It is proper that our democratic society have policies and procedures that encourage a broad range of lifestyles and ensure that the civil rights of poor and nonconventional as well as traditional households are respected. Nevertheless, the law must not sanction lifestyles that are unhealthy or dangerous to family members, especially children.

Public policy on state intrusion into families has vacillated. The modern juvenile court began at about the same time as compulsory school attendance in the early twentieth century (Morse, 1979). Juvenile courts were established to give assistance to troubled children and their families, to be the "good parent" their biological parents were unable to be. The tendency to see poor or immigrant families as inadequate, along with the deliberately informal court procedures thought necessary for the best interests of children, resulted in many children in the first six decades of this century being removed unnecessarily from their homes, sometimes permanently.

The backlash to this period and the current trend of American legal efforts is toward reducing the scope of intrusion into families by limiting the objectives of child protection to concentrate almost solely on purely physical protection. Simply stated, avoidable or preventable neglect or abuse are the grounds for intervention; the availability of "better" alternative care for children of poor or deficient parents is not.

The state has enormous power over the presenting family and must exercise its authority consistently and in keeping with its goals for improving troubled families. The decisions of all juvenile court judges in such cases are the same: Did abuse or neglect occur? Where will the child live? Should parental rights be terminated? What services will the family receive? When can state intervention into the family cease? (American Bar Association, 1981).

Sample rules for preventing children from being lost in foster care have been developed by the American Bar Association (Hardin & Shalleck, 1985). The stated goal of the rules was to help achieve stable and secure homes for foster children by first avoiding unnecessary removal from the original family, then returning children to their families as soon as possible after removal, and finally securing permanent homes for foster children when they cannot be returned to their families within a reasonable time.

By the American Bar Association's ideal standards, a decision to remove should take into account not only the present danger but also whether preventive services might keep the family together. When a child must be removed, it is important that the court evaluate thoroughly the plan for reunification and look periodically at how well that plan is being implemented. If it becomes clear that the family is not to be reunified, finding a permanent home for the child without unnecessary delays is crucial, because children must know that someone is committed to caring for them for as long as they need care.

This leads to a consideration of how effective permanency planning actually is. This policy was enunciated in the Adoption Assistance and Child Welfare law of 1980. It followed studies that showed that foster care of children was often ineffective and that, many times, children who had been removed from their own families were "adrift" in a number of placements with no accurate records kept of their whereabouts, history, or agency plans for their future. Permanency planning studies in the 1970s revealed that intensive services to the child's own family, goal-oriented written case plans, and assertive social work could often facilitate family reunification. Other forms of permanency planning include the adoptive placement of children who, because of their race or physical or mental handicaps, had been previously considered hard to place (Stein, 1987).

Human service work in preventing child placement or reuniting youngsters with their biological families has included case management to assist families in obtaining the many services they often need: legal, medical, child care, psychological, employment, and income assistance. Although there is considerable official enthusiasm for the permanency planning approach, its effectiveness depends on a number of factors including the availability and quality of these services as well as the family's ability and willingness to use them. Thus, this approach is apt to be far more useful in some well-endowed communities than in other, more meager ones and with some highly motivated and more advantaged families than with others who have low motivation to change or suffer from a multitude of financial, educational, physical, and/or psychosocial problems.

Questions must be raised about the value of permanency planning as a universal policy with its emphasis on keeping or reuniting children with their biological parents—parents who have been found to be seriously inadequate in the care of their children. Although it is clearly desirable to keep children in their homes and to work to improve the total family situation, positive outcomes of these efforts are far from assured. As Stein (1987) reports, there are only a few studies as to how effective permanency planning actually is. For instance, one study showed that one-third of children reunited with their own families had to be placed again in foster homes. He, among other specialists in the field, calls for skilled evaluation of this planning and its component treatment methodologies as well as intensive follow-up services to families after reunification occurs.

Throughout this discussion of permanency planning, the dollar factor has been present, if not altogether obvious. One suspects that at least some of the official enthusiasm for permanency planning stems from the fact that keeping children with their own severely troubled families is apt to be much cheaper than placing them with foster families or in residential facilities. However, the long-term effects of short-changing abused and neglected children through lack of adequate services may be enormously expensive over the years.

Pressure for adoption of hard-to-place children is also part of the permanency planning legislation. Here again, longitudinal research is lacking in respect to the effects of these adoptions on both the children and the adoptive parents. However, one can suspect that this may be also a money-saving device in many instances, and one can also urge further well-designed studies to learn more about the outcomes of these placements and pathways to improved policies and procedures.

DIVORCED AND SEPARATED FAMILIES

Divorce and child custody law are areas with which many Americans have first-hand experience. Divorces in one year will affect the lives of 1.2 million American children. Our society is approaching a point where nearly half of its children will live with neither or only one of their biological parents (United States House of Representatives, 1984).

Contested Child Custody

Court battles over custody should occur only when one parent represents a threat to the welfare of the children or when negotiating is made impossible by a lack of fair dealing. Unless parents cannot agree on the important postdivorce arrangements for their children, the divorce courts will play a perfunctory role. When the children are supported by welfare, the court will oversee support orders to ensure that the state is reimbursed as fully as possible. However, the courts fail to secure support from the noncustodial parent for 20% of the children of divorce, and only 59% of eligible mothers receive child support awards (Garfinkel, 1987). (See also Volume 3, Chapter 3.)

Custody contests seem to happen most often when one or both parents are using the divorce court to play out frustration with the divorce or when one is afraid of losing control or contact with the children. In other cases the primary custodian may feel she or he has no option but to defend the right to continue a parenting arrangement against an angry or dangerous ex-spouse or the threat of loss of financial support. If a threat to child safety and welfare is not involved, a conscientious attorney should encourage parents to decide the outcome. The client must understand the risks of the court "solution," especially if the family is at all out of the ordinary because most judges hold to older standard values and many judges dislike trying such cases.

Once a lawsuit is under way, it is very difficult to forget the allegations that are made prior to and during court proceedings. Each parent listens to the other's testimony and hears their mutual memories of vacations and family events recast into something unrecognizable. The testifier is "proving" that the other parent is cold and detached or too emotional and smothering. Emotionally battered and financially drained, the parents have little left for the considerable needs of the children for whom they struggle.

For the guidance of attorneys representing divorcing parents and the judges who must make custodial decisions, most states employ a multifactor "best interests" test. By evaluating a list of objective and behavioral criteria, they try to determine with which parent the child has the best relationship and the best chance for secure, moral growth and development following the disruption of the family. Particular emphasis is placed on continuing the child in an "established custodial environment," the home maintained by that parent to whom the child has come to look for his or her routine guidance, comfort, and care. Difficult cases involve circumstances where, following the breakup of the family unit, lives are so disrupted that neither parent has been able to establish such an environment or where that environment has been acquired by trick, kidnapping, or contempt of court.

Financial ability to support the children is also listed as a factor in child custody law. However, courts do not interpret this to allow the more financially secure spouse to obtain custody unless he or she is the parent who, on balance, is best suited to be custodian. Where low- or nonwage earners are the preferred custodians, support awards are used to equalize financial ability.

Other factors include the preference of the child, if mature enough to express one, the health and morals of the parents, the ability of each parent to cooperate with the other to foster an ongoing relationship of the child with the other parent, and any other factor that the court finds will affect the physical or emotional health or well-being of the child. Human service professionals are often called upon by the courts to help sort out these factors.

Joint Custody: Legal Policy Affecting Divorcing Families

Joint custody legislation is emerging as a strong trend around the nation, thought by family and court professionals to encourage the maintenance of contact by noncustodial parents with their children. Legislators cite data that indicate that children who continued to have regular contact with both parents after an amicable divorce were better adjusted and more likely to be adequately supported (Wallerstein & Huntington, 1983). With these premises joint custody legislation has been enacted in about half of the states to require that the trial court consider an award of joint custody, although about 90% of children of divorce remain in their mother's custody (see Chapter 3). Model standards for evaluating joint custody are under development by the American Bar Association, Section on Family Law (Horowitz & Dodson, 1985).

The term "joint custody" can be confusing. Joint *legal* custody gives one parent primary possession while requiring that both be involved in major decisions affecting the child's health, education, or welfare. Judges consider the ability of the two parents to make important decisions together and to foster in the children a good continuing relationship with the other parent. Where there is actual joint *possession* of children, each parent has physical care for significant periods of time, for example, alternate weeks or months (if proximity allows) or school year with one parent and summer vacation with the other.

Generations from now social scientists will have had an opportunity to complete longitudinal studies of the policy's effects on children and to study trends in predivorce negotiations and settlements, postdivorce parental contact, levels of child support orders, and compliance with those orders. Careful analysis will be needed to learn whether ordering shared parenting after bitter opposition or over one parent's objections will be found to have left children in continued tense environments. Some research suggests that latency-age children benefit from joint custody under certain conditions (see Chapter 3).

Although intended to foster more secure and well-supported children, there is some evidence emerging that joint custody is being used to place a heavy thumb on the scales of justice by parents willing to use the demand for it as a weapon. Examples include situations where the preseparation marital relationship may have been characterized by a heavily controlling father who earns most of the family's income and a weak or docile mother. Another example involves the family in which the father is very uninvolved with the children and perhaps very involved with his career and acquisitions. In either instance a disingenuous claim for sole or joint custody by such a father can be intimidating to the mother, perhaps causing her to reduce her support or property demands (Weitzman, 1986).

In developing its model joint custody statute, the American Bar

Association is debating whether joint custody should be permitted over one parent's objection and what factors would militate against such orders, for example, child or spousal abuse or the likelihood of parental kidnaping (American Bar Association, 1986). However, data on the impact of joint custody when one parent objects are lacking.

Increase in Custody Disputes: A Function of Changing Policy?

Social policy has set the stage for modern custody litigation. Nineteenth-century fathers had virtually absolute control over children, who were viewed as their property. If the parents divorced, it was presumed that the father would be granted custody. As fathers' work became less home-based and mothers were more often alone at home caring for children, the "tender years" doctrine arose. Women were felt to be more closely in tune with the developmental needs of children. This led to mothers being favored for the care of young children upon divorce, unless they were shown to be unfit. Unfitness as a legal test was not often described in terms of actual ability to raise a child. Rather, it was defined moralistically, including sexual misconduct, alcoholism, or unusual lifestyle or sexual preference.

The trend now is away from sexual preference or moralistic definitions of fitness. Extramarital affairs are not the automatic custodial disqualifier they once were so long as the parent's conduct does not adversely affect the child, as difficult as this often is to determine. Enlightened courts also apply this standard to custodial decisions when one of the parents is involved in a homosexual relationship, although this is an area in which the courts may surreptitiously find enough other negative criteria upon which to base a finding against awarding custody to a homosexual parent.

Custody decisions have become vastly more difficult. Families once knew before they even decided to divorce who would be the custodian. With the "best interests" of the children, as reflected in sexually neutral custody laws, either parent or even both are free to seek custody. Although this is certainly an advance over knee-jerk awards of children to the parent of one sex or the other, the lack of certainty has added new tensions to the process. Everyone, including children, is left wondering who will be the custodian. The potential for conflict is far greater, and the decision process for courts more complex.

Because of our culture's tendency to treat families as intensely private, many judges regard it as strange that parents would elect to have a judge resolve something as important to them as custody of their children. This is not a bad question to raise with disputing parents, because it can help them think about whether they can trust themselves better than a strange judge and process. Couples need advice about how to think through their own solutions so that the parents can carry on when the attorneys and judges are not readily available. This is a role that social workers, psychologists, psychiatrists, family therapists, and other professionals, particularly those with specialized training in the mediation of family disputes, may play.

DISTURBED FAMILY RELATIONSHIPS

Divorce and postdivorce modifications and enforcement actions comprise the single largest class of lawsuits in any given state, with over half of all suits filed each year dealing with divorce. Courts must determine such charged issues as alimony; the distribution of marital property, including professional degrees earned by one partner while the other supported the family; family-owned businesses and pensions; and disputes about the custody and support of children. The mere mention of some of these concepts can induce tremendous anxiety. The sight of a summons or the necessary language of a complaint or court order, while common to a lawyer, can be traumatic to a client.

Yet the terms of most divorces are not resolved in the courts. Rather, they are achieved by each side disclosing or discovering the assets and positions of the other and then negotiating a settlement, which the court approves. Effective communication is important to this process. Still, husband and wife are now plaintiff and defendant. Therefore, legal discovery techniques such as interrogatories, depositions, and subpoenas often are used to augment the couple's reduced ability to communicate openly so that finances and issues of child rearing, which may have contributed to marital discord, can be resolved.

Those divorcing individuals who seek professional help must be encouraged to differentiate their emotions about the spouse from the necessity of cooperating with him or her for the good of postseparation arrangements. However difficult, restraint and reason in the short term is the wisest long-term course. When possible, legal action should be delayed until high emotions begin to wane.

Selection of an attorney can be critical. An attorney who specializes in family law is apt to be best informed about the ever-changing law and better able to avoid worsening a potentially volatile situation. A "hired gun" who does what his or her client demands may give that client some avenging satisfaction but frequently does not achieve the best result or leave the family in good shape to handle their many future decisions. The best choice is the attorney who listens carefully, provides information about the process and the law, and helps the client reach decisions at the right time. In a working partnership the client is able to make progress in the emotional divorce that is apace with the legal one.

Regrettably, some lawyers still load complaints and court arguments with allegations of adultery or cruelty despite modification of most states' divorce laws to remove "fault" as grounds for divorce. Most states now allow dissolution upon the sworn testimony of one spouse that there has been an irremediable breakdown of the marriage relationship. Fault can be a factor in determining who is the proper parent for child custody or in awarding spousal support to the "wronged" spouse, but even in these determinations other criteria are apt to be more important. Fault, unless pertinent to other issues, serves only to perpetuate ill feelings that will hamper future contacts.

Court processes, with their rules about who speaks when in court and what is and is not admissible evidence, create a very alien environment for most families. So much of the process seems disconnected from the participants that the result can be immense frustration. The courtroom experience can become justification for continued resentment and bewilderment.

Modern divorce law is being redesigned to reduce opportunities for discord through the development of objective criteria for determinations of custody and of spousal and child support. (Custody criteria were addressed earlier in this chapter.)

Child support standards, consistent within each state, are mandated by federal law and should be fully implemented by 1988. The 1984 legislation requires states to withhold child support from the wages of absent parents whose payments are delinquent and creates financial incentives for states to collect child support.

Finally, it authorizes the state of Wisconsin to use federal funds to finance a demonstration of a child support insurance program that, among other features, provides a percentage-of-income standard that judges may use in determining child support obligation—17% of gross income for one child, 25% for two children, 29% for three children, 31% for four children, and 34% for five or more children. Later judges in Wisconsin will be required to use the standard unless they make a written finding that justifies its nonuse (Garfinkel, 1987, Child Support Enforcement Amendments, 1984).

Although individual circumstances may vary results, in most states the process begins with a mathematical calculation based on each parent's income and some standard of the child's basic needs. Detailed support policies that can be explained to a client may facilitate agreements, because attorneys for both spouses presumably will come up with similar estimations of appropriate support.[1]

The struggle in many states is to see that support guidelines provide adequate financial support for the children of divorce, many of whom are living in conditions of poverty. Family advocates are also seeking effective policy to guide the courts and parents with the various arrangements needed to effectuate sole custody and non-traditional custody. For example, both the courts and parents will be helped by carefully drafted guidelines for longer-term, overnight visitations in sole custody cases and, in shared custody cases, relative contributions for transportation, medical care, education, child care, and clothing.

In determining child support, courts must take into account such factors as the financial condition of the parents, their job stability, and the presence of other dependents to be supported. Adequate and regular child support correlates, not surprisingly, with full employment of the nonprimary parent. Payment of support also correlates with the payor having predictable and significant contact with the children. Involved nonprimary parents are more apt to help with "extras" such as camp, music lessons, and the like. Therefore, courts are striving to ensure that the parent who is not the primary caregiver have ample opportunity to be with and parent the children.

Joint custody involving recipients of AFDC benefits requires special care. Federal law conditions AFDC eligibility on the "continued absence" of a parent and whether the child is "living in the home" of a parent claiming the AFDC benefits. So that poor families are not forced to choose between financial support or the benefits of shared parenting, California has enacted legislation to minimize the risks, nominating one joint custodial parent as the primary caregiver and one home as the primary home for purposes of determining eligibility for AFDC benefits (California Civil Code, Section 4600.5 [h]). Without legislation other states' courts could be asked to make similar findings.

Some jurisdictions have established guidelines for determining the validity and value of claims for spousal support or alimony. Again, these criteria and mathematic formulas have the advantage of reducing the opportunity for discord between the spouses by making what is nearly always a charged issue a matter of court policy with which both sides must live. Ranges are established where alimony will be unlikely; where short-term, rehabilitative alimony will be likely; or where long-term traditional alimony will be likely. In addition, the guidelines may address how to apportion the spouses' financial resources fairly, given the strength of the applicant's claim.

Problems sometimes spill over into postdivorce contests. Problems in enforcement of support are probably the most frequent complaint, with visitation and custody interferences following in rate of incidence. States receiving federal funds for AFDC benefit programs must have routine support enforcement, as when court action is automatic and certain, compliance will be more likely. However, in many cases the noncustodial parent is unemployed, underemployed, or so burdened with other family financial responsibilities (as in the case of remarriage) that he or she is unable to contribute significant amounts of support (Wilson & Neckerman, 1985).

There is considerable range to visitation violations and interferences. The primary parent may remove the child from the jurisdiction or may hide the whereabouts of the children. He or she may not cooperate in arranging visits when the court order states "reasonable" rights of visitation or may refuse to allow alternative visitation if the scheduled visit must be missed. The custodial parent may convey such negative views of the noncustodial parent that the children do not wish to visit.

Custodial parents also offer a range of complaints about visiting parents. The visiting parent may not visit at all or may fail to arrange for visits in advance. The visiting parent may neglect to be on time for pickup and return of the children without giving advance notice. Indeed, he or she may not show up for a scheduled visit. Visitations may be conspicuously luxurious and overstimulating. In extreme situations the child may not be returned or the visiting parent may show up for the visitation intoxicated or on drugs or may abuse or upset the child during the visit or use the visitation as an opportunity to harass or abuse the custodial parent.

Remedies for visitation violations include finding the violating parent in contempt of court orders. He or she may be fined or jailed or otherwise coerced to allow the visits to take place as ordered. Compensatory "banking" of denied visitation days allows the noncustodial parent to obtain court assistance in making up lost visits.

Bonds may be utilized to secure future compliance, and courts may award costs to the aggrieved parent who had to seek assistance.

Where the custodial parent establishes that some aspect of visits are detrimental to the child, the court may modify the visitation order to provide specific conditions such as limited hours for visits or orders against appearing in an intoxicated condition or driving during the visits. In severe situations the court may require visits under supervision in a neutral setting. Because contact by the child with his or her parent is presumed to be beneficial and because the cessation of contact is often viewed by the child as the fault of the child, the court will almost never curtail visitation completely. Similarly, because the child's needs are ongoing, support cessation is almost never used by the courts to coerce compliance with visitation orders.

In some states once a court has ordered custody and visitation, parents who fail to return a child can be charged with kidnapping. Federal law permits the prosecution of the parent for kidnapping if the child is taken from the home state contrary to a custody or visitation order. Some states permit injunctive orders for the protection of former spouses against acts of violence or custody interference.

The best means to avoid postdivorce conflict is to minimize conflict in the divorce process. A humane divorce in which the spouses are helped to plan respectful postdivorce relations is best, one that does not destroy the couple's residual caring and puts the needs of the children ahead of individual grievances. If the divorce has been destructive but both parties are ready to find a better approach to matters, they could learn techniques to identify needs and find solutions. Even one spouse can be effective in changing the tenor of relations if he or she is taught what to expect and how to avoid falling into old ineffective behavior patterns.

For example, even if only one spouse resists demanding or giving instant responses, the other will have to allow time for decisions. Time to give a response improves it and lessens the propensity for hostility. Establishing firm "rules" about all the aspects of contact, such as when telephone calls are not acceptable, how school notices and reports are to be shared, and when and how documents for health insurance or medical receipts are exchanged, can reduce sources of irritation. Although the effort to plan for problem areas may seem artificial and demeaning, the peace it can bring is worth the effort.

DEVELOPMENTS IN COURTS HANDLING FAMILY MATTERS

How can justice systems better address the needs of families in trouble? There seem to be several strong trends. One is to improve the existing system, including using more behavioral scientists in the decision process, establishing reasonable limits for how long cases may remain undecided, and developing family courts that can address in one court all the various circumstances that bring families into courts. The other trend is to take family legal determinations out of the courts, replacing them with alternative dispute resolution methods such as mediation and arbitration.

Behavioral Sciences in the Courts

Family therapists and other human service professionals are often called upon in today's courts to help the judge make a decision that is right for the child's developmental stage and that offers the child the most chance for continuity with parents and extended family members. To the extent that mental disturbances are noted, these must be evaluated. By modern standards the mental or physical health of a parent is one factor that must be assessed to know to what extent it might impede adequate parenting. Other important psychosocial factors beneficial to evaluating custodial decisions are those of the child in relation to parents, home, school, and community and the child's preferences.

To be effective witnesses, psychiatrists, psychologists, social workers, and family therapists must be familiar with the legal standards applied in the particular family court in which testimony is to be given. Often the testimony of an evaluating or treating therapist is the only evidence offered by a witness other than the parents and their close family members, all of whom may be seen as too biased to give much guidance in what is best for the child.

For their part human service professionals are not immune to the multitude of cultural and professional biases that beset domestic decisions, and they are not thought of by judges or lawyers as entirely objective. Indeed, there is debate within the social and behavioral sciences on "correct" theory and the effectiveness of various psychotherapeutic approaches. Thus, when called to give professional testimony in family matters, especially when retained by one parent, the testimony of the evaluator or therapist can be very controversial, and there may be intensive cross-examination by the other parent's lawyer. Therapists can maximize their impact in such cases by insisting on seeing all the pertinent family members and reviewing the applicable research before drawing conclusions. Their testimony should very carefully relate the factors in the case to the relevant research findings. The series of volumes of which this chapter is a part is intended to provide assistance to human service professionals in this regard.

Some therapists see the judicial process as antithetical to therapeutic goals and therefore refuse any connection with the courts. However, their clients may be involved, voluntarily or involuntarily, in court processes for which they need support and reassurance. Being familiar with the processes would enhance the therapist's ability to help.

Family Courts

In most states there is a separate court that deals with matters of delinquency, abuse, and neglect; another handles divorce, custody, paternity, and family support; and a third deals with orphans and children in need of guardians. It is possible to have one family within the jurisdiction of two such courts at the same time. Usually there are court rules for avoiding more than one court giving a ruling. However, legal scholars and judges take exception to a situation that arguably allows disputants to secure contrary results depending on which court gets jurisdiction first. It is this dichotomy that the gathering movement for family courts is meant to address. All matters concerning children would be handled in one court by judges specializing in family law using one set of procedures and standards.

The disadvantages of such a court are thought to be a propensity for the judges elected or nominated to these courts to be less well-qualified than are the judges of the states' highest trial courts, which are usually where divorce, paternity, and family support matters are heard. Also, the steady diet of divorce, custody, abuse, neglect, and delinquency is predicted to produce a numbing, or burnout, of judges, making them even more ill suited to the needs of families than their predecessors in the general jurisdiction courts.

Few states have such courts, and some that do have not been able to overcome state constitutional issues of jurisdiction to create a truly consolidated court. Rather, they have established a new family division in an existing court without eliminating overlapping jurisdictions. Early indications are promising where true consolidation has been effected and discouraging where the change is one of title only (Moore & Bassett, 1986).

Alternatives to Trial Courts

In some areas crowded trial dockets have resulted in intolerably long court cases affecting children and their parents adversely. Any resolution might be preferable to the limbo of 2- and 3-year pendencies. One effective technique for shortening the length of time cases await trial is the summary trial. These take place before a judge, with each attorney presenting his or her client's case without calling witnesses or introducing physical evidence. Legal theories and facts are summarized, and the judge then gives an advisory opinion that, if accepted, becomes final. If the opinion is objected to, the case goes on to trial. Alternative dispute resolution (ADR), including mediation and arbitration (concepts borrowed from labor law and applied with some success to other disputes), represent other techniques to which courts and litigants turn for a more speedy result.

Both ADR concepts involve the presence of a third party who assists the disputants in identifying areas of agreement and disagreement and in fashioning possible solutions to the disagreements. A contract or agreement often is the result of a successful effort. The document might take the place of court determination, as with separating unmarried cohabitants. Or, it might become the basis for a judgment, as in a custody and property settlement attached to a divorce judgment.

ADR terminology is not precise. Some mediations, for example, are no more than skilled interventions, as where police separate disputing spouses. Most court mediations in which the mediator makes a recommendation if the parties cannot agree are not true mediations. Where someone else has the power to influence a court's decision, disputants tend to build their case for that person; their communications are geared as much for effect as content.

Mediation differs from arbitration most significantly in that it requires that the entire process be voluntary. It is said to enhance the participants' decision-making abilities and their sense of participation in the planning for their postdivorce family relations. The third party is to be a neutral facilitator without any more authority than the disputants are mutually willing to give him or her. This helps ensure that the communications will be more honest as the disputants, not someone else, must create the agreement (Blades, 1984; Milne, 1983).

Arbitration gives the arbitrator the authority to make or recommend a decision in the event that the disputants cannot agree.

Should the arbitrator have to make the determination, he or she is likely to seek a solution somewhere between the two sides, so each side usually overstates its position. Its advantage is that an arbitrator can cut quickly to the real issues for settlement. Grounds for overturning the arbitrator's decision are strict and have the potential for leading to the arbitrator's abuse of authority, wittingly or unwittingly. Because arbitration shares many attributes of the court process without the considerable protections of the court, this method of reaching decisions works best where both sides desire a speedy solution and can be comfortable knowing that neither will be entirely happy or unhappy with the outcome.

Alternative dispute resolution in family matters is either lauded or lambasted in the literature. One way to evaluate the potential of out-of-court resolution is to discern first who decided that the controversy should be settled out of court, the disputants, the judicial system, or the legislature. Globally overstated, those alternatives to the courts, which have been created by the courts (or legislatures at the beckoning of the courts), often have a coercive quality that seriously jeopardizes weaker, less knowledgeable or more fearful disputants who must speak for themselves in such a system. ADR should not be permitted where obvious power imbalances exist. For example, sending an abused spouse off to mediate with an abuser, which some criminal courts are doing, seems especially wrong-headed and even dangerous. Victims cannot bargain freely and have no reason to believe they will not suffer for having honestly expressed their needs.

Couples with relatively balanced communication abilities who want to resolve their family problems in a less alienating environment than the courts may choose mediation. Done skillfully, the process can help people learn to handle their problems more effectively. It remains to be seen whether court-ordered mediation can be structured in a way that protects the integrity of the disputants and balances their bargaining strength.

Perhaps the most far-reaching concern about alternative dispute resolution in family matters is the current lack of training standards or accreditation for private family mediators. Training requirements literally do not exist yet in most states. Organizations advancing family mediation are involved in spirited debate over whether lay or professional qualifications should be required, what standards should apply, and how to monitor or enforce those standards for the protection of the consuming public. If and when standards are established, many who presently practice family mediation will likely be allowed to continue whether they meet those standards or not. Some couples are thus left vulnerable to inadequate assistance.

The available research on the mediation process, although limited, is worth noting. Pearson and Thoenes (1981) found that about half of those referred for mediation did not accept the offer. Of those who did, 58% came to an agreement and, of those who did, more were likely to report a good relationship with a former spouse as time passed. Many felt some satisfaction in having made the effort to settle differences through mediation, even if the process was unsuccessful. They identified the following factors associated with successful mediation: (a) an experienced mediator, (b) spouses with some interest in communicating with each other, (c) low-intensity conflict, and (d) disputes that did not involve extended family members or other third parties. More research is necessary to reach high-level confidence in such conclusions.

CONCLUSION

It is hoped that social scientists and mental health professionals will be available when called upon to assist the courts in making difficult custody determinations; in developing treatment plans for juvenile delinquents, batterers, and family violence victims; in developing plans for dysfunctional families involved in abuse or neglect of their children; and in establishing goals for the reunification of families.

Communities bear some responsibility to assess what they are doing to support family life. Judges and lawyers involved in the administration of family law, social scientists, family therapists, and others with special knowledge and skills in dealing with families, together with ordinary citizens, are needed to make communities better, safer places for children and families to thrive. By applying the best knowledge available and marshaling the political support necessary to try out potentially effective approaches, improvements may be possible.

NOTES

1. While I am certain that having a child support standard and mandatory enforcement will be important to many states that have been less effective in this area, for states like Michigan the effect of the new standard seems to portend an overall

reduction in funds available for the support of children of divorce. This may be particularly true for middle-class and upper-middle-class families. In a few years one may find that the new guidelines, because of their complexity, will have benefited attorneys more than any other class of individuals involved with divorcing families.

The problem arises from this question: Do the quoted percentages of income pertain to the gross income of the *payor* parent or to the gross income for *both* parents? The effect of the latter approach, which is Michigan's, can be dramatic. For example, consider the situation where the payor parent earns $750.00 per week and the custodial parent has no income. With one child the custodial parent receives $127.50 per week toward the support of the child. Next, consider the same income but split between the parents with the payor parent earning $500.00 per week and the custodial parent earning $250.00 per week. Support falls to $85.00 per week for the child of that relationship. These numbers correspond to the new Michigan guidelines. Is the custodial parent, with little better than marginal employment, able effectively to make up the difference through his or her wages?

The percentages that are being used in the new standardized guidelines are often well below standards that had previously existed. In Washtenaw County, Michigan, support for one child has been 26% of the noncustodial parent's net income up to $500.00 per week and an average of 17% of net dollars above that amount. For two children the schedule computed 35% of the noncustodial parent's net income and 19% above $500.00. Three, four, and five children were computed on a basis of 40%, 45% and 50%, respectively. Reducing factors were applied where custodians had income, but never more than 30%. The Wisconsin schedule uses gross income whereas Michigan's former schedule used net income. Still, at low- to moderate-income levels, the effect is a reduction in child support.

References

Abidin, R.R. (Ed.) (1980). *Parent education and intervention handbook*. Springfield, Il: Thomas.

Ackerman, N. (1958). *The psychodynamics of family life*. New York: Basic Books.

Ackerman, N. (1970). Family psychotherapy and psychoanalysis: The implication of difference. In N. Ackerman (Ed.), *Family Process*. New York: Basic Books.

Aguiree, B.E. (1985). Why do they return? Abused wives in shelters. *Social Work, 30*(4), 350–354.

Ahrons, C. (1983). Predictors of paternal involvement postdivorce: Mothers' and fathers' perceptions. *Journal of Divorce, 6*(3), 55–69.

Ahrons, C.R. (1980a). *The continuing coparental relationship between divorced spouses*. Paper presented at the 1980 annual meeting of the American Orthopsychiatric Association, Toronto, Canada.

Ahrons, C.R. (1980b). Joint custody arrangements in the postdivorce family. *Journal of Divorce, 3*(3), 189–206.

Ainsworth, F., & Fulcher, L.C. (Eds.) (1981). *Group care of children: Concepts and issues*. London and New York: Tavistock Publications.

Ainsworth, M., Blehar, M., Waters, E., & Wall, S. (1978). *Patterns of attachment*. Hillsdale, NJ: Erlbaum.

Aldgate, J. (1980). Identification of factors influencing children's length of stay in care. In J. Triseliotis (Ed.), *New developments in foster care and adoption* (pp. 22–40). London and Boston: Routledge and Kegan Paul.

Alexander, J.F., & Barton, C. (1976). Behavioral systems therapy for families. In D.H. Olsen (Ed.), *Treating relationships*. Lake Mills, IA: Graphic.

Alexander, J.F., & Parsons, B.V. (1982). *Functional family therapy*. Monterey, CA: Brooks/Cole.

Alexander, J.F., & Parsons, B.V. (1973). Short-term behavioral intervention with delinquent families: Impact on family process and recidivism. *Journal of Abnormal Psychology, 81*, 219–225.

Allen, C.M., & Straus, M.S. (1980). Resources, power, and husband–wife violence. In M.A. Straus & G.T. Hotaling (Eds.), *The social causes of husband–wife violence* (Ch. 12). Minneapolis: University of Minnesota Press.

Allen, F.H. (1942). *Psychotherapy with children*. New York: Norton.

Allen, M.L., Golubock, C., & Olson, L. (1983). A guide to the Adoption Assistance and Child Welfare Act of 1980. In M. Hardin (Ed.), *Foster children in the courts* (pp. 575–609). Boston: Butterworth Legal Publishers.

Allerhand, M.E., Weber, R., & Haug, M. (1966). *Adaptation and adaptability: The Bellefaire follow-up study*. New York: Child Welfare League of America.

American Association for Protecting Children (1986). *Highlights of official child neglect and abuse reporting 1984*. Denver: Author.

American Bar Association (1981). *Child abuse and neglect litigation: A manual for judges*. National Legal Resource Center for Child Advocacy and Protection.

American Bar Association (1986). *Revised draft of model joint custody statute*. Annual Meeting Compendium, Section on Family Law.

Anderson, S.A.; Russell, C.S.; & Schumm, W.R. (1983). Perceived marital quality and family life-cycle categories: A further analysis. *Journal of Marriage and the Family, 47,* 127–139.

Andrews, F., & Withey, S. (1976). *Social indicators of well-being: Americans' perceptions of life quality.* New York: Plenum.

Archer, D., & Garter, R. (1984). *Violence and crime in cross-national perspective.* New Haven, CT: Yale University Press.

Armentrout, J., & Burger, C. (1972). Children's reports on parental childrearing behavior at five grade levels. *Developmental Psychology, 7,* 44–48.

Atkeson, B.M., & Forehand, R. (1978). Parent behavioral training for problem children: An examination of studies using multiple outcome measures. *Journal of Abnormal Child Psychology, 6*(4), 449–460.

Bakan, D. (1971). *Slaughter of the innocents: A study of the battered child phenomenon.* Boston: Beacon Press.

Baker, L. (1981). *The transition to divorce: Discrepancies between husbands and wives.* Unpublished doctoral dissertation, Purdue University.

Ball, P.G., & Wyman, E. (1978). Battered wives: Barriers to identification and treatment. *American Journal of Orthopsychiatry, 2*(3–4), 545–552.

Bane, M.J. (1976). Marital disruption and the lives of children. *Journal of Social Issues, 32,* 103–117.

Bannon, J. (1975). *Law enforcement problems with intra-family violence.* Unpublished manuscript. Detroit Police Department. (Summarized in *Violence against women* (1981), United States Department of Health and Human Services).

Baron, L., & Straus, M.A. (1988, in press). Cultural and economic sources of homicide. *Sociological Quarterly.*

Baron, L., Straus, M.A., & Jaffee, D. (1988, in press). Legitimate violence, violent attitudes, and rape: A test of the cultural spillover theory. *Annals of the New York Academy of Sciences.*

Barrett, C.L., Hampe, I.E., & Miller, L.C. (1978). Research on child psychotherapy. In S.L. Garfield & A.E. Bergin (Eds.), *Handbook of psychotherapy and behavior change* (2nd ed.). New York: Wiley.

Barth, R.P., & Berry, M. (in press). Outcomes of child welfare services under permanency planning. *Social Service Review.*

Barton, C., Alexander, J.F., Wandron, H., Turner, C.W., & Warburton, J. (1985). Generalizing treatment effects of functional family therapy: Three replications. *American Journal of Family Therapy, 13*(3), 16–26.

Bateson, G. (1971). *Steps to an ecology of mind.* New York: Ballantine Books.

Bateson, G., Jackson, D., Haley, J., & Weakland, Jr. (1956). Toward a theory of schizophrenia. *Behavioral Science, 1*(4), 251–264.

Baucom, D., & Hoffman, J. (1986). The effectiveness of marital therapy: Current status and application to the clinical setting. In N. Jacobson, & A. Gurman (Eds.), *Clinical handbook of marital therapy.* New York: Guilford.

Baucom, D., & Lester, G. (November 1982). *The utility of cognitive restructuring as a supplement to behavioral marital therapy.* Paper presented at the annual meeting of the Association for the Advancement of Behavior Therapy, Los Angeles.

Baumrind, D. (1973). The development of instrumental competence through socialization. In A. Pick (Ed.), *Minnesota Symposium on Child Psychology, 7,* University of Minnesota Press.

Belsky, J. (1984). The determinants of parenting: A process model. *Child Development, 55,* 83–96.

Benedek, E.P., & Benedek, R.S. (1979). Joint custody: Solution or illusion? *American Journal of Psychiatry, 136,* 1540–1544.

Benn, R. (1985). *Factors associated with security of attachment in dual career families.* Paper given at biennial conference of the Society for Research in Child Development, Toronto.

Bernstein, B. (1977). Lawyer and counselor as an interdisciplinary team: Preparing the father for custody. *Journal of Marriage and Family Counseling, 3,* 29–40.

Billings, A. (1979). Conflict resolution in distressed and nondistressed married couples. *Journal of Consulting and Clinical Psychology, 47,* 368–376.

Birchler, G.R., Weiss, R.L., & Vincent, J.P. (1975). Multimethod analysis of social reinforcement exchange between distressed and nondistressed spouse and stranger dyads. *Journal of Personality and Social Psychology, 31,* 349–366.

Bird, H.W., Schuham, A.I., Benson, L., & Gans, L.L. (1981). Stressful life events and marital dysfunction. *Hospital & Community Psychiatry, 32,* 386–490.

Blackstone, Sir W. (1768). *Commentaries on the laws of England.* London: Houghton Mifflin.

Blades, J. (1984). Mediation: An old art revitalized. *Mediation Quarterly, 3,* 59–98.

Bloom, B.L., Asher, S.J., & White, S.W. (1978). Marital disruption as a stressor: A review and analysis. *Psychological Bulletin, 85,* 867–894.

Bloom, B.L., White, S.W., Asher, S.J. (1979). Marital disruption as a stressful life event. In G. Levinger, & O.C. Moles (Eds.), *Divorce and separation: Context, causes, and consequences.* New York: Basic Books.

Blumenthal, K., & Weinberg, A. (Eds.) (1984). *Establishing parent involvement in foster care agencies.* New York: Child Welfare League of America.

Boelens, W., Emmelkamp, P., MacGillavry, D., & Markvoort, M. (1980). A clinical evaluation of marital treatment: Reciprocity counseling vs. system-theoretic counseling. *Behavioral Analysis and Modification, 4,* 85–96.

Bograd, M. (1984). Family systems approach to wife battering: A feminist critique. *American Journal of Orthopsychiatry, 54,* 558–568.

Boothe, A. (1979). Does wives' employment cause stress for husbands? *The Family Coordinator, 28,* 486–490.

Boszormenyi-Nagy, I., & Spark, G.M. (1973). *Invisible loyalties.* New York: Harper & Row.

Boulding, E. (1979). Family wholeness: New conceptions of family rules. In K. Feinstein (Ed.), *Working women and their families.* Beverly Hills: Sage.

Bowen, M. (1960). Family concept of schizophrenia. In D. Jackson (Ed.), *The etiology of schizophrenia.* New York: Basic Books.

Bowen, M. (1961). Family psychotherapy. *American Journal of Orthopsychiatry, 31,* 40–60.

Bowen, M. (1978). *Family therapy in clinical practice.* New York: Jason Aronson.

Bowker, L.H. (1983). *Beating wife-beating.* Lexington, MA: Heath.

Brocki, S. (1979). *Marital status, sex and mental well-being.* Unpublished doctoral dissertation, Vanderbilt University, Nashville, TN.

Bronfenbrenner, U. (1958). Socialization and social class through time and space. In E.E. Maccoby, T. Newcomb, & E. Hartley (Eds.), *Readings in social psychology* (pp. 400–425). New York: Holt.

Bronfenbrenner, U., Moen, P., & Garbarino, J. (1984). Child, family and community. In R. Parke (Ed.), *The family.* Chicago: University of Chicago Press. *Review of Child Development Research, 7,* 283–328.

Brown, B.F. (1980, April). A study of the school needs of children in one-parent families. *Phi Delta Kappan*, 537–540.

Brown, E.M. (1976). Divorce counseling. In D.H. Olson (Ed.), *Treating relationships* (pp. 399–429). Lake Mills, IA: Graphic.

Brown, J.H., Finch, W.A., Northen, H., Taylor, S.H., & Weil, M. (1982). *Child, family, neighborhood: A master plan for social service delivery*. New York: Child Welfare League of America.

Brown, M.D. (1985). Creating new realities for the newly divorced: A structural strategic approach for divorce therapy with an individual. In D.H. Sprenkle (Ed.), *Divorce therapy* (pp. 101–120). New York: Haworth Press.

Browne, A. (1987). *When battered women kill*. New York: Free Press.

Brutz, J., & Ingoldsby, B.B. (1984). Conflict resolution in Quaker families. *Journal of Marriage and the Family, 46*(1), 21–26.

Bryce, M., & Lloyd, C. (Eds.) (1981). *Treating families in the home: An alternative to placement*. Springfield, IL: Thomas.

Buckley, W. (1968). Society as a complex adaptive system. In W. Buckley (Ed.), *Modern systems research for the behavioral scientist*. Chicago: Aldine.

Burke, E.W., & Weir, T. (1976). Relationship of wives' employment status to husband, wife, and pair satisfaction and performance. *Journal of Marriage and the Family, 38*, 279–287.

Burke, R.J., Weir, T., & DuWors, R.E. (1979). Type A behavior of administrators and wives' reports of marital satisfaction and well-being. *Journal of Applied Psychology, 64*, 57–65.

Burr, W.R. (1970). Satisfaction with various aspects of marriage over the life cycle: A random middle class sample. *Journal of Marriage and the Family, 32*, 29–37.

Butchorn, L. (1985). *Social networks and the battered woman's decision to stay or leave*. Unpublished doctoral dissertation, Boston University, Boston.

Cadoret, R., & Cain, C. (1980). Sex differences in predictors of antisocial behavior in adoptees. *Archives of General Psychiatry, 17*, 1171–1175.

Caffey, J. (1946). Multiple fractures in the long bones of infants suffering from chronic subdural hematoma. *American Journal of Roentgenology, Radium Therapy, and Nuclear Medicine, 56*, 163–173.

California Civil Code. Section 4600.5 [h].

Campbell, A. (1980). *The sense of well-being in America*. New York: McGraw-Hill.

Campbell, A., Converse, P.E., & Rodgers, W.L. (1976). *The quality of American life*. New York: Russell Sage Foundation.

Cantor, D.W., & Drake, E.A. (1984). *Divorced parents and their children: A guide for mental health professionals*. New York: Springer.

Caplan, G. (Ed.) (1955). *Emotional problems of early childhood*. New York: Basic Books.

Carbino, R. (1980). *Foster parenting—An updated review of the literature*. New York: Child Welfare League of America.

Carbino, R. (1981). Developing a parent organization: New roles for parents of children in substitute care. In A.N. Maluccio, & P.A. Sinanoglu (Eds.), *The challenge of partnership: Working with parents of children in foster care* (pp. 165–186). New York: Child Welfare League of America.

Carlo, P. (1985). The children's residential treatment center as a living laboratory for family members: A review of the literature and its implications for practice. *Child Care Quarterly, 14*, 156–170.

Carmody, D.C., & Williams, K.R. (1987, in press). Wife assault and perceptions of sanctions. *Violence and Victims.*

Carter, E., & McGoldrick, M. (1980). *The family life cycle: A framework for family therapy.* New York: Gardner Press.

Cate, R.M., Henton, J.M., Joval, K., Christopher, F.S., & Lloyd, S. (1982). Premarital abuse: A social psychological perspective. *Journal of Family Issues, 3,* 79–90.

Cherlin, A.J. (1981). *Marriage, divorce, remarriage.* Cambridge, MA: Harvard University Press.

Child Support Enforcement Amendments (1984). PL 98–378.

Chilman, C. (1968). Fertility and poverty in the United States: Some implications for family planning programs, policy and research. *Journal of Marriage and the Family, 30*(2), 207–228.

Chilman, C. (1979). Parent satisfactions–disatisfactions and their correlates. *Social Service Review, 53* (2), 195–213.

Chilman C. (1980). Parent satisfactions, concerns and goals for their children. *Family Relations, 29*(3), 339–345.

Chilman, C. (1983). *Adolescent sexuality in a changing American society: Perspectives for human service professionals.* New York: Wiley.

Chodorow, N. (1978). *The reproduction of mothering.* Berkeley: University of California Press.

Clarke-Stewart, A. (1977). *Child care in the family.* New York: Academic Press.

Cleary, P.D., & Mechanic, D. (1983). Sex differences in psychological distress among married people. *Journal of Health and Social Behavior, 24,* 111–121.

Clingembeel, W.G., & Reppucci, N.D. (1982). Joint custody after divorce: Major issues and goals for research. *Psychological Bulletin, 91,* 102–127.

Coates, R.B.; Miller, A.D.; & Ohlin, L.E. (1978). *Diversity in a youth correctional system.* Cambridge, MA: Ballinger.

Cohen, N.J., Sullivan, J., Minde, K., Novak, C., & Helwig, C. (1981). Evaluation of the relative effectiveness of methylphenidate and cognitive behavior modification in the treatment of kindergarten-aged hyper-active children. *Journal of Abnormal Child Psychology, 9*(1), 43–54.

Cohen, S.N. (1985). Divorce mediation: An introduction. In D.H. Sprenkle (Ed.), *Divorce therapy* (pp. 69–84). New York: Haworth Press.

Cole, C.L., Cole, A.L., & Dean, D.G. (1980). Emotional maturity and marital adjustment: A decade replication. *Journal of Marriage and the Family, 42,* 533–539.

Coleman, D.H., & Straus, M.A. (1983). Alcohol abuse and family violence. In E. Gottheil, K.A. Druley, T.E. Skolada, & H.M. Waxman (Eds.), *Alcohol, drug abuse and aggression.* Springfield, Il: Thomas.

Coleman, J.C. (1980). Friendship and the peer groups in adolescence. In J. Adelson (Ed.), *Handbook of adolescent psychology.* New York: Wiley.

Coleman, K.H. (1980). Conjugal violence: What 33 men report. *Journal of Marital and Family Therapy, 6*(2), 207–213.

Coletta, N. (1983). At risk for depression: A study of young mothers. *Journal of Genetic Psychology, 142,* 301–310.

Conger, J. (1973). *Adolescence and youth.* New York: Harper & Row.

Conger, R., McCarthy, J., Yang, R., Lake, B., & Kropp, J. (In press). Perception of child, childrearing values, and emotional distress. *Child Development.*

Conn, J.H. (1939). The child reveals himself through play: The method of the play interview. *Mental Hygiene, XXIII,* 46–49.

Coopersmith, S. (1967). *The antecedents of self-esteem*. San Francisco: Freeman.

Crohn, H., Brown, H., Walker, L., & Beir, J. (1981). Understanding and treating the child in the remarried family. In I.R. Stuart & L.E. Abt (Eds.), *Children of separation and divorce: Management and treatment*. New York: Van Nostrand Reinhold.

Crowe, M. (1978). Conjoint marital therapy: A controlled outcome study. *Psychological Medicine, 8,* 623–636.

Cvetkovich, G., & Grote, B. (1975). *Antecedents of responsible family formation*. Progress report paper presented at a conference sponsored by the Population Division, National Institute of Child Health and Human Development, Bethesda, MD.

Davidson, B. (1984). A test of equity theory for marital adjustment. *Social Psychology Quarterly, 47*(1), 36–42.

Davidson, B., Balswick, J., & Halverson, C. (1983). Affective self-disclosure and marital adjustment: A test of equity theory. *Journal of Marriage and the Family, 45,* 93–113.

Davies, L., & Bland, D. (1978). The use of foster parents as role models for parents. *Child Welfare, 57,* 380–386.

Davis, E.G. (1971). *The first sex*. New York: Putnam.

Dean, D.G. (1966). Emotional maturity and marital adjustment. *Journal of Marriage and the Family, 28,* 454–457.

De Mause, L. (1974). *The history of childhood*. New York: Psychohistory Press.

De Mause, L. (Ed.) (April 1975). Our forebearers made childhood a nightmare. *Psychology Today,* 5–87.

Derdeyn, A.P. (1975). Child custody consultation. *American Journal of Orthopsychiatry, 45,* 791–801.

Derdeyn, A.P. (1976). Child custody contests in historical perspective. *American Journal of Orthopsychiatry, 133,* 1369–1376.

Derdeyn, A.P. (1978). Child custody: A reflection of cultural change. *Journal of Clinical Child Psychology, 7,* 169–173.

Deschner, J.P. (1984). *The hitting habit: Anger control for battering couples*. New York: Free Press.

de Shazer, S. (1982). *Patterns of brief family therapy: An ecosystemic approach*. New York: Guilford.

de Shazer, S. (1984). Death of resistance. *Family Process, 23*(1), 11–21.

de Shazer, S. (1985). *Keys to solution in brief therapy*. New York: Norton.

de Shazer, S., & Berg, I. (1985). A part is not apart: Working with one of the partners present. In A. Gurman (Ed.), *Casebook of marital therapy*. New York: Guilford.

de Shazer, S., Berg, I.K., Lipchik, E., Nunnally, E., Molnar, A., Gingerich, W., & Weiner-Davis, M. (1986). Brief therapy: Focused solution development. *Family Process, 25*(2), 207–223.

de Shazer, S., Gingerich, W., & Weiner-Davis, M. (1985). *Coding family therapy interviews: What does the therapist do that is worth doing?* Paper presented at the annual conference of the American Association for Marriage and Family Therapy, New York.

De Witt, K.N. (1978). The effectiveness of family therapy: A review of outcome research. *Archives of General Psychiatry, 35*(5), 549–561.

Dhir, K., & Markman, H.J. (1984). Application of social judgement theory to understanding and treating marital conflict. *Journal of Marriage and the Family, 46,* 597–610.

Dobash, R.E., & Dobash, R. (1979). *Violence against wives: A case against patriarchy.* New York: Free Press.

Doherty, G. (1975). Basic life-skills and parent effectiveness training with the mothers of acting-out adolescents. *Journal of Clinical Child Psychology, 31,* 3–6.

Doherty, W.J., & Colangelo, N. (1984). The family FIRO model: A model proposal for organizing family treatment. *Journal of Marital and Family Therapy, 10*(1), 19–31.

Dollard, J., & Miller, N. (1950). *Personality and psychotherapy.* New York: McGraw-Hill.

Douvan, E., & Elder, G. (Eds.) (1975). *The adolescence and the life cycle.* New York: Wiley.

Dubey, D.R., O'Leary, S.G.; & Kaufman, K.F. (1983). Training parents of hyperactive children in child management: A comparative outcome study. *Journal of Abnormal Child Psychology, 11*(2), 229–245.

Dumas, J.E. (1984). Interactional correlates of treatment outcome in behavioral parent training. *Journal of Consulting and Clinical Psychology, 52*(6), 946–954.

Dumas, J.E., & Wahler, R.G. (1983). Predictors of treatment outcome in parent training: Mother insularity and socioeconomic disadvantage. *Behavioral Assessment, 5,* 301–313.

Durkin, R.P., & Durkin, A.B. (1975). Evaluating residential treatment programs for disturbed children. In M. Guttentag & E.L. Struening (Eds.), *Handbook of evaluation research* (Vol. 2). Beverly Hills, CA: Sage.

Dyer, E. (1963). Parenthood as crisis: A restudy. *Marriage and Family Living, 25,* 196–201.

Eastman, K.S. (1985). Foster families: A comprehensive bibliography. *Child Welfare, 64,* 565–585.

Elder, G. (1974). *Children of the great depression.* Chicago: University of Chicago Press.

Elder, G. (1984). Families, kin, and the life course. In R. Parke (Ed.), *The family.* Chicago: University of Chicago Press, 1984. *Review of Child Development Research, 7,* 329–350.

Elder, G., Caspi, A., & Downey, G. (1986). Problem behavior and family relationships: A multi-generational analysis. In A. Sorenson, F. Weinert, & L. Sherrod (Eds.), *Human development: Interdisciplinary perspectives* (pp. 293–340). New York: Harper & Row.

Elkind, D. (1967). Egocentrism in adolescence. *Child Development, 38*(4), 1025–1034.

Elster, A., & Lamb, M. (1986). Adolescent fathers: The under-studied side of adolescent pregnancy. In J. Lancaster & B. Hamburg (Eds.), *School-age pregnancy and parenthood.* New York: Aldine De Gruyter.

Ely, A., Guerney, B., & Stover, L. (1973). Efficacy of the training phase of conjugal therapy. *Psychotherapy: Therapy, Research and Practice, 10,* 201–207.

Emery, R.E. (1982). Interparental conflict and children of discord and divorce. *Psychological Bulletin, 92,* 310–330.

Eno, M.M. (1985). Sibling relationships in families of divorce. In D.H. Sprenkle (Ed.), *Divorce therapy* (pp. 139–156). New York: Norton.

Entwisle, D., & Doering, S. (1981). *The first birth.* Baltimore: Johns Hopkins University Press.

Epstein, N., & Jackson, F. (1978). An outcome study of short-term communication training with married couples. *Journal of Consulting and Clinical Psychology, 46,* 207–212.

Eysenck, H.J. (1960). Learning theory and behavior therapy. In H.J. Eysenck (Ed.), *Behavior therapy and the neuroses.* London: Pergamon Press.

Fein, E., Maluccio, A.N., Hamilton, V.J., & Ward, D.L. (1983). After foster care: Outcomes of permanency planning for children. *Child Welfare, 62,* 485–562.

Feldman, H., & Feldman, M. (1975). The family life cycle: Some suggestions for recycling. *Journal of Marriage and the Family, 37,* 227–284.

Feldman, L. (1976). Goals of family therapy. *Journal of Marrige and Family Counseling, 2,* 103–113.

Feldman, L.B. (1985). Integrative multi-level therapy: A comprehensive interpersonal and intrapsychic approach. *Journal of Marital and Family Therapy, 11*(4), 357–373.

Felner, R.D., Stolberg, A.L., & Cowen, E.L. (1975). Crisis events and school mental health referral patterns of young children. *Journal of Consulting and Clinical Psychology, 43,* 303–310.

Field, M.H., & Field, H.F. (1973). Marital violence and the criminal process: Neither justice nor peace. *Social Service Review, 47*(2), 221–240.

Field, T. (1984). Early interactions between infants and their post-partum depressed mothers. *Infant Behavior and Development, 7,* 517–523.

Field, T., & Widmayer, S. (1982). Motherhood. In B. Wolman (Ed.), *Handbook of developmental psychology* (pp. 681–701). Englewood Cliffs, NJ: Prentice-Hall.

Finkelstein, N.E. (1981). Family-centered group care—The children's institution, from a living center to a center for change. In A.N. Maluccio & P.A. Sinanoglu (Eds.), *The challenge of partnership: Working with parents of children in foster care* (pp. 89–105). New York: Child Welfare League of America.

Fisher, B. (1981). *Rebuilding: When your relationship ends.* San Luis Obispo, CA: Impact.

Fitzharris, T.L. (1985). *Profiles of 10,000 children in residential care.* Sacramento, CA: Children's Services Foundation.

Fleischmann, M.J. (1981). A replication of Patterson's "intervention for boys with conduct disorder problems." *Journal of Consulting and Clinical Psychology, 49,* 343–351.

Fleuridas, C., Nelson, T.S., & Rosenthal, D.M. (1986). The evaluation of circular questions: Training family therapists. *Journal of Marital and Family Therapy, 12,* 113–128.

Floyd, F.J., & Markman, H.J. (1983). Observational biases in spouse observation: Toward a cognitive/behavioral model of marriage. *Journal of Consulting and Clinical Psychology, 51*(3), 450–457.

Forehand, R., Griest, D.L., & Wells, I.C. (1979). Parent behavioral training: An analysis of the relationship among multiple outcome measures. *Journal of Abnormal Child Psychology, 7*(3), 229–242.

Forman, B., Hagan, D., & Brian, J. (1984). Measures for evaluating total family functioning. *Family Therapy, 11*(1), 1–36.

Francke, L.B. (1983). *Growing up divorced.* New York: Linden Press.

Fraser, J.S. (1984a). Process level integration: Corrective vision for a binocular view. *Journal of Strategic and Systemic Therapies, 3*(3), 43–57.

Fraser, J.S. (1984b). Paradox and orthodox: Folie a deux? *Journal of Marital and Family Therapy, 10,* 361–372.

Fraser, J.S. (1986a). The crisis intervention: Strategic rapid intervention. *Journal of Strategic and Systemic Therapies, 5*(1–2), 71–87.

Fraser, J.S. (1986b). Integrating system based therapies: Similarities, differences, and some critical questions. In D.E. Efron (Ed.), *Journeys: Expansion of the strategic-system therapies* (pp. 125–149). New York: Brunner/Mazel.

Freed, D.J., & Foster, H.H. (1974). The shuffled child and divorce court. *Trial, 10,* 11–24.

Freud, A. (1946). *The psychoanalytic treatment of children.* London: Imao.

Freud, S. (1955). *Analysis of a phobia in a five-year-old boy* (J. Strachey, Ed. & Trans.). London: Hogarth Press. (Original work published 1909.)

Furstenberg, F., Jr. (1976). *Unplanned parenthood: The social consequences of teen-age childbearing.* New York: Free Press.

Furstenberg, F., Jr. (1982). Conjugal succession: Reentering marriage after divorce. In P.B. Baltes & O.G. Brim (Eds.), *Life-span development and behavior* (Vol. 4). New York: Academic Press.

Gagnon, J., & Simon, W. (1973). Youth, sex, and the future. In H. Gottlieb (Ed.), *Youth in contemporary society.* Beverly Hills, CA: Sage.

Gambrill, E.D., & Stein, T. J. (Eds.) (1985). Permanency planning for children: Special issue. *Children and Youth Services Review, 7*(2/3), 38, 77–281.

Gaquin, D.A. (1978). Spouse abuse: Data from the national crime survey. *Victimology, 2,* 632–643.

Gardner, R.A. (1971. *The boys and girls book about divorce.* New York: Bantam Books.

Gardner, R.A. (1976). *Psychotherapy and children of divorce.* New York: Jason Aronson.

Gardner, R.A. (1978). *The boys and girls book about one-parent families.* New York: Bantam Books.

Gardner, R.A. (1982). *Family evaluation in child custody litigation.* Cresskill, NJ: Creative Therapeutics.

Garfield, S.L., & Bergin, A.E. (1986). *Handbook of psychotherapy and behavior change* (3rd ed.). New York: Wiley.

Garfinkel, I. (1987). Child support. *Encyclopedia of Social Work, Vol. 1* (18th ed., pp. 260–265). Silver Spring, MD: National Association of Social Workers.

Gelles, R.J. (1974). *The violent home: A study of physical aggression between husbands and wives.* Beverly Hills, CA: Sage.

Gelles, R.J., & Straus, M.A. (1979). Determinants of violence in the family: Toward a theoretical integration. In W.R. Burr, R. Hill, F.I. Nye & I.L. Reiss (Eds.), *Contemporary theories about the family* (pp. 549–581). New York: Free Press.

Gelles, R.J., & Straus, M.A. (1987). Is violence toward children increasing? A comparison of 1975 and 1985 national survey rates. *Journal of Interpersonal Violence 2,* 212–222.

Giles-Sims, J. (1983). *Wife battering: A systems theory approach.* New York: Guilford.

Girodo, M., Stein, S., & Dotzenroth, S. (1980). The effects of communication skills training and contracting on marital relations. *Behavioral Engineering, 6,* 61–76.

Goetting, A. (1980). *The effects of divorce on adults and children in contemporary American society: A review of research.* Paper presented at the annual meeting of the National Council on Family Relations, Portland, OR.

Goffman, J.M. (1984). *Batterers anonymous: Self-help counseling for men who batter women*. Homes Beach, FL: Learning Publications.

Goldstein, H.S. (1974). Reconstructed families: The second marriage and its children. *Psychiatric Quarterly, 48*, 433–440.

Goldstein, J., Freud, A., & Solnit, A. (1973). *Beyond the best interests of the child*. New York: Free Press.

Goldstein, J., Freud, A., & Solnit, A.J. (1979). *Before the best interests of the child*. New York: Free Press.

Goldstein, M. (1978). Further data concerning the relation between premarital adjustment and paranoid symptomatology. *Schizophrenia Bulletin, 4*, 236–243.

Goldzband, M.G. (1980). *Custody cases and expert witnesses: A manual for attorneys*. New York: Harcourt Brace Jovanovich.

Gondolf, E.W. (1985). *Men who batter: An integrated approach for stopping wife abuse*. Homes Beach, FL: Learning Publications.

Goode, W.J. (1974). Force and violence in the family. In S.K. Steinmetz & M.A. Straus (Eds.), *Violence in the family* (pp. 25–43). New York: Harper & Row.

Gordon, C. (1972). Social characteristics of early adolescence. In J. Kagan & R. Coles (Eds.), *Twelve to sixteen: Early adolescence*. Toronto: George J. MacLead.

Gove, W.R., Hughes, M., & Style, C.B. (1983). Does marriage have positive effects on the psychological well-being of the individual? *Journal of Health and Social Behavior, 24*, 122–131.

Granvold, D.K. (1983). Structured separation for marital treatment and decision-making. *Journal of Marital and Family Therapy, 9*, 403–412.

Green, B.L., Lee, R.R., & Lustig, N. (1973). Transient structured distance as a maneuver in marital therapy. *Family Coordinator, 20*, 15–22.

Greenblatt, C.S. (1983). A hit is a hit is a hit . . . or is it? Approval and tolerance of the use of physical force by spouses. In D. Finkelhor, R.J. Gelles, G.T. Hotaling, & M.A. Straus (Eds.), *The dark side of families*. Beverly Hills, CA: Sage.

Griest, D.L., & Wells, K.C. (1983). Behavioral family therapy with conduct disorders in children. *Behavior Therapy, 14*, 37–53.

Group for the Advancement of Psychiatry (1980). *Child custody and the family*. New York: Mental Health Materials Center.

Gurman, A.S., & Kniskern, D.P. (1981). Family therapy outcome research: Knowns and unknowns. In A.S. Gurman & D.P. Kniskern (Eds.), *Handbook of family therapy*. New York: Brunner/Mazel.

Gurman, A.S., Kniskern, D.P., & Pinsof, W.M. (1986). Research on the process and outcome of marital and family therapy. In S.L. Garfield & A.E. Bergin (Eds.), *Handbook of psychotherapy and behavior change* (3rd ed.). New York: Wiley.

Haeuser, A.A. (June 1985). *Social control over parents' use of physical punishment: Issues for cross-national child abuse research*. Paper presented at the United States–Sweden Joint Seminar on Physical and Sexual Abuse of Children, Satra Bruck, Sweden.

Hahlweg, K., Revenstorf, D., & Schindler, L. (1982). Treatment of marital distress: Comparing formats and modalities. *Advances in Behavior Research and Therapy, 4*, 57–74.

Hahlweg, K., Schindler, L., Revenstorf, D., & Brengelmann, J. (1984). The Munich marital therapy study. In K. Hahlweg & N. Jacobson (Eds.), *Marital interaction: Analysis and modification*. New York: Guilford.

Haley, J. (1963). *Strategies of psychotherapy*. New York: Grune & Stratton.

Haley, J. (1973a). Strategic therapy when a child is presented as a problem. *Journal of American Academy of Child Psychology, 12,* 64–74.

Haley, J. (1973b). *Uncommon therapy: The psychiatric techniques of Milton H. Erikson, M.M.* New York: Norton.

Haley, J. (1976). *Problem solving therapy.* San Francisco: Jossey-Bass.

Haley, J. (1980). *Leaving home: The therapy of disturbed young people.* New York: McGraw-Hill.

Hansen, J.C. (Ed.) (1982). *Therapy with remarriage families.* Rockville, MD: Aspen Systems.

Hardin, M., & Shalleck, A. (1985). *Court rules to achieve permanency for foster children: Sample rules and commentary.* Washington, DC: American Bar Association.

Harper, G. (1983). Varieties of parenting failure in anorexia nervosa: Protection and paretectomy, revisited. *Journal of American Academy of Child Psychology, 22*(2), 134.

Hartman, A., & Laird, J. (1983). *Family-centered social work practice.* New York: Free Press.

Hartup, W. (1978). Perspectives on child and family interaction: Past, present and future. In R. Lerner & G. Spanier (Eds.), *Child influences on family and marital interaction.* New York: Academic Press.

Hawkins, J.D. (1985). Executive summary. *Drug abuse, mental health and delinquency.* Washington, DC: Office of Juvenile Justice and Delinquency Prevention.

Hawkins, J.D., & Fraser, M. (1983). Social support networks in delinquency prevention and treatment. In J.D. Whittaker & J. Garbarino (Eds.), *Social support networks.* New York: Aldine.

Haynes, J.M. (1981). *Divorce mediation: A practical guide for therapists and counselors.* New York: Springer.

Heinicke, C. (1985). *Prebirth couple functioning and the quality of mother-infant relationships.* Paper presented at the Biennial Meetings of the Society for Research in Child Development, Toronto.

Henton, J., Cate, R., Koval, J., Lloyd, S., & Christopher, S. (1983). Romance and violence in dating relationships. *Journal of Family Issues, 4,* 467–482.

Hess, R.D., & Camara, K.A. (1979). Post-divorce relationships as mediating factors in the consequences of divorce for children. *Journal of Social Issues, 35,* 79–96.

Hetherington, E. (1979). Divorce: A child's perspective. *American Psychology, 34,* 79–96.

Hetherington, E., Cox, M., & Cox, R. (1978). The aftermath of divorce. In H. Stevens & M. Mathews (Eds.), *Mother–child relations.* Washington, DC: National Association for the Education of Young Children.

Hetherington, E.M., Cox, M., & Cox, R. (1981). The aftermath of divorce. In E.M. Hetherington & R.D. Parke (Eds.), *Contemporary readings in child psychology* (pp. 234–249). New York: McGraw-Hill.

Hetherington, E.M., Cox, M., & Cox, R. (1982). Effects of divorce on parents and children. In M.E. Lamb (Ed.), *Nontraditional families: Parenting and child development.* Hillsdale, NJ: Lawrence Erlbaum Associates.

Hetherington, M. (1984). Stress and coping in children and families. In A. Doyle, D. Gold, & D. Moskowitz (Eds.), *Children in families under stress.* San Francisco: Jossey-Bass.

Hetherington, M., Cox, M., & Cox, R. (1979). The development of children in mother-headed families. In H. Hoffman & D. Reiss (Eds.), *The American family: Dying or developing?* New York: Plenum.

Hilbert, C.H., & Hilbert, H.C. (1984). Battered women leaving shelter: Which way do they go? A discriminant function analysis. *Journal of Applied Social Sciences, 8*(2), 291–297.

Hobbs, D. (1963). Parenthood as crisis: A third study. *Journal of Marriage and the Family, 27,* 367–372.

Hoffman, L., & Manis, J. (1978). Influence of children on marital interaction and parental satisfactions and dissatisfactions. In R. Lerner & G. Spanier (Eds.), *Child influences on marital and family interaction: A lifespan perspective.* New York: Academic Press.

Hoffman, L., Thornton, A., & Manis, J. (1978). The value of children to parents in the United States population. *Journal of Population, 1,* 91–131.

Homans, G. (1961). *Social behavior: Its elementary forms.* New York: Harcourt Brace.

Homatidis, S., & Konstantareas, M.M. (1981). Assessment of hyperactivity: Isolating measures of high discriminant ability. *Journal of Consulting and Clinical Psychology, 49*(4) 533–541.

Hoover, C.F., & Fitzgerald, R.G. (1981). Dominance in the marriages of affectional patients. *Journal of Nervous and Mental Disease, 160*(11), 624–628.

Horejsi, C.R., Bertsche, A.V., & Clark, F.W. (1981). *Social work practice with parents of children in foster care: A handbook.* Springfield, IL: Thomas.

Hornung, C.A., McCullough, B.C., & Sugimoto, T. (1981). Status relationships in marriage: Risk factors in spouse abuse. *Journal of Marriage and the Family, 43,* 675–692.

Horowitz, R., & Dodson, G. (1985). *Child support, custody and visitation: A report to state child support commissions.* American Bar Association, Section on Family Law, 1986 Annual Meeting Compendium.

Huggins, M.D., & Straus, M.A. (1980). Violence and the social structure as reflected in children's books from 1850 to 1970. In M.A. Straus & G.T. Hotaling (Eds.), *The social causes of husband-wife violence* (pp. 51–67). Minneapolis: University of Minnesota Press.

Hughes, M., & Gove, W. (1981). Living alone, social integration and mental health. *American Journal of Sociology, 87,* 48–74.

Huntington, D.S. (1982). Divorce and the development needs of children. In *Mediation of child custody and visitation disputes.* California: Association of Family and Conciliation Courts, Institute for Training and Research.

Ilfeld, F.W. (1980). Understanding marital stressors: The importance of coping styles. *Journal of Nervous and Mental Disease, 168*(6), 375–381.

Ilfeld, F.W., Jr., Ilfeld, H.Z., Alexander, J.R. (1982). Does joint custody work: A first look at outcome data of relitigation. *American Journal of Psychiatry, 139,* 62–66.

Imber-Black, E. (1986). *Family rituals.* Presentation at the annual meeting of the Indiana Association for Marital and Family Therapy, Indianapolis.

Irving, H.H. (1980). *Divorce mediation: A rational alternative to the adversary system.* New York: Universe Books.

Isaacs, M. (1982). Helping mom fail: A case of a stalemated divorcing process. *Family Process, 21,* 225–234.

Jackson, A.D., & Dunne, M.J. (1981). Permanency planning in foster care with the ambivalent parent. In A.N. Maluccio & P.A. Sinanoglu (Eds.), *The challenge of partnership: Working with parents of children in foster care* (pp. 39–51). New York: Child Welfare League of America. (M)

Jacobs, J.W. (1982). The effect of divorce on fathers: An overview of the literature. *American Journal of Psychiatry, 139*, 1235–1241.

Jacobson, D. (1978a). The impact of marital separation/divorce on children: I. Parent–child separation and child adjustment. *Journal of Divorce, 1*, 341–360.

Jacobson, D. (1978b). The impact of marital separation/divorce on children: II. Interparent hostility and child adjustment. *Journal of Divorce, 2*, 3–20.

Jacobson, D. (1978c). The impact of marital separation/divorce on children: III. Parent–child communication and child adjustment, and regression analysis of findings from overall study. *Journal of Divorce, 2*, 175–194.

Jacobson, D.S. (1983). *Conflict, visiting and child adjustment in the stepfamily: A linked family system.* Paper presented at annual meeting of the American Orthopsychiatric Association, Boston.

Jacobson, N., & Margolin, G. (1979). *Marital interaction.* New York: Brunner/Mazel.

Jacobson, N.S. (1985). Family therapy outcome research: Potential pitfalls and prospects. *Journal of Marital and Family Therapy, 11*(2), 149–159.

Jacobson, N.S., Waldron, H., & Moore, D. (1980). Toward a behavioral profile of marital distress. *Journal of Consulting and Clinical Psychology, 48*(6), 696–702.

Janchill, M.P. (1981). *Guidelines to decision making in child welfare.* New York: Human Services Workshops.

Janis, I.L. (1983). *Short-term counseling, guidelines based on recent research.* New Haven, CT: Yale University Press.

Janis, I.L., & Mann, L. (1977). *Decision making: A psychological analysis of conflict, choice, and commitment.* New York: Free Press.

Jansen, M.A., & Myers-Abell, J. (1980). Assertion training for battered women: A pilot program. *Social Work, 25*, 1964–1965.

Jenkins, S. (1981). The tie that binds. In A.N. Maluccio & P.A. Sinanoglu (Eds.), *The challenge of partnership: Working with parents of children in foster care* (pp. 39–51). New York: Child Welfare League of America.

Jenkins, S., & Norman, E. (1975). *Beyond placement: Mothers view foster care.* New York: Columbia University Press.

Jenson, J.M., Hawkins, J.D., & Catalano, R.L. (1986). *Social support in aftercare services for troubled youth.* Unpublished manuscript, University of Washington, Center for Social Welfare Research, Seattle.

Jenson, J., and Whittaker, J.K. (1987). Parental involvement in children's residential treatment: From placement to aftercare. *Children and Youth Services Review*, 81–100.

Jessor, S., & Jessor, R. (1975). Transition from virginity to nonvirginity among youth: A social-psychological study over time. *Development Psychology, 11*, 473–484.

Johnson, S., & Greenberg, L. (1985a). Differential effects of experiential and problem-solving interventions in resolving marital conflict. *Journal of Consulting and Clinical Psychology, 53*, 175–184.

Johnson, S., & Greenberg, L. (1985b). Emotionally focused couples therapy: An outcome study. *Journal of Marital and Family Therapy, 11*, 313–316.

Johnson, S.M. (1977). *First person singular.* New York: Lippincott.

Jones, M.A., Neuman, R., & Shyne, A. (1976). *A second chance for families.* New York: Child Welfare League of America.

Jones, R.R., Weinrott, M.R., & Howard, J.R. (1981). *Impact of the teaching-family model on troublesome youth: Findings from the national evaluation.* Rockville, MD: National Institutes of Mental Health.

Jorgensen, S.R. (1977). Societal class heterogamy, status striving, and perception of marital conflict: A partial replication and revision of Pearlin's Contingency Hypothesis. *Journal of Marriage and the Family, 39,* 653–689.

Jouriles, E.N., & O'Leary, K.D. (1985). Interspousal reliability of reports of marital violence. *Journal of Consulting and Clinical Psychology, 53,* 419–421.

Kalter, N. (1977). Children of divorce in an outpatient psychiatric population. *American Journal of Orthopsychiatry, 47,* 40–51.

Kamerman, S. (1987). Family: Nuclear. *Encyclopedia of Social Work. Vol. 1* (18th ed., pp. 540–548). Silver Spring, MD: National Association of Social Workers.

Kamerman, S., & Kahn, A. (1978). *Family policy: Government and family in fourteen countries.* New York: Columbia University Press.

Kantor, D., & Neal, J.H. (1985). Integrative shifts for the theory and practice of family systems therapy. *Family Process, 24*(1), 13–40.

Kaplan, L. (1986). *Working with multiproblem families.* Lexington, MA: Lexington Books, Heath.

Kaslow, F.W. (1981). Divorce and divorce therapy. In A.S. Gurman & D.P. Kniskern (Eds.), *Handbook of family therapy.* New York: Brunner/Mazel.

Kaslow, F.W. (1984). Divorce: An evolutionary process of change in the family system. *Journal of Divorce, 7,* 21–39.

Kaslow, F.W., & Steinburg, J. (1981). Ethical divorce therapy and divorce proceedings: A psycho-legal perspective. In L. L'Abate (Ed.), *Values, ethnics, legalities, and the family therapist.* Rockville, MD: Aspen Systems.

Katz, A.J., Krasinski, M., Philip, E.; & Wieser, C. (1975). Change in interactions as a measure of effectiveness in short term family therapy. *Family Therapy, 2*(1), 31–56.

Kaufman Kantor, G., & Straus, M.A. (1987). *Stopping the violence: Battered women, police utilization, and police response.* Paper presented at the 1987 annual meeting of the American Society of Criminology, Montreal.

Kazdin, A.E. (1981). Acceptability of child treatment techniques: The influence of treatment efficacy and adverse side effects. *Behavior Therapy, 12,* 493–506.

Kelly, J.B. (1981). The visiting relationships after divorce: Research findings and clinical implications. In I.R. Stuart & L.E. Abt (Eds.), *Children of separation and divorce: Management and treatment.* New York: Van Nostrand Reinhold.

Kelly, J.B., & Wallerstein, J.S. (1976). The effects of parental divorce: Experiences of the child in early latency. *American Journal of Orthopsychiatry, 46,* 20–32.

Kelly, J.B., & Wallerstein, J.S. (1979). The divorced child in the school. *National Principal, 59,* 51–58.

Kerr, M. (1981). Family systems theory and therapy. In A.S. Gurman & D.P. Kniskern (Eds.), *Handbook of family therapy* (Ch. 7). New York: Brunner/Mazel.

Kessler, J. (1966). *Psychopathology of childhood.* Englewood Cliffs, NJ: Prentice-Hall.

Kinney, J., Madsen, B., Fleming, T., & Haapala, D.A. (1977). Homebuilders: Keeping families together. *Journal of Consulting and Clinical Psychology, 45,* 667–673.

Kirsten, G., & Robertiello, R. (1978). *Big you, little you.* New York: Pocket Books.

Kitson, G.C., & Raschke, H.J. (1981). Divorce research: What we know; what we need to know. *Journal of Divorce, 4*(3), 1–38.

Klein, M. (1955). The psychoanalytic play technique. *American Journal of Orthopsychiatry, XXV,* 223–238.

Kohlberg, L. (1964). Development of moral character and moral ideology. In L. Hoffman & M. Hoffman (Eds.), *Child development research* (Vol. 1). New York: Russell Sage.

Kohn, M., & Schooler C. (1983). *Work and personality: An inquiry into social stratification.* Norwood, NJ: Ablex.

Koss, M.P., & Butcher, J.N. (1986). Rsearch on brief psychotherapy. In S.L. Garfield & A.E. Bergin (Eds.), *Handbook of psychotherapy and behavior change* (3rd ed.). New York: Wiley.

Kressel, K., & Deutsch, M. (1977). Divorce therapy: An in-depth survey of therapists' views. *Family Process, 16,* 413–444.

Kruger, M.A. (1983). The child care learning center: A practitioner-designed training and staff development program for child and youth care workers. *Child Care Quarterly, 12,* 152–159.

Kurdek, L.A. (Ed.) (1983). *New directions for child development: Children and divorce.* San Francisco: Jossey-Bass.

L'Abate, L., Anderson, J.S., & Baggett, M.S. (1984). Linear and circular interventions with families of children with school related problems. In *Family therapy with school related problems.* Rockville, MD: Aspen Systems.

Laird, J. (1979). An ecological approach to child welfare: Issues of family identity and continuity. In C.B. Germain (Ed.), *Social work practice: People and environments* (pp. 174–209). New York: Columbia University Press.

Lamb, M. (1978). The father's role in the infant's social world. In J. Stevens & M. Mathews (Eds.), *Mother/child, father/child relationships.* Washington, DC: National Association for the Education of Young Children.

Lamb, M. (1981). *The role of the father in child development* (2nd ed.). New York: Wiley.

Lambert, J.M., Shapiro, D.A., & Bergin, A.E. (1986). Effectiveness of psychotherapy. In S.L. Garfield & A.E. Bergin (Eds.), *Handbook of psychotherapy and behavior change* (3rd ed.). New York: Wiley.

Lane, K.E., & Gwartney-Gibbs, P.A. (1985). Violence in the context of dating and sex. *Journal of Family Issues, 6,* 45–59.

Laner, M.R., & Thompson, J. (1982). Abuse and aggression in courting couples. *Deviant Behavior: An Interdisciplinary Journal, 3,* 229–244.

LaRossa, R.E. (1980). And we haven't had any problem since: Conjugal violence and the politics of marriage. In M.A. Straus & G.T. Hotaling (Eds.), *The social causes of husband-wife violence* (pp. 157–175). Minneapolis: University of Minnesota.

Lazarus, A.A. (1960). The elimination of children's phobias by deconditioning. In H.J. Eysenck (Ed.), *Behavior therapy and the neuroses.* London: Pergamon Press.

Lea, R.C. (1983). *Acting-up disorders in children: An evaluation of an intervention.* Unpublished dissertation, Harvard University.

Lebow, J. (1981). Issues in the assessment of outcome in family therapy. *Family Process, 19*(2), 177–178.

Lebow, J. (1986). Research. *AFTA Newsletter, 26,* 1–2.

LeCroy, C.W. (1984). Residential treatment services; A review of some current trends. *Child Care Quarterly, 13,* 83–97.

Ledingham, J., Schwartzman, A., & Serbin, L. (1984). Current adjustment and family functioning of children behaviorally at risk for adult schizophrenia. In A. Doyle, D. Gold, & D. Moskowitz (Eds.), *Children and families under stress.* San Francisco: Jossey-Bass.

Lee, J.A.B., & Park, D.N. (1980). *Walk a mile in my shoes: A manual on biological parents for foster parents.* West Hartford: University of Connecticut, School of Social Work.

LeMasters, E. (1957). Parenthood as crisis. *Marriage and Family Living, 19,* 352–355.

Leon, A.M., Mazur, R., Montalvo, E., & Rodrieguez, M. (1984). Self-help support groups for Hispanic mothers. *Child Welfare, 63,* 261–268.

Lerman, L. (1981). *Prosecution of spouse abuse: Innovations in criminal justice response.* Washington, DC: Center for Women Policy Studies.

Lerner, R., & Spanier, G. (1983). *Child influences on marital and family interaction.* New York: Academic Press.

Levonson, R.W., & Gottman, J.M. (1983). Marital interaction: Physiological linkage and affective exchange. *Journal of Personality and Social Psychology, 45*(3), 587–597.

Levy, D. (1938). Release therapy in young children. *Psychiatry, I,* 387–89.

Lewis, W.W. (1982). Ecological factors in successful residential treatment. *Behavioral Disorders, 7*(3), 149–155.

Libman, E., Takefman, J., & Brender, W. (1980). A comparison of sexually dysfunctional, maritally disturbed and well-adjusted couples. *Personality and Individual Differences, 1*(3), 219–227.

Lindemann, E. (1944). Symptomatology and management of acute grief. *American Journal of Psychiatry, 101,* 141–148.

Lipchik, E., & de Shazer, S. (1986). The purposeful interview. *Journal of Strategy and Systemic Therapies, 5*(1–2), 88–99.

Luftman, S., & Kirschenbaum, M. (1974). *The dynamic family.* Palo Alto, CA: Science and Behavior Books.

Makepeace, J.M. (1983). Life events stress and courtship violence. *Family Relations, 32,* 101–109.

Maluccio, A.N. (1977). Community-based child placement services: Current issues and trends. *Child and Youth Services, 1,* 2–12.

Maluccio, A.N. (1981a). An ecological perspective on practice with parents of children in foster care. In A.N. Maluccio & P.A. Sinanoglu (Eds.), *The challenge of partnership: Working with parents of children in foster care* (pp. 22–35). New York: Child Welfare League of America.

Maluccio, A.N. (Ed.) (1981b). *Promoting competence in clients: A new/old approach to social work practice.* New York: Free Press.

Maluccio, A.N., Fein, E., & Olmstead, K.A. (1986). *Permanency planning for children: Concepts and methods.* London and New York: Travistock Publications and Methuen.

Maluccio, A.N., & Sinanoglu, P.A. (Eds.) (1981). *The challenge of partnership: Working with parents of children in foster care.* New York: Child Welfare League of America.

Marcia, J. (1980). Identity in adolescence. In J. Adelson (Ed.), *Handbook of adolescent psychology.* New York: Wiley.

Margolin, G. (1981). Behavior exchange in happy and unhappy marriages: A family life cycle perspective. *Behavior Therapy, 12,* 329–343.

Margolin, G., & Wampold, B.E. (1981). Sequential analysis of conflict and accord in distressed and non-distressed marital partners. *Journal of Consulting and Clinical Psychology, 49*(4), 554–567.

Markman, H.J. (1979). The application of a behavioral model of marriage in predicting relationship satisfaction for couples planning marriage. *Journal of Consulting and Clinical Psychology, 47,* 743–749.

Markman, H.J. (1981). The prediction of marital distress: A five-year follow-up. *Journal of Consulting and Clinical Psychology, 49,* 760–762.

Martin, D. (1976). *Battered wives.* San Francisco: Glide.

Maruyama, M. (1968). The second cybernetics: Deviation-amplifying mutual causal processes. In W. Buckley (Ed.), *Modern systems research for the behavioral scientist.* Chicago: Aldine.

Masnick, G., & Bane, M.J. (1980). *The nation's families: 1960–1990.* Cambridge: Joint Center for Urban Studies of the Massachusetts Institute of Technology and Harvard University.

Matteson, D. (1975). *Adolescence today: Sex roles and search for identity.* Homewood, IL: Dorsey Press.

Maybanks, S., & Bryce, M. (Eds.) (1979). *Home-based services for children and families.* Springfield, IL: Thomas.

McAdoo, H. (1982). Levels of stress and family support in black families. In H. McCubbin, E. Cauble, & J. Patterson (Eds.), *Family Stress, coping and social support.* Springfield, IL: Thomas.

McGowan, B., & Meezan, W. (Eds.) (1983). *Child welfare: Current dilemmas—future directions.* Itasca, IL: Peacock.

McIntyre, D. (1984). Domestic violence: A case of the disappearing victim? *Australian Journal of Family Therapy, 5*(4), 249–258.

McMahon, R.J., & Forehand, R.L. (1983). Consumer satisfaction in behavioral treatment of children: types, issues, and recommendations. *Behavior Therapy, 14,* 209–225.

Mech, E.V. (1983). Out-of-home placement rates. *Social Service Review, 57,* 659–667.

Menaghan, E. (1982). Measuring coping effectiveness: A panel analysis of marital problems and coping efforts. *Journal of Health and Social Behavior, 23,* 220–234.

Menaghan, E. (1983). Marital stress and family transitions: A panel analysis. *Journal of Marriage and the Family, 45,* 371–386.

Merikangas, K.R., Ranelli, C.J., & Kupfer, D.J. (1979). Marital interaction in hospitalized depressed patients. *Journal of Nervous and Mental Disease, 167*(11), 689–695.

Miller, B.C. (1976). A multivariate developmental model of marital satisfaction. *Journal of Marriage and the Family, 38,* 643–657.

Miller, I.W., Epstein, N.B., Bishop, D.S., & Keitner, G.I. (1985). The McMaster family assessment device: Reliability and validity. *Journal of Marital and Family Therapy, 11*(4), 345–357.

Miller, K., Fein, E., Howe, G.W., Gaudio, C.P., & Bishop, G.V. (1984). Time-limited, goal-focused parent aide service. *Social Casework, 65,* 472–477.

Milne, A. (1983). Divorce mediation. The state of the art. *Mediation Quarterly, 1,* 15–32.

Minuchin, S. (1974). *Families and family therapy.* Cambridge, MA: Harvard University Press.

Minuchin, S., & Fishman, H.C. (1981). *Family therapy techniques.* Cambridge, MA: Harvard University Press.

Mitchell, R.E., Cronkite, R.C., & Moos, R.H. (1983). Stress, coping and depression among married couples. *Journal of Abnormal Psychology, 92*(4), 433–448.

Mnookin, R.H., & Kornhauser, L. (1979). Bargaining in the shadow of the law: The case of divorce. *Yale Law Journal, 88,* 950–997.

Money, J., & Ehrhardt, A. (1972). *Man and woman, boy and girl.* Baltimore: Johns Hopkins University Press.

Moore v. City of Cleveland. (1977). 431 US 494.

Moore, P., & Bassett, S. (1986). A family court for Michigan. A survey evaluating the effectiveness of family courts with comprehensive jurisdiction. *Michigan Family Law Journal, 14,* 8–9.

Morrison, A.L. (1982). *A prospective study of divorce: Its relation to children's development and parental functioning.* Unpublished dissertation, University of California at Berkeley.

Morse, S. (1979). Family law in transition: From traditional families to individual liberties. In V. Tufte & B. Myerhoff (Eds.), *Changing images of the family.* New York and London: Yale University Press.

Mowrer, O.H. (1950) *Learning theory and personality dynamics.* New York: Ronald Press.

Moynihan, P. (1986). *Family and nation.* San Diego, CA: Harcourt Brace Jovanovich.

Murstein, B.I., & MacDonald, M.G. (1983). The relationships of "exchange-orientation" and "commitment" scales to marriage adjustment. *International Journal of Psychology, 18*(3/4), 297–311.

Mussen, P., Conger, J., & Kagan, J. (1979). *Child development and personality.* New York: Harper & Row.

Napier, A., & Whitaker, C. (1978). *The family crucible.* New York: Harper & Row.

National Center for Health Statistics (27 June 1983). *Monthly Vital Statistics Report,* Table 6. *32*(3), 9.

Neidig, P.H., & Friedman, P.H. (1984). *Spouse abuse: A treatment program for couples.* Champaign, IL: Research Press.

Nelson, B.J. (1984). *Making an issue of child abuse: Political agenda setting for social problems.* Chicago: University of Chicago Press.

Newberger, E.H. et al. (1977). Pediatric social illness: Toward an etiologic classification. *Pediatrics, 60,* 178–185.

Newman, G. (1981). *101 ways to be a long distance super-dad.* Mountain View, CA: Blossom Valley Press.

Newson, J., & Newson, E. (1963). *Patterns of infant care in an urban community.* London: Allen & Unwin.

Nicarthy, G., Merriam, K., & Coffman, S. (1984). *Talking it out: A guide to groups for abused women.* Seattle: Seal Press.

Nichols, W.C. (1984). Therapeutic needs of children in family system reorganization. *Journal of Divorce, 7*(4), 23–44.

Nichols, W.C. (1985). Family therapy with children of divorce. In D.H. Sprenkle (Ed.), *Divorce therapy* (pp. 55–68). New York: Haworth Press.

Norton, A.J. (1980). The influence of divorce on traditional life cycle measures. *Journal of Marriage and the Family, 42,* 63–69.

O'Farrell, T., Cutter, H., & Floyd, F. (1983). *The class of alcoholism and marriage (CALM) project: Results on marital adjustment and communication from before to after therapy* (Tech. Rep. No. 4–1). Brockton, MA: Brockton/West Roxbury Veterans Administration Medical Center.

O'Leary, K.D., & Curley, A. (1986). Assertion and family violence: Correlates of spouse abuse. *Journal of Marital and Family Therapy, 12*(3), 281–289.

O'Leary, K.D., Curley, A., Rosenbaum, A., & Clarke, C. (1985). Assertion training for abused wives: A potentially hazardous treatment. *Journal of Marital and Family Therapy, 11*(3), 319–322.

Oakland, T. (1984). *Divorced fathers: Reconstructing a quality of life.* New York: Human Sciences Press.

Offer, D., & Offer, J. (1969). *The psychological world of the teenagers.* New York: Basic Books.

Ollendick, T.H. (1986). Child and adolescent behavior therapy. In S.L. Garfield & A.E. Bergin (Eds.), *Handbook of psychotherapy and behavior change* (3rd ed.). New York: Wiley.

Olsen, L. (1982). Services for minority children in out-of-home care. *Social Services Review, 56,* 572–585.

Olson, D., McCubbin, H., & Associates (1983). *Families: What makes them work.* Beverly Hills, CA: Sage.

Olson, D.H., Russell, C.S., & Sprenkle, D.H. (1980). Marital and family therapy: A decade review. *Journal of Marriage and the Family, 42,* 973–993.

Orden, S., & Bradburn, N. (1968). Dimensions of marriage happiness. *American Journal of Sociology, 73,* 715–731.

Osofsky, J. & Osofsky, H. (1984). Psychological and developmental perspectives on expectant and new parenthood. In R. Parke (Ed.), R. Emde, H. McAdoo, G. Sackett (Associate Eds.), *The family.* Chicago: University of Chicago Press.

Page, R., & Clark, G.A. (Eds.) (1977). *Who cares?* London: National Children's Bureau.

Pagelow, M.D. (1981). *Women battering: Victims and their experience.* Beverly Hills, CA: Sage.

Pagelow, M.D. (1984). *Family violence.* New York: Praeger.

Palisi, B. (1984). Marriage companionship and marriage well-being: A comparison of metropolitan areas in three countries. *Journal for Comparative Family Studies, XV,* 43–57.

Pappenfort, D.M., Kilpatrick, D.M., & Roberts, R.W. (Eds.) (1973). *Child care: Social policy and the institution.* Chicago: Aldine.

Pappenfort, D.M., Young, T.M., & Marlow, C.R. (1983). *Residential group care: 1981: 1966 and preliminary report of selected findings from the national survey of residential group care facilities.* Chicago: University of Chicago, School of Social Service Administration.

Parke, R. (1979). Perspectives on father-infant interaction. In J. Osofsky (Ed.), *Handbook of infant development.* New York: Wiley.

Parke, R., & O'Leary, S. (1976). Father–mother–infant interaction in the newborn period. In K. Riegel & J. Meachman (Eds.), *The developing individual in a changing world* (Vol. 2). The Hague: Morton.

Parnas, R.I. (1967). The police response to the domestic disturbance. *Wisconsin Law Review, 914* 914–960.

Parton, N. (1985). *The politics of child abuse.* New York: St. Martin's Press.

Patterson, G., Littman, R., & Bricker, W. (1967). Assertive behavior in children: A step toward a theory of agression. *Monographs of the Society for Research in Child Development, 32*(5), 1–43.

Patterson, G.R. (1974). Retraining of aggressive boys by their parents. Review of recent literature and follow-up evaluation. *Canadian Psychiatric Association Journal, 19,* 142–161.

Patterson, G.R., Chamberlain, P., & Reid, J.B. (1982). A comprehensive evaluation of a parent-training program. *Behavior Therapy, 13,* 636–650.

Patterson, G.R., & Fleischmann, M.J. (1979). Maintenance of treatment effects: Some considerations concerning family systems and follow-up date. *Behavior Therapy, 10,* 168–185.

Pearlin, L., & Schooler, C. (1982). The structure of coping. In H. McCubbin, A. Cauble, & J. Patterson, J. (Eds.), *Family stress, coping and social support* (pp. 109–136). Springfield, IL: Thomas.

Pearlin, L.I., Schooler, C. (1978). The structure of coping. *Journal of Health and Social Behavior, 19,* 2–21.

Pearson, J., & Thoennes, N. (1981). The decision to mediate: Profiles of individuals who accept and reject the opportunity to mediate contested child custody and visitation disputes. *Journal of Divorce, 1*(3), 17–33.

Pearson, J., & Thoennes, N. (1982). The benefits outweigh the costs. *The Family Advocate 4,* 26–32.

Pearson, J., Thoennes, N., & Vanderkooi, L. (1982). The decision to mediate: Profiles of individuals who accept and reject the opportunity to mediate contested child custody and visitation issues. In E.O. Fisher, & M.S. Fisher (Eds.), *Therapists, lawyers, and divorcing spouses.* New York: Haworth Press.

Pederson, F., Cain, R., Zaslow, M., & Anderson, B. (1981). Variation in infant experience associated with alternative family role organization. In L. Laesa & I. Sigel (Eds.), *Families as learning environment for children.* New York: Plenum.

Pfohl, S.J. (1977). The discovery of child abuse. *Social Problems, 24,* 310–323.

Philips, I. (1983). Opportunities for prevention in the practice of psychiatry. *American Journal of Psychiatry, 140,* 389–395.

Pietrowski, C. (1979). *Work and the family system.* New York: Free Press.

Pinsof, W. (1980). *The family therapy coding system (FTCS) coding manual.* Evanston, IL: Northwestern University Medical School, Center for Family Studies, Department of Psychiatry.

Pinsof, W.M. (1983). Integrative problem-centered therapy: Toward the synthesis of family and individual psychotherapies. *Journal of Marital and Family Therapy, 9,* 19–35.

Pizzey, E. (1974). *Scream quietly or the neighbors will hear.* London: Penguin.

Plass, P. (1986). *Patterns in spousal homicide: An analysis of racial, regional, and gender variations.* Durham: University of New Hampshire, Family Research Laboratory.

Plass, P., & Straus, M.A. (1987). *Intra-family homicide in the United States: Incidence rates, trends, and differences by region, race and gender.* Paper presented at the Third National Family Violence Research Conference, University of New Hampshire, Family Research Laboratory, Durham.

Pleck, E., Pleck, J.H., Grossman, M., & Bart, P.B. (1977). The battered data syndrome: A comment on Steinmetz' article. *Victimology: An International Journal, 2,* 680–683.

Pope, H., & Mueller, C.W. (1979). The intergenerational transmission of marital instability: Comparisons of race and sex. In G. Levinger & O.C. Moles (Eds.), *Divorce and separation: Context, causes and consequences.* New York: Basic Books.

Powers, D., & Powell, J. (1983). A role for residential treatment in preparation for adoption. *Residential Group Care and Treatment, 2,* 31–44.

Presser, H. (1974). Early motherhood. Ignorance or bliss? *Family Planning Perspectives, 6*(2), 8–14.

Price-Bonham, S., & Balswick, J.O. (1980). The noninstitutions: Divorce, desertion and remarriage. *Journal of Marriage and the Family, 42,* 959–972.

Radbill, S.X. (1974). A history of child abuse and infanticide. In R.E. Helfer & C.H. Kempe (Eds.), *The battered child* (2nd ed., pp. 3–34). Chicago: University of Chicago Press.

Rankin, R.P., & Maneker, J.S. (1983). The duration of marriage in a divorcing population: The impact of children. *Journal of Marriage and the Family, 47,* 43–52.

Renne, K.S. (1971). Health and marital experience in an urban population. *Journal of Marriage and the Family, 33,* 338–350.

Rice, J.M., & Rice, R.C. (1986). *Divorce therapy.* New York: Norton.

Richards, M.P.M. (1982, April). *Marital separation and children: Some problems of method and theory.* Paper presented at Fourth Rugby Research Seminar of the National Marriage Guidance Council, Great Britain.

Rofes, E. (Ed.) (1982). *The kids' book of divorce: by, for and about kids.* New York: Vintage Books.

Rollins, B.C., & Cannon, K.L. (1974). Marital satisfaction over the family life cycle: A reevaluation. *Journal of Marriage and the Family, 36*(2), 271–282.

Rollins, B.C., & Feldman, H. (1970). Marital satisfaction over the family life cycle. *Journal of Marriage and the Family, 32,* 20–28.

Rollins, B.C., & Galligan, R. (1978). The developing child and marital satisfaction of parents. In R.M. Lerner & G.B. Spanier (Eds.), *Child influences on marital and family interaction* (pp. 71–105). New York: Academic Press.

Rosen, S.M., Fanshel, D., & Lutz, M.E. (Eds.) (1987). *Face of the nation 1987.* Statistical supplement to *Encyclopedia of Social Work* (18th ed.). Silver Spring, MD: National Association of Social Workers.

Rosenbaum, A., & O'Leary, K.D. (1981). Marital violence: Characteristics of abusive couples. *Journal of Consulting and Clinical Psychology, 49,* 63–71.

Ross, C.J. (1977). *Society's children: the care of indigent youngsters in New York City, 1875–1903.* Unpublished doctoral dissertation, Yale University.

Rowe, J., Cain, H., Hundleby, M., & Keane, A. (1984). *Long-term foster care.* London: Batsford Academic and Educational.

Rutter, M. (1970). Sex differences in children's responses to family stress. In E.J. Anthony & C. Koupernik (Eds.), *The child in his family.* New York: Wiley.

Rutter, M. (1979). Protective factors in children's responses to stress or disadvantage. In M. Kent & J. Rolf (Eds.), *Primary prevention of psychopathology* (Vol. III). Hanover, NH: University Press of New England.

Rutter, M. (1983). Developmental psychopathology. In M. Hetherington (Ed.), *Handbook of child psychology: Socialization, personality and social development, 4.* New York: Wiley.

Ryan, P., McFadden, E.J., & Warren, B.L. (1981). Foster families: A resource for helping parents. In A.N. Maluccio & P.A. Sinanoglu (Eds.), *The challenge of partnership: Working with parents of children in foster care* (pp. 189–199). New York: Child Welfare League of America.

Ryder, R. (1974). Longitudinal data relating marriage satisfaction and having a child. *Journal of Marriage and the Family, 35,* 604–608.

Sabatelli, R.M., & Cecil-Pigo, E.F. (1985). Relational interdependence and commitment in marriage. *Journal of Marriage and the Family, 47,* 931–937.

Sack, A.R., Keller, J.F., & Howard, R.D. (1982). Conflict tactics and violence in dating situations. *International Journal of Sociology of the Family, 12*, 89–100.

Sager, C.J., Brown, H.S., Crohn, H., Engel, T., Rodstein, E., & Walker, L. (1983). *Treating the remarried family.* New York: Brunner/Mazel.

Salts, C.J. (1979). Divorce process: Integration of theory. *Journal of Divorce, 2*, 233–240.

Salts, C.J. (1985). Divorce stage theory and therapy: Therapeutic implications throughout the divorcing process. In D.H. Sprenkle (Ed.), *Divorce therapy* (pp. 13–23). New York: Haworth Press.

Santrock, J.W., & Warshak, R.A. (1979). Father custody and social development in boys and girls. *Journal of Social Issues, 35*, 112–125.

Saposnek, D.T. (1983). *Mediating child custody disputes.* San Francisco: Jossey-Bass.

Satir, V. (1964). *Conjoint family therapy.* Palo Alto, CA: Science and Behavior Books.

Satir, V. (1983). *Conjoint family therapy* (3rd ed.). Palo Alto, CA: Science and Behavior Books.

Satir, V., & Baldwin, M. (1983). *Satir step by step: A guide to creating change in families.* Palo Alto, CA: Science and Behavior Books.

Satir, V., & Baldwin, M. (1985). *Step by step: A guide to creating change in families.* Palo Alto, CA: Science and Behavior Books.

Scanzoni, J. (1978). *Sex roles, women's work, and marital conflict.* Lexington, MA: Lexington Books.

Schafer, R.B., & Keith, P.M. (1980). Equity and depression among married couples. *Social Psychology Quarterly, 43*(4), 430–435.

Schaffer, E. (1972). Children's reports of parental behavior. *Child Development, 43*, 413–424.

Schorr, A. (1986). *Common decency.* New Haven, CN: Yale University Press.

Schumm, W.R., & Bugaighis, M.A. (1986). Marital quality over the marital career: Alternative explanations. *Journal of Marriage and the Family, 48*, 165–168.

Schumm, W.R., Martin, M.J., Bollman, S.R., & Jurich, A.P. (1982). Classifying family violence: Whither the woozel? *Journal of Family Issues, 3*, 319–340.

Schwartz, I.M., Jackson, Beelk, M., & Anderson, R. (1983). Minnesota's "hidden" juvenile control system: Inpatient psychiatric and chemical dependency treatment. Unpublished manuscript, University of Minnesota, Hubert H. Humphrey Institute of Public Affairs.

Sears, R. (1970). Relation of early experiences to self-concept and gender role in middle childhood. *Child Development, 41*, 267–269.

Select committee on children, youth, and families: A report. (1983). Washington, DC: U.S. Government Printing Office.

Selvini-Palazzoli, M., Boscolo, L., Cecchin, G.F., & Prata, G. (1978). *Paradox and counterparadox.* New York: Jason Aronson.

Selvini-Palazzoli, S. (1986). Toward a model of psychotic family games. *Journal of Marital and Family Therapy, 12*(4), 339–351.

Shapiro, T.J., & Caplan, M.S. (1983). *Parting sense: A couple's guide to divorce mediation.* Lutherville, MD: Greenspring Publications.

Shaw, C.R., & McKay, H.D. (1969). *Juvenile delinquency and urban areas.* Chicago: University of Chicago Press.

Shepherd-Look, D. (1982). Sex differentiation and the development of sex roles. In B. Wolman (Ed.), *Handbook of developmental psychology.* Englewood Cliffs, NJ: Prentice-Hall.

Shereshefsky, P., & Yarrow, L. (1973). *Psychological aspects of a first pregnancy and early parenthood adaptation*. New York: Raven Press.

Sherman, E.A., Neuman, R., & Shyne, A.W. (1973). *Children adrift in foster care*. New York: Child Welfare League of America.

Sherman, L.W., & Berk, R.H. (1984). The specific deterrent effects of arrest for assault. *American Sociological Review, 49*, 261–272.

Shields, C. (1986a). *An analysis of family therapy interaction in the initial interview: Testing a stochastic process model of family therapy interview*. Unpublished doctoral dissertation proposal, Purdue University, Indiana.

Shields, C.G. (1986b). Critiquing the new epistemologies: Toward minimum requirements for a scientific theory of family therapy. *Journal of Marital and Family Therapy, 12*(4), 359–373, 379–383.

Shyne, A.W., & Schroeder, A.G. (1978). *National study of social services to children and their families*. Washington, DC: National Center Child Advocacy.

Sinanoglu, P.A., & Maluccio, A.N. (Eds.). (1981). *Parents of children in placement: Perspectives and programs*. New York: Child Welfare League of America.

Slavson, S.R. (1952). *Child psychotherapy*. New York: Columbia University Press.

Snyder, D.K., & Fruchtman, L. (1981). Differential patterns of wife abuse: A data-based typology. *Journal of Consulting and Clinical Psychology, 49*(6), 878–885.

Solomon, B. (1976). *Black empowerment: Social work in oppressed communities*. New York: Columbia University Press.

Solow, R.A., & Adams, P.L. (1977). Custody by agreement: Child psychiatrist as child advocate. *Journal of Psychiatry and Law, 5*, 77–100.

Sonkin, D.J., & Durphy, M. (1982). *Learning to live without violence: A handbook for men*. San Francisco: Volcano Press.

Spanier, G.B., & Lewis, R.A. (1980). Marital quality: A review of the seventies. *Journal of Marriage and the Family, 42*, 825–840.

Sprenkle, D.H. (1985). Introduction: Divorce therapy. In D.H. Sprenkle (Ed.), *Divorce therapy* (pp. 5–11). New York: Haworth Press.

Sprenkle, D.H., & Cyrus, C. (1983). Abandonment: The sudden stress of divorce. In C.R. Figley & H.I. McCubbin (Eds.), *Stress and the family* (Vol. 2). New York: Brunner/Mazel.

Sprenkle, D.H., & Piercy, F.P. (1986). Divorce therapy, In F.P. Piercy & D.H. Sprenkle, (Eds.), *Family therapy sourcebook* (Ch. 6). New York: Guilford.

Sprenkle, D.H., & Storm, C.L. (1983). Divorce therapy outcome research: A substantive and methodological review. *Journal of Marital and Family Therapy, 9*, 239–258.

Springer, C., & Wallerstein, J.S. (1983). Young adolescents' responses to their parents' divorces. In L.A. Kurdek (Ed.), *Children and divorce*. San Francisco: Jossey-Bass.

Stachura, J., & Teske, R. (1979). *A special report on spouse abuse in Texas*. Huntsville, TX: Sam Houston State University, Criminal Justice Center.

Star, B. (1987). Domestic violence. *Encyclopedia of Social Work. Vol. 1* (18th ed., pp. 463–476). Silver Spring, MD: National Association of Social Workers.

Steffensmeier, R.H. (1982). A role model of the transition to parenthood. *Journal of Marriage and the Family, 44*, 319–334.

Stein, T. (1987). Foster care. In *Encyclopedia of Social Work* (Vol. I). Silver Spring, MD: National Association of Social Workers.

Stein, T., & Rzepnicki, T. (1983). *Decision making at child welfare intake*. New York: Child Welfare League of America.

Stein, T.J., Gambrill, E.D., & Wiltse, K.T. (1978). *Children in foster homes: Achieving continuity of care*. New York: Praeger.

Steiner, G. (1981). *The futility of family policy*. Washington, DC: Brookings.

Steinman, S. (1981). The experience of children in a joint custody arrangement: A report of a study. *American Journal of Orthopsychiatry, 51,* 403–414.

Steinmetz, S.K. (1977). *The cycle of violence: Assertive, aggressive, and abusive family interaction*. New York: Praeger.

Steinmetz, S.K. (1978a). Services to battered women: Our greatest need. A reply to Field and Kirchner. *Victimology: An International Journal, 3,* 222–226.

Steinmetz, S.K. (1978b). The battered husband syndrome. *Victimology, 2*(3–4), 499–509.

Steinmetz, S.K., & Straus, M. (1974). *Violence in the family*. New York: Harper & Row.

Stets, J.E., and Straus, M.A. (1988). The marriage license as a hitting license: A comparison of dating, cohabiting, and married coupled. In M.A. Pirog-Good and J.E. Stets (Eds.), *Violence in Dating Relationships: Emerging Social Issues*. New York: Praeger.

Stevens, J. (1986). *Parenting skill: Does social support matter?* Unpublished manuscript, Georgia State University.

Stevenson, H.W., & Siegel, A.E. (1984). *Child development research and social policy*. Chicago: University of Chicago Press.

Stierlin, H. (1977). *Psychoanalysis and family therapy*. New York: Jason Aronson.

Storm, C.L., & Sprenkle, D.H. (1982). Individual treatment in divorce therapy: A critique of an assumption. *Journal of Divorce, 5,* 87–97.

Storm, C.L., Sprenkle, D.H., & Williamson, W. (1985). Innovative divorce approaches developed by counselors, conciliators, mediators, and educators. In R. Levant (Ed.), *Psychoeducational approaches to family therapy*. New York: Springer.

Straus, M.A. (1973). A general systems theory approach to a theory of violence between family members. *Social Science Information, 12*(3), 105–125.

Straus, M.A. (1976). Sexual inequality, cultural norms, and wife-beating. *Victimology, 1,* 54–76.

Straus, M.A. (1977a). Wife-beating: How common, and why? *Victimology, 2,* 443–458.

Straus, M.A. (1977b). Societal morphogenesis and intrafamily violence in cross-cultural perspective. *Annals of the New York Academy of Sciences, 285,* 719–730.

Straus, M.A. (1979). Family patterns and child abuse in a nationally representative American sample. *Child Abuse and Neglect, 3,* 213–225.

Straus, M.A. (1980a). Social stress and marital violence in a national sample of American families. In F. Wright, C. Bahn, & R. Rieber (Eds.), *Forensic psychology and psychiatry* (pp. 229–250). New York: Annals of the New York Academy of Sciences (Vol. 347).

Straus, M.A. (1980b). Victims and aggressors in marital violence. *American Behavioral Scientist, 23,* 681–704.

Straus, M.A. (1983). Ordinary violence versus child abuse and wife beating: What do they have in common? In D. Finkelhor, G.T. Hotaling, R.J. Gelles, & M.A. Straus (Eds.), *Issues and controversies in the study of family violence*. Beverly Hills, CA: Sage.

Straus, M.A. (1985). *The index of legitimate violence*. [Mimeograph].

Straus, M.A. (1987a). Medical care costs of intrafamily assault and homicide. *Bulletin of the New York Academy of Medicine, 62*(5), 556–561.

Strauss, M.A. (1987b). *Primary group characteristics and intra-family homicide.* Paper presented at the Third National Family Violence Research Conference, University of New Hampshire, Family Research Laboratory, Durham.

Straus, M.A., & Gelles, R.J. (1986). Societal change and change in family violence from 1975 to 1985 as revealed by two national surveys. *Journal of Marriage and the Family, 48,* 465–479.

Straus, M.A., and Gelles, R.J. (Eds.) (1989). *Physical violence in American families: Risk factors and adaptation to violence in 8,145 families.* New Brunswick, NJ: Transaction Press.

Straus, M.A.; Gelles, R.J.; & Steinmetz, S.K. (1980). *Behind closed doors: Violence in the American family.* New York: Doubleday/Anchor.

Straus, M.A., & Hotaling G.T. (Eds.) (1980). *The social causes of husband–wife violence.* Minneapolis: University of Minnesota Press.

Straus, M.A., & Lincoln, A.J. (1985). A conceptual framework for understanding crime and the family. In A.J. Lincoln & M.A. Straus (Eds.). *Crime and the family* (pp. 5–23). Springfield, IL: Thomas.

Stuart, I.R., & Abt, L.E. (1981). *Children of separation and divorce: Management and treatment.* New York: Van Nostrand Reinhold.

Stuart, R. (1980). *Helping couples change: A social learning approach to marital therapy.* New York: Guilford.

Sutton, P., & Sprenkle, D.H. (1985). Criteria for a constructive divorce: Theory and research to guide the practitioner. In D.H. Sprenkle (Ed.), *Divorce therapy* (pp. 39–51). New York: Haworth Press.

Swenson, C.H., Eskew, R.W., & Kohlhepp, K.A. (1981). Stage of family life cycle, ego development, and the marriage relationship. *Journal of Marriage and the Family, 43,* 841–853.

Szinovacz, M.E. (1983). Using couple data as a methodological tool: The case of marital violence. *Journal of Marriage and the Family, 45*(3), 633–644.

Tall, J., & Johnston, J. (1982). Mandatory mediation without a court setting. Paper presented at annual meeting of American Orthopsychiatric Association, San Francisco.

Taylor, D.A., & Alpert, S.W. (1973). *Continuity and support following residential treatment.* New York: Child Welfare League of America.

Taylor, R.B. (1981). *The kid business.* Boston: Houghton Mifflin.

Terkelson, K. (1980). Toward a theory of the family life cycle. In E. Carter & M. McGoldrick (Eds.), *The family life cycle.* New York: Gardner Press.

Tessman, L.H. (1977). *Children of parting parents.* New York: Jason Aronson.

Tomlinson, R., & Peters, P. (1981). An alternative to placing children: Intensive and extensive therapy with "disengaged" families. *Child Welfare, 60,* 95–104.

Tomm, K. (1986). On incorporating the therapist in a scientific theory of family therapy. *Journal of Marital and Family Therapy, 12*(4), 373–379.

Tooley, K. (1976). Antisocial behavior and social alienation post divorce: The "man of the house" and his mother. *American Journal of Orthopsychiatry, 46,* 33–42.

Toomin, M.K. (1972). Structured separation with counseling: A therapeutic approach for couples in conflict. *Family Process, 11,* 299–310.

Turkewitz, H., & O'Leary, K. (1981). A comparative outcome study of behavioral marital therapy and communication therapy. *Journal of Marital and Family Therapy, 7,* 159–169.

Turner, C. (1980). Resources for helping in parenting. *Child Welfare, 59,* 179–187.

Turner, N.W. (1980). Divorce in mid-life: Clinical implications and applications. In W. Norman & I. Scaramella (Eds.), *Mid-life: Developmental and clinical issues*. New York: Brunner/Mazel.

Turner, N.W. (1985). Divorce: Dynamics of decision therapy. In D.H. Sprenkle (Ed.), *Divorce therapy* (pp. 27–38). New York: Haworth Press.

U.S. Children's Bureau (1983). *Child welfare research note #1*. Washington, DC: Department of Health and Human Services.

Ullman, D.G., Egan, D., Fiedler, N., Jurenec, G., Pliske, R., Thompson, P., & Doherty, M.E. (1981). The many faces of hyperactivity: Similarities and differences in diagnostic policies. *Journal of Consulting and Clinical Psychology*, 49(5), 649–704.

United States Attorney General, Task Force on Family Violence (1984). *Final report*. Washington, DC: Government Printing Office.

United States Bureau of the Census, Current Population Reports. (1982a). *Characteristics of American children and youth: 1980* (Series P–23, No. 114). Washington, DC: Government Printing Office.

United States Bureau of the Census, Current Population Reports (1982b). *Marital status and living arrangements: March 1981* (Series P–20, No. 372). Washington, DC: Government Printing Office.

United States House of Representatives. Committee on Ways and Means, Subcommittee on Public Assistance and Unemployment Compensation (1984). *House hearings on child support enforcement legislation, July 14, 1983: 27*. Washington, DC: Government Printing Office.

Vanfossen, B.E. (1981). Sex differences in the mental health effects of spouse support and equity. *Journal of Health and Social Behavior, 22*, 130–143.

Varderkooi, L. & Pearson, J. (1983). Mediating divorce disputes: Mediator behavior, styles, roles. *Family Relations, 32*, 557–566.

Vener, A., & Stewart, C. (1974). Adolescent sexual behavior in middle America revisited: 1970–1973. *Journal of Marriage and the Family, 36*(4), 728–735.

Veroff, J., Douvan, E., & Kulka, R. (1981). *The inner American: A self-portrait from 1957 to 1976*. New York: Basic Books.

Visher, E.B., & Visher, J.S. (1979). *Stepfamilies: A guide to working with stepparents and stepchildren*. New York: Brunner/Mazel.

Volgy, S.S., & Everett, C.A. (1985). Systemic assessment criteria for joint custody. In D.H. Sprenkle (Ed.), *Divorce therapy* (pp. 85–98). New York: Haworth Press.

von Bertalanffy, L. (1968). *General systems theory: Foundation, development, application*. New York: George Braziller.

Voydanoff, P. (1983). Unemployment: Family strategies for adaptation. In C.R. Figley & H.I. McCubbin (Eds.), *Stress and the family: Vol II, Coping with catastrophe* (Ch. 6). New York: Brunner/Mazel.

Wahler, R.G., Afton, A.D., & Fox, J.J. (1979). The multiple entrapped parent: Some new problems in parent training. *Education and Treatment of Children, 2*(4), 279–286.

Wald, M., Goldstein, J., Freud, A., & Solnit, A.J. (1980). Before the best interests of the child. *Michigan Law Review, 78*(5), 645–694.

Walker, L.E., (1979). *The battered woman*. New York: Harper & Row.

Wallerstein, J.S. (1977). Responses of the pre-school child to divorce: Those who cope. In M.F. McMillan & S. Henao (Eds.), *Child psychiatry: Treatment and research*. New York: Brunner/Mazel.

Wallerstein, J.S. (1978). Children of divorce: Preliminary report of a ten-year follow-up. In J. Anthony & C. Chilland (Eds.), *The child in his family* (Vol. 5). New York: Wiley.

Wallerstein, J.S. (1982). *Current environments for young children in separating and divorced families.* Paper presented at the MacArthur Conference on Child Care: Growth Fostering Environments for Young Children, Chicago.

Wallerstein, J.S. (1983). Children of divorce: The psychological tasks of the child. *American Journal of Orthopsychiatry, 53,* 230–243.

Wallerstein, J.S. (1985). Parent–child relationships following divorce. In E.J. Anthony & G. Pollock (Eds.), *Parental influences in health and disease* (pp. 317–348). Boston: Little, Brown.

Wallerstein, J.S., & Huntington, D. (1983). Bread and roses: Nonfinancial issues related to fathers' economic support of their children following divorce. In J. Cassetty (Ed.), *The parental child support obligation: Research, practice and social policy.* Lexington, MA: Lexington Books. Heath.

Wallerstein, J.S., & Kelly, J.B (1974). The effects of parental divorce: The adolescent experience. In J. Anthony & C. Koupernik (Eds.), *The child in his family: Children at psychiatric risk* (Vol. 3). New York: Wiley.

Wallerstein, J.S., & Kelly, J.B. (1975). The effects of parental divorce: The experiences of the preschool child. *American Journal of Orthopsychiatry, 46,* 256–269.

Wallerstein, J.S., & Kelly, J.B. (1977). Divorce counseling: A community service for families in the midst of divorce. *American Journal of Orthopsychiatry, 47,* 4–22.

Wallerstein, J.S., & Kelly, J.B. (1980a). *Surviving the breakup: How children and parents cope with divorce.* New York: Basic Books.

Wallerstein, J.S., & Kelly, J.B. (1980b). Effects of divorce on the father–child relationship. *American Journal of Psychiatry, 137,* 1534–1539.

Walters, J., & Stinett, N. (1971). Parent–child relationships: A decade review. *Journal of Marriage and the Family, 33,* 70–111.

Ward, M. (1984). Sibling ties in foster care. *Child Welfare, 63,* 321–332.

Warshak, R.A., & Santrock, J.W. (1983). The impact of divorce in father-custody and mother-custody homes: The child's perspective. In L.A. Kurdek (Ed.), *Children and divorce.* San Francisco: Jossey-Bass.

Washington Cofo Memo (1986). December, VI, 4. Newsletter of the Coalition of Family Organizations. (Available from National Council on Family Relations, 1910 W. County Road B, St. Paul, MN 55113.)

Watson, A. (1969). The children of Armageddon: Problems of children following divorce. *Syracuse Law Review, 21,* 231–239.

Watson, K.W. (1982). A bold, new model for foster family care. *Public Welfare, 40,* 14–21.

Watzlawick, P., Beavin, J., & Jackson, D. (1967). *Pragmatics of human communication: A study of interactional patterns, pathologies, and paradoxes.* New York: Norton.

Watzlawick, P., Weakland, J., & Fisch, R. (1974). *Change: Principles of problem formation and problem resolution.* New York: Norton.

Weakland, J., Fisch, R., Watzlawick, P., & Bodin, A. (1974). Brief therapy: Focused problem resolution. *Family Process, 13,* 141–168.

Webster-Stratton, C. (1985). Predictors of treatment outcome in parent training for conduct disordered children. *Behavior Therapy, 16,* 223–243.

Weingarten, H.R. (1985). Marital status and well-being: A national study comparing first-married, currently divorced, and remarried adults. *Journal of Marriage and the Family, 47,* 653–662.

Weiss, R.S. (1975). *Marital separation.* New York: Basic Books.

Weiss, R.S. (1979a). *Going it alone: The family life and social situation of the single parent.* New York: Basic Books.

Weiss, R.S. (1979b). Growing up a little faster. *Journal of Social Issues, 35,* 97–111.

Weissman, H.H. (1978). *Integrating services for troubled families.* San Francisco: Jossey-Bass.

Weissman, M., Playkel, E., & Klerman, G. (1972). The depressed woman as a model. *Social Psychiatry, 7,* 98–108.

Weitzel, W.J. (1980). From residential treatment to adoption: A permanency planning service. *Child Welfare, 63,* 361–365.

Weitzman, L. (1986). *The divorce revolution: The unexpected social and economic consequences for women and children in America.* New York: Free Press.

Wells, R., & Gianetti, V. (1986). Individual marital therapy: A critical reappraisal. *Family Process, 25*(1), 43–51.

Weltner, J.S. (1982). A structural approach to the single-parent family. *Family Process, 21,* 203–210.

Whitaker, C.A., & Miller, M.S. (1971). Evaluation of "psychiatric" help when divorce impends. In J. Haley (Ed.), *Changing families: A family therapy reader.* New York: Grune & Stratton.

Whittaker, J.K. (1979). *Caring for troubled children: Residential treatment in a community context.* San Francisco, CA: Jossey-Bass.

Whittaker, J.K. (1981). Family involvement in residential treatment: A support system for parents. In A.N. Maluccio & P.A. Sinanoglu (Eds.), *The challenge of partnership: Working with parents of children in foster care* (pp. 67–88). New York: Child Welfare League of America.

Whittaker, J.K. (1986). Formal and informal helping in child welfare services: Implications for management and practice. *Child Welfare, 65*(1), 17–25.

Whittaker, J.K., & Garbarino, J. (1983). *Social support networks: Informal helping in the human services.* New York: Aldine.

Whittaker, J.K., & Maluccio, A.N. (in press). Changing paradigms in substitute services for children and youth: Retrospect and prospect. In R.P. Hawkins & J. Breiling (Eds.), *Issues in implementing foster family-based treatment.* Rockville, MD: National Institute of Mental Health.

Whittaker, J.K., & Maluccio, A.N. (November 1986). *Position paper on out-of-home care.* Paper prepared for the resolutions committee, biennial meeting of the Child Welfare League of America.

Whittaker, J.K., & Pecora, P. (1984). Outcome evaluation in residential child care: A selective North American perspective. *Community Care* (UK), Business Press International, 71–87.

Whittaker, J.K., Schinke, S.P., & Gilchrist, L. (in press). The ecological paradigm in child, youth and family services: Implications for policy and practice. *Social Service Review.*

Wiener, N. (1954). *The human use of human beings.* New York: Anchor Books.

Wilson, J., & Neckerman, K. (1985). Poverty and family structure. In S. Danziger & D. Weinberg (Eds.), *Fighting poverty* (pp. 232–259). Cambridge, MA: Harvard University Press.

Wiltse, K. (1981). *Education and training for child welfare services.* Unpublished paper, School of Social Welfare, University of California, Berkeley.

Winn, M. (8 May 1983). The loss of childhood. *The New York Times Magazine.*

Wolpe, J. (1958). *Psychotherapy and reciprocal inhibition.* London: Oxford University Press.

Wolraich, M.L. (1979). Behavior modification therapy in hyperactive children: Research and clinical implications. *Clinical Pediatrics, 18*(9), 563–570.

Wooden, K. (1976). *Weeping in the playtime of others.* New York: McGraw-Hill.

Wynne, L., Ryckoff, I., Day, J., & Hirsch, S. (1958). Pseudomutuality in the family relations of schizophrenia. *Psychiatry, 21,* 205–221.

Yager, J., Grant, I., & Bolus, R. (1984). Interaction of life events and symptoms in psychiatric patient and nonpatient married couples. *Journal of Nervous and Mental Disease, 172*(1), 21–25.

Yllo, K. (1978). Nonmarital cohabitation: Beyond the college campus. *Alternative Lifestyles, 1,* 37–54.

Yllo, K.A., & Straus, M.A. (1981). Interpersonal violence among married and cohabiting couples. *Family Coordinator, 30,* 339–345.

Zeits, C., & Prince, R. (1982). Child effects on parents. In D. Wolman (Ed.), *Handbook of developmental psychology* (pp. 751–770). Englewood Cliffs, NJ: Prentice-Hall.

Zelnik, M., Kantner, J., & Ford, K. (1982). *Adolescent pathways to pregnancy.* Beverly Hills, CA: Sage.

Zigler, E.F., Kagan, S.L., & Klugman, E. (1983). *Children, families, and government.* Cambridge (U.K.): Cambridge University Press.

Zill, N. (22 March 1983). *Divorce, marital conflict, and children's mental health: Research findings and policy recommendations.* Testimony before Subcommittee on Family and Human Services, United States Senate Subcommittee on Labor and Human Resources.

Zimmerman, S. (1982). Confusions and contradictions in family policy developments: Applications of a model. *Family Relations, 31,* 445–455.

INDEX

About the Editors and Authors

Insoo K. Berg, Co-Founder and Director of Training at the Brief Family Therapy Center of Milwaukee, Wisconsin, has been active in clinical practice, teaching, and writing in the area of marriage and family therapy. She provides consultation for various social service programs and public schools and has conducted seminars in Europe, Japan, Hong Kong, and the United States. President of the Wisconsin Association for Marriage and Family Therapy, Ms. Berg is a native of Korea and received her M.S.S.W. from the University of Wisconsin-Milwaukee.

Catherine S. Chilman, Professor Emeritus and part-time instructor at the School of Social Welfare, University of Wisconsin–Milwaukee, has her M.A. in social work from the University of Chicago and Ph.D. in psychology from Syracuse University. Her work experience includes direct service, administration, teaching, and research in the field of the family. Among other organizations, Dr. Chilman has served on National Council on Family Relations, the Council of Social Work Education, the International Conference of Social Work, the American Psychological Association, and the Groves Conference on Marriage and the Family, of which she has been President. Her books include *Growing Up Poor, Your Child 6–12,* and *Adolescent Sexuality in a Changing American Society: Social and Psychological Perspectives for the Human Services Professions.*

Fred M. Cox is Dean and Professor of Social Work at the University of Wisconsin–Milwaukee School of Social Welfare. He earned the M.S.W. degree from the University of California in 1954 and the D.S.W. from the University of California at Berkeley in 1968. From 1954 through 1957 he was employed as a social worker with the Family Service Bureau in Oakland, California. His specialties are social welfare policy and community organization practice. He is principal editor of two works, *Strategies of Community Organization,* now in its fourth edition, and *Tactics and Techniques of Community Practice,* now in its second edition. He served as Secretary–Treasurer of the National Association of Deans and Directors of Schools of Social Work between 1985 and 1987 and was recently reelected to the Board of Directors of the Council on Social Work Education.

J. Scott Fraser is currently Director of the Crisis/Brief Therapy Center at the Good Samaritan Hospital Community Mental Health Center in Dayton, Ohio. He is also Clinical Associate Professor at the Wright State University School of Professional Psychology and Medicine in Dayton and served as Adjunct Associate Professor of Psychology at Miami University in Oxford, Ohio. Since receiving his Ph.D. in Clinical Psychology at Miami University in 1976, he has actively practiced, taught,and written on the theory and practice of Strategic Brief Therapy and Rapid Intervention.

Richard J. Gelles is Dean of the College of Arts and Sciences and Professor of Sociology and Anthropology at the University of Rhode Island and Lecturer on Pediatrics at the Harvard Medical School. He directs the Family Violence Research Program at the University of Rhode Island and has published extensively on the topics of child abuse, wife abuse, and family violence. Dr. Gelles is the author of *The Violent Home* and *Family Violence;* co-author of *Behind Closed Doors: Violence in the American Family* and *Intimate Violence;* and co-editor of *The Dark Side of Families, International Perspectives on Family Violence,* and *Child Abuse and Neglect: Biosocial Dimensions.*

Eve Lipchik has been associated with the Brief Family Therapy Center in Milwaukee, Wisconsin, for 8 years and is presently its Associate Director. Before moving to Milwaukee she worked with the Primary Mental Health Project in Rochester, New York. Ms. Lipchik received her M.S.W. from the University of Wisconsin–Milwaukee and is a Clinical Member of the American Association for Marriage and Family Therapy as well as an Approved Supervisor. Besides her clinical work and teaching at the Center, she writes about her special interest, interviewing, and guest edited a special issue of the *Journal of Strategic and Systemic Therapy* on this topic as well as one of the Family Therapy Collection volumes published by Aspen.

Anthony N. Maluccio, Professor at the School of Social Work, University of Connecticut, received his A.B. from Yale University and his M.S. and D.S.W. in social work from Columbia University. He also serves as Director of the School's Center for the Study of Child Welfare. After recently completing a major study of children in long-term foster care, Dr. Maluccio's present research activities focus on permanency planning for children and youth, services to adolescents in foster care, and competence-centered social work practice. His publications include *Permanency Planning for Children, The Chal-*

lenge of Partnership: Working with Parents of Children in Foster Care, and *Parents of Children in Placement.*

Margaret J. Nichols has been a family lawyer since 1977 and is currently in private practice with the firm of Harris, Lax, Guenzel & Dew in Ann Arbor, Michigan. A graduate of Kalamazoo College and Western Michigan University, she received her law degree from Wayne State University and worked for 5 years with the Legal Aid Office of Detroit, concentrating on cases involving divorce, welfare benefits, and domestic assault. Recently she trained in divorce mediation techniques and has lectured widely on joint custody, divorce mediation, and property distribution in divorce. Ms. Nichols also currently supervises a University of Michigan legal clinic devoted to the legal needs of indigent victims of domestic violence.

Elam W. Nunnally is a family life educator who is a co-designer of the (Minnesota) Couple Communication Program. He is also a marriage and family therapist who assisted in the development of solution-focused brief therapy at the Brief Family Therapy Center in Milwaukee, where he has his practice. He is Associate Professor in the School of Social Welfare, University of Wisconsin–Milwaukee, where he teaches marriage and family therapy, family development, and courses in parenting and parent education. During his summers he teaches Couple Communication and brief therapy in Scandinavia. He co-authored *Alive and Aware, Talking Together, Straight Talk,* and articles on communication and brief therapy.

Candyce S. Russell, Ph.D., is Professor, Marriage and Family Therapy Program, Department of Human Development and Family Studies, Kansas State University, Manhattan, Kansas. Her publications include a series of articles and chapters on the Circumplex Model of Marital and Family Systems in the *1980 Decade Review of Marriage and Family Therapy Literature* (with David Olson and Douglas Sprenkle), research on the transition to parenthood, marital satisfaction over the family life cycle, and evaluation of family therapy outcome. She serves as Secretary of the American Association for Marriage and Family Therapy.

Douglas H. Sprenkle is Professor and Director of the Marriage and Family Therapy Program in the Department of Child Development and Family Studies at Purdue University. He received his Ph.D. in Family Social Science from the University of Minnesota and is a Fellow and Approved Supervisor in the American Association for Marriage and Family Therapy. The author of over 50 articles and book chapters related to marriage and family therapy, Dr. Sprenkle is the editor of *Divorce Therapy* and the co-author, with Fred Piercy, of *Family Therapy Sourcebook*. With David Olson and Candyce Russell, he is the co-developer of the Circumplex Model of Marital and Family Systems.

Murray A. Straus is Professor of Sociology and Director of the Family Research Laboratory, University of New Hampshire. He is the author or co-author of over 100 articles on the family, research methods, and South Asia and 10 books, including *Social Stress in the United States, Crime and the Family, The Dark Side of Families, The Social Causes of Husband–Wife Violence,* and *Behind Closed Doors: Violence in the American Family.* His professional affiliations include President of the National Council on Family Relations, Vice President of the Eastern Sociological Society, and Member of the Council, American Association for the Advancement of Science.

Judith S. Wallerstein, Executive Director of the Center for the Family in Transition, School of Social Welfare at the University of California at Berkeley, has her M.A. in social work from Columbia University and her Ph.D. in psychology from the University of Lund, Sweden. She is widely recognized as one of the country's leading researchers on children and divorce, having reported her research in over 40 articles that have appeared in such periodicals as the *Family Law Quarterly, American Journal of Orthopsychiatry, Journal of the American Academy of Child Psychiatry, Behavioral Science and the Law,* and *Mediation Quarterly.* She is the author of *How Children and Parents Cope with Divorce.*

Carolyn Kott Washburne, who received her M.S.W. in community organization from the University of Pennsylvania School of Social Work, worked as a social worker for 15 years. She is now a freelance writer and editor and teaches English part time at the University of Wisconsin–Milwaukee.

James K. Whittaker is presently Professor of Social Work and Director, Social Welfare Ph.D. Program at the University of Washington, Seattle. He began his career in 1962 as a child care worker with emotionally disturbed children at the Walker Home & School in Needham, Massachusetts, and since that time has been continuously involved in the child, youth, and family services field as a clinician, researcher, and consultant. His five books on child and youth care and social work practice have been translated into four languages. His research in progress includes identifying predictors of success in residential youth care and treatment and developing and evaluating social support interventions with high-risk families.